Doing Fieldwork
at Home

Doing Fieldwork at Home

The Ethnography of Education in Familiar Contexts

Edited by
Loukia K. Sarroub and Claire Nicholas

ROWMAN & LITTLEFIELD
Lanham • Boulder • New York • London

Published by Rowman & Littlefield
An imprint of The Rowman & Littlefield Publishing Group, Inc.
4501 Forbes Boulevard, Suite 200, Lanham, Maryland 20706
www.rowman.com

6 Tinworth Street, London SE11 5AL, United Kingdom

British Library Cataloguing in Publication Information Available

Library of Congress Cataloging-in-Publication Data Available

ISBN 978-1-4758-5744-3 (cloth)
ISBN 978-1-4758-5745-0 (pbk.)
ISBN 978-1-4758-5746-7 (electronic)

Contents

v

To Georgia, Kader, Sef, and Sofia—my family who helped ground my research at "home," and to friends, colleagues, and young people and their families near and far who have helped shape and facilitate the doing of ethnographic fieldwork over the years—Loukia K. Sarroub

To my family, whose patience with the blurred boundaries of home and field has enabled me to do meaningful work; and to my partners, collaborators, and interlocutors for sharing their worlds and worldviews in what are truly joint efforts—Claire Nicholas

We thank Bob Jeffrey and Lisa Russel for organizing the synergistic session of ethnographers that inspired this volume during the 2018 Oxford Ethnography and Education Conference in the UK. We appreciate Sef Sarroub-Le Sueur's help in copy-editing an early draft of the book manuscript during his high school senior year.

Introduction

In the Field at Home

Loukia K. Sarroub and Claire Nicholas

In this volume, we attempt to better understand ethnographic research on education in local contexts wherein the researcher has regular contact and social relationships with the intended research participants. Recent disciplinary trends find ethnographers increasingly engaged in research in settings familiar to them, such as their own workplaces, leisure spaces, neighborhoods, and communities. The study of such practices illuminates interconnected methodological, ethical, and analytical dilemmas. It also offers opportunities for methodological innovation, explicates and challenges the effects of educational policies and practices, and interrogates and develops theories about educational structures, policies, and experiences. Our aim is to highlight the agency of educational actors and provide accounts of how the everyday practices of those engaged in education are instrumental in social reproduction.

With the same spirit that undergirded Annette Lareau and Jeffrey Schultz's (1996) edited book *Journeys through Ethnography: Realistic Accounts of Fieldwork*, we foreground ethnographers' narratives and research processes of discovery as well as the resolution of practices, dilemmas, and innovations involved in doing fieldwork. The chapters present an array of "home" contexts across the world, thus engaging readers in similar and contrasting fieldwork experiences that illuminate what it means to do research in familiar contexts. In connection to the advantages and disadvantages of doing such fieldwork, we seek to address the conditions under which people do what they do and to ask if there is such a thing as being "too close to home" in one's fieldwork.

Many ethnographies published since the mid-1980s include rich, thick descriptions of ethnographers' (familiar and strange) fieldwork experiences, but these are usually presented as appendices or methodological sections of monographs. Our collection of chapters is focused on a growing number of studies and scholars of education who do fieldwork where they live as opposed to faraway places. We are invested in providing different audiences more nuanced understandings of the phenomena they study in such circumstances in connection to the relational contexts of conducting such research.

The authors examine concerns related to conducting research "at home" that are particular to educational research settings. These concerns both overlap with and diverge from other conversations and writings about insider/outsider ethnography, home as field site, and the like. Anthropology as a discipline has been reckoning with these issues since at least the 1980s and 1990s, when a number of seminal publications questioned the politics and poetics of ethnographic writing, the positionality of ethnographers in the field, and the influence of researcher and interlocutor identities on the nature of ethnographic encounters (Brettell 1993; Clifford and Marcus 1986/2010; Gupta and Ferguson 1997; Wolf 1992). Since that time, while doing ethnography "at home" has become increasingly commonplace across disciplines, the specificity of what that looks like in diverse educational contexts has received little sustained attention.

This book contributes multiple entry points into the consideration of doing "home" fieldwork, more specifically with regard to better understanding the localities wherein interaction and relations are ongoing and simultaneous with research agendas. In other words, the chapters in this collection include researchers' responses to the particular challenges of doing fieldwork at home in proximal sites in which interpersonal relationships and research are sustained over time.

In these contexts, home emerges as a category that is not a given from the start. It is instead negotiated over the course of designing, conducting, and writing up ethnography among researchers and participants who relate to one another according to degrees of affinity and difference (social, political, cultural, ethnic, linguistic, racial, educational, gendered, and other). We argue that these alignments and frictions deserve close, critical examination and can lead to rich, methodologically innovative, and ethically sound ethnographic work.

This book aims to inform a wide audience, ranging from educational researchers to university students, to community and school leaders invested in doing research in the contexts of their own "homes." As such, each chapter provides a window into a familiar world that draws from research and researchers of various backgrounds and disciplines around the world. For example, in their chapter, Vibeke Røn Noer and Camilla Kirketerp Nielsen discuss conducting fieldwork at their places of work in Denmark wherein they both teach—nursing and veterinary educational contexts—and how student-nurses and veterinary pre-professional experiences shape the strategies by which their lives are lived. Noer and Nielsen provide insight into the lives as well as the professionalization of their students and argue that doing field-work "at home" fosters this insight.

In their fieldwork, Phillip Ryan and Mary Anne Poe also study their work-place in the American South. They question what it means for two White university faculty administrators in a predominantly White institution (PWI) to examine their university's racial climate and the impact of its lack of diver-sity on Black community members. As faculty administrators in social work and intercultural studies, they focus on how the construct of race manifests as lived experience within this context.

Elizabeth Pérez-Izaguirre's chapter offers an analysis of the interactions between Basque educators and non-autochthonous students in a Basque public school. She examines her positionality as a Basque teacher and educa-tional ethnographer in connection to an educational milieu which includes a high percentage of studentship from immigrant families who are expected to learn Basque. In her chapter, Tricia Gray examines how to leverage the eth-nographer's own local experiences in the context of meatpacking plants and demographic change in her community and school, where she was a teacher. She discusses the subversive tactics the school district and its teachers deployed to stay under the radar of alienating city ordinances that ultimately did not serve all students in a vitriolic sociopolitical context.

The next set of chapters center on resolving relational and methodologi-cal dilemmas in high school and middle school classrooms. In the chapter by Loukia K. Sarroub, she explores high school classroom literacy prac-tices and discourse in a U.S. Midwestern city in connection to low socio-economic status in an intervention reading program. Focusing in particular on an incident that inadvertently and literally positions the teacher and a young Black male student at odds with one another highlights how doing fieldwork at home changes and brings together social actors over time. In Charlotta Rönn's classroom ethnography in Sweden, she studies students' informal talk in order to understand the role of peer-to-peer learning in lesson-related tasks. Her chapter examines how to gain access to students' informal interactions with their friends and explains their hidden, collab-orative coping strategies when doing schoolwork outside of the teacher's hearing.

Chapter 7 in this volume offers ethnographer perspectives of doing fieldwork in home contexts that connect multiple institutions in the same Midwestern community. For example, Claire Nicholas and Surin Kim, two university researchers, engage in a crafts and entrepreneurship workshop series with a local community center in order to foster cross-cultural con-nections and contribute to the "micro-ecology" of entrepreneurship for local immigrant and refugee communities. They discover and delve into what it means to be accountable while doing research at home, especially in negotiating relational aspects of the research and community involvement.

In Jen Stacy's chapter, she explores how, as a university professor and researcher who is bilingual in English and Spanish in a California university, she negotiated entry into her study with her students. She addresses how as a researcher she represented herself to her undergraduate student-parents in the teacher education program at her university. Her discussion highlights the cultural and academic realities of undergraduate student-parents studying to be teachers and how teacher education programs can be more responsive to student-parents' cultural practices.

The chapter by Stig-Börje Asplund, Nina Kilbrink, and Jan Axelsson combines variation theory with conversation analysis when planning and analyzing the learning processes that take place when a Swedish vocational teacher and secondary students interact in a welding class. The authors focus their attention on the collaboration between the two university researchers and the vocational education teacher who becomes a researcher-teacher in an upper secondary vocational school, thus turning the ethnographic lens inward to flesh out methodological processes. In turn, Thijs Jan van Schie, in his chapter, examines being a teacher and graduate student who becomes a researcher and ethnographer in a Waldorf school in the Philippines. He discusses the challenges of participant observation and gaining access as a researcher in a Waldorf education site, which is familiar to him in his own country, the Netherlands, but also features cultural differences in the Filipino setting.

The final chapter in this volume, written by Sarah Staples-Farmer, a high school English teacher, examines the challenges of fieldwork focused on court-affiliated youth and their teachers in three detainment settings in the U.S. Midwest. She studies youth, who, upon being released and labeled "youth offenders," make the transition from confinement in locked cells monitored by cameras and juvenile detention officers to high school classrooms. She focuses on how she and their teachers and schools accommodate them to support their success.

Our book engages readers via international contributions from "home" field sites around the world and international authors. The chapters also feature work from early career researchers and those who are more established. Importantly, the various chapters address a wide spectrum of educational contexts—ranging from higher education to K–12 public and private schools to prison schools. The realistic accounts portrayed in each chapter address how local collaborations are instantiated through the research process—from access and data collection to the write-up phases. The major themes that emerge across the chapters highlight (1) positionality and negotiation of multiple roles, that is, researcher, educator, colleague, friend, community member; (2) reconciling multiple, hybrid, and intersectional identities with varying insider/outsider statuses vis-à-vis research participants; (3) resulting power dynamics in connection to relational identities—sometimes conflicting, consolidating, equalizing, and/or elevating; (4) innovative methodological responses to these dilemmas; and (5) integrated research designs and research ethics, offering possibilities for participation and insights on the social impact of research findings. The book's chapters thus individually and collectively treat and resolve local ways of doing fieldwork at home and highlight the creation and sharing of knowledge among researchers and research participants.

REFERENCES

Brettell, Caroline B. (ed). 1993. *When They Read What We Write: The Politics of Ethnography*. Westport, CT: Bergin & Garvey.

Clifford, James and George E. Marcus (eds). 1986/2010. *Writing Culture: The Poetics of Ethnography*. Berkeley, CA: University of California Press.

Gupta, Akhil and James Ferguson (eds). 1997. *Anthropological Locations: Boundaries and Grounds of a Field Science*. Berkeley, CA: University of California Press.

Lareau, Annette and Jeffrey Schultz (eds). 1996. *Journeys Through Ethnography: Realistic Accounts of Fieldwork*. Westview Press.

Wolf, Marjory. 1992. *A Thrice Told Tale: Feminism, Postmodernism, and Ethnographic Responsibility*. Palo Alto: Stanford University Press.

Chapter 1

Fieldworking at Home

Exploring the Experiences and Strategies of Student Nurses and Veterinary Students

Vibeke Røn Noer and Camilla Kirketerp Nielsen

An increasing number of ethnographic studies are conducted in profession-oriented educational settings. In many cases, the research projects are formulated by the educational institutions themselves, and the related fieldwork is carried out by researchers who have backgrounds as professionals (teachers, nurses, doctors, pedagogues, etc.) and educators in the profession-oriented educational institutions. As such, the fieldwork that is carried out can be termed "fieldwork done at home"—that is, conducted in the researchers' local contexts. The fieldwork that is described in this chapter was carried out among students and former, present, and potential future colleagues (and educators) of the researchers. Undoubtedly, this constitutes a relational web with imperative embedded challenges and dilemmas that require attention, reflection, and careful handling during the entire research process—that is, prior to entering the field and until the end of fieldwork—with a possible return to the field as a professional and educator.

Conducting fieldwork, especially in local contexts, can be a lonely journey through both points of departure and during periods of intensive fieldwork. Fieldworking researchers rarely have the possibilities and opportunities to engage and invest time in ongoing, in-depth discussions on the practical aspects of the fieldwork. They deal with continuous challenges associated with fieldwork and the choices to-be-made that inevitably form the fieldwork.

This chapter explores fieldworking practice and refers to long-term fieldwork that is carried out independently by authors at home in nursing and veterinary educational settings. Drawing on examples from the fieldwork, the chapter explores and discusses some common challenges that were encountered and resolved by both authors. The fieldworking researchers had to make choices associated with these challenges. In practical terms, these choices have subsequently (post-fieldwork) been identified as being pivotal in relation to alterations in the relationship between participants and researchers.

The chapter does not provide guidelines on how to conduct fieldwork in familiar local settings, nor does it attempt to cover all aspects, stages, complexities, and perspectives on fieldwork that is carried out at home. However, by drawing on selected concrete examples and in-common experiences, it points out possible unforeseen challenges that are associated with fieldwork conducted at home and elaborates on the consequences of the choices made by fieldworking researchers. The chapter seeks to provide insight into how being situated as a researcher "at home" in local contexts can be balanced and, in some cases, even emphasized positively.

FIELDWORK IN TWO SETTINGS

The chapter refers to two independent projects for which researchers conducted ethnographic fieldwork in nursing education and veterinary education with a focus on students, teachers, and their educational interplay (Nielsen 2018; Noer 2016). Hence, the studies refer to the educational fields of future nurses and future veterinarians. The ethnographic studies were conducted by the authors as part of their doctoral work. In both cases, the research projects were formulated within the educational institutions. Both researchers are professionals (certified nurse and certified veterinarian) and, prior to the beginning of the fieldwork, they had worked as educators in nurse and veterinary education in Denmark.

In methodological terms, the research projects share a common approach that is inspired by educational ethnography (Atkinson, 2015; Borgnakke, 1996a,b; Hammersley and Atkinson, 2007) and the Nordic tradition of classroom research (Lindblad and Sahlström, 2003). Further, the projects were commonly inspired by Marcus (1995) and the notion of "multi-sited" ethnography. In both projects, the Marcus inspiration was brought into play as the methodological principle of "following-the-field," "following-the-case," and "following-the-learners."

Hence, students in both projects were followed in real educational time and rhythm as they alternated between different learning contexts ranging from university campus classrooms to workplaces at hospitals and commercial pig farms over a period of two years. As such, the chapter refers to long-term fieldwork that was conducted in diverse educational settings and contexts. The empirical material was generated using a mix of qualitative methods ranging from traditional ethnographic methods, participant observation, spontaneous dialogue, photos, and the collection of documents and interviews to the experimental use of new ethnographic methods, including videos and video diaries (Borgnakke, 1996a,b; Brinkmann, 2012; Hammersley and Atkinson, 2007; Hastrup, 2010; Noer, 2014).

FOLLOWING NURSING EDUCATION

The starting point for the ethnographic studies in the nursing education environment was an alternative educational model based on the principle of "practice before theory." In this full-scale study, the researcher followed students enrolled in this alternative program through all learning contexts in the final eighteen months of the nursing program until six months after their graduation and their entrance into the nursing field as professional nurses. The aim of the study was to produce new knowledge about how students handle the fundamental conditions and challenges of the nurse training program as a vocational education that involves the inherent alternation between theory and practice (Noer, 2016).

FOLLOWING VETERINARY EDUCATION

In the veterinary educational environment, a pedagogical development project on game-based learning as a possible way to strengthen the interplay between practice and theory undergirded the educational ethnographic research. The ethnographic study followed veterinary students through alternating learning contexts, referring to both academic classrooms and commercial pig herds, as well as to group-work sessions and game-based situations in a mandatory master's course. The fieldwork spanned two years, and more than 300 students and 15 teachers were followed. The aim of the research was to produce new knowledge on how game-based learning functions as a didactic activity within the current teaching and learning practices of an existing veterinary course (Nielsen, 2018).

The two projects were designed and conducted independently; consequently, the empirical material that was generated was dispersed in time and space. The authors were, however, fortunate to have been given the opportunity to engage in discussions for extended periods during the research process. These ongoing discussions form the basis of this chapter.

ENTERING THE HOME CONTEXT

"Ethnographic fieldwork always involves a degree of participation in the chosen field" (Atkinson 2015, 34). In doing fieldwork, the researcher becomes his or her own research tool, and the mutual influences of the researcher and the field are regarded as a basic condition for the qualitative researcher (Hammersley and Atkinson, 2007; Hastrup, 2010). Thus, the researcher's personal presence in the field is a cardinal point in any fieldwork, and both on arrival in the field and during the fieldwork, he or she must reflect on his or her role and its significance with regard to the fieldwork relationships. In fieldwork that is conducted at home—that is, in the institutional workplace —the researcher must bring him- or herself into play (again) while utilizing his or her sensitivity, experience, and relationships within the field.

In these particular cases, the researchers were educated as a nurse and as a veterinarian, respectively, and were recently educators in the associated educational institutions. As such, the field sites were well known in both cases. Thus, immediate and easy access to all places such as university classrooms, clinical settings in hospitals, and bio-secured commercial pig herds was common to the projects. The language and workflow were well known to the researchers; therefore, access was apparently unproblematic. The experiences of the researchers, however, are that fieldwork in home fields requires not only access to the field—that is, the negotiation of first access—but also a keen awareness of the need to renegotiate access as an ongoing practical matter during the fieldwork.

In both projects, the researchers arrived with known identities as both professionals and experienced teachers, but when entering the classroom, their new identities as field researchers immediately took form. The researchers were no longer behind the teacher's desk in front of the students; rather, they were now situated among the rows of students. As the field researchers sat among the students, the importance of researchers' perspective and position was markedly noticeable, and although the researchers were known in their own fields, the fieldwork began with a significant change in their roles and perspectives as shown in the following field note excerpt.

One of the things that struck me when I started fieldworking was the importance of perspective and position. [. . .] Sitting among the students with no teaching, supervision, or examination obligations, for example, I did not consider what should be on the curriculum list, but rather whether the curricula were more loaded than good. However, writing away from the teaching and nursing perspective and getting closer to the students' perspective did not mean that I had become like them. As a 40+ years, married, mother of two without a Facebook profile, I was miles away from the young students.

At the same time, I was very "close." Trained as a nurse back in 1997, I worked as a nurse in Oncology and in the Intensive Care Unit before completing a master's degree in nursing science. After that, I taught at the Nursing Training Program for more than 10 years. Being close to the field, therefore, in my case, meant that I had a deep insight into the profession and the decade's way of pursuing education. Thus, I knew the field and was able to evoke my own emotions and memories associated with my time as a nursing student/nurse, as a teacher, and now as a PhD student. (Noer 2016, 33)

The reflections on the significance of the researchers' backgrounds and the ongoing discussions with the participants are linked to the fieldwork and to the everyday practice of participant observation. However, they are also linked to issues of proximity and distance in relation to the actors in the field. As a newly arrived researcher in the home field, the first reflection centers on how the researcher can approach the field while distancing him- or herself from well-known roles and positions in the field at the same time, thus approaching both the field and participants with a new agenda. In both studies, the choice was a fully open approach, and when asked, the researchers never hid their professional identities. Similarly, it was obvious to both educators and students why the researchers were present in the classrooms and in the clinical practices.

Despite the researchers' openness about their own relationships to the field, it was striking how, from the very beginning of the fieldwork, students and teachers categorized the researchers into positions such as "like us" and "not quite like us." During the fieldwork, the "like us" position often gave researchers the acceptance, trust, and confidence of participants, thereby assigning the researchers a place in the community. It was evident in both studies that the participants found relief in the fact that the researchers were not foreign to the field. "No matter how I introduced myself and my project to the research participants, their first question would always be 'But you are a veterinarian, right?' Their relief was similarly noticeable as I said yes, causing me both a sense of cohesion and concern at the same time" (Field notes, Nielsen 2015).

The concerns were mainly related to the recurring anthropological question of degrees of familiarity (Hammersley and Atkinson, 2007). Undoubtedly, the researcher must reflect on the importance of degrees of nativeness and researcher positions. However, such reflections must never undermine the empirical points that the fieldwork reveals. Further, and of importance to the aspects of fieldwork discussed in this chapter, the reflections must seek to embrace and highlight the potential that, in the authors' views, is linked to conducting fieldwork at home.

The well-known and familiar can be regarded as fruitful, as familiarity enables researchers to quickly capture precise, detailed, and accurate contextualizing descriptions of specific settings (in this case, hospitals and commercial pig herds). Familiarity allows researchers to commit to more active engagement with the practices of the participants and to maintain a focus on the participants' actions and interactions. Embracing and highlighting the potential of fieldwork conducted at home also means that the researchers' open approaches are given attention and positively credited as the essential points of departure for accepting the researchers' presence. Being accepted is crucial to establishing trust and confidence between participants and researchers.

FIELDWORKING AT HOME

"If participation is fundamental, so too is the element of observation" (Atkinson 2015, 40). Participant observation is, in this sense, the methodological hallmark of ethnography (Atkinson, 2015; Hammersley and Atkinson, 2007; Walford, 2008) and serves as the researchers' ethnographic anchor in both authors' studies (Nielsen, 2018; Noer, 2016). Thus, participant observation was always given priority, even when other methods, such as video observation, were involved along the way. The proximity to situations, events, and participants in the projects were characteristic of the intense phases of the fieldwork.

Initially, the fieldwork entailed getting close to the participants, their class communities, and their agendas. In hindsight, the students gave the researchers an incredible degree of access to their lives. Following students on campus, in the clinic, in pig herds, or in their apartments quickly became a part of the researchers' everyday fieldwork. Coming close meant that the students not only talked about educational matters and life as students but also shared private stories with the researchers—for instance, stories of grief after a miscarriage or details about a family member's life-threatening disease.

Hence, being close to the students for two years meant that in several cases, the relationships with individual students resembled friendships rather than researcher–informant relationships, and this was a constant and continuous challenge for the researcher. From the students' perspectives, it became increasingly difficult to relate to the researcher as a researcher. Initially, this was expressed by the fact that the students often directed questions about specific academic content to the researchers.

The students later approached the researchers to seek answers to questions related to not only academic content but also their doubts regarding whether their programs of study were right for them and whether they could handle what was expected of them in their professional lives. The appeal from the students to the researchers was to answer all the questions that were directed at them—the academic and the personal. The challenge, from the researcher's perspective, is found in balancing proximity and distance—that is, managing the proximity and not betraying the confidence of participants that is embedded in letting the researcher get close, but at the same time being able to establish an analytical distance from the field and actors.

The following example featuring Anett is one of many contained in the field notes, and it is clear that the relationships with the participants and the way in which the researcher is involved were constantly challenged and changing. The ways in which such changes and challenges are handled become crucial for the relationship and the fieldwork.

> I had a clear agreement with the students. After graduation, I would follow them into their first jobs and, hence, continue to follow them as a researcher. Every other week for six months, they sent me their diaries, which were often accompanied by an email saying, "Diary uploaded, kind regards, X." However, the email from Anett was different: she asked for my help not as a researcher but as an experienced teacher and nurse. She framed the diary by stating that this diary was extraordinary.
>
> She pointed out that she might have betrayed the principle of confidentiality and that she really had no excuse other than the fact that she really needed my help. When she started her shift this morning, the little boy whom she had recently cared for had died. She felt lost, and she asked me, just this one time, to help her.
>
> Looking at the email and the diary, my first instinct was to give her a call. However, at the same time, I thought about how very hard I had worked to situate myself as a researcher within the setting. What would happen if I called her? I had this feeling that any dispassionate reaction—as in, doing nothing—would compromise the fieldwork and, not least, leave Anett alone in a vulnerable situation.
>
> I ended up sending her an email asking her to give me a call. We talked about the diary and about what had happened that morning. It all came down to one question—she asked me for advice about whom to call and where to go for help in situations where a new nurse faces death, life, and everything in between for the first time. (Field notes, Noer 2013)

Although the researcher can plan, design, and conduct field studies according to methods books, the relationship with the participants changes over time, and the choices that are "the right ones" according to the books and papers will be challenged—sometimes to a breaking point. The question of proximity and distance also arose in relation to the teachers. Here, however, the movement was the opposite: close relationships became more distant as fieldwork progressed, and confidentiality and collaboration were transformed into "I am the teacher; you are the researcher."

Teachers were no longer like-minded colleagues. Now, one was in a position to observe the other. What had previously been collaborative was no longer a common starting point. From the teachers' perspectives, being observed was clearly transcendent, and although many of the teachers willingly opened their classrooms to the researchers, it was with some skepticism, and at times, the welcome was not warm. The example below makes it clear that the requirement for the researcher is to be able to handle the position that the participants assign to him or her:

> My long-term colleague turned to me and said: "Oh my—you are really snoopy." Although he sent me a smile, I sensed that he wasn't happy with me observing his lecture today. (Noer 2016, 61)

Situations such as these require the researcher to decide—very often in a split second—how to handle both the comment and the reference. The choice seems to be to either ignore the teacher's covert reference to the researcher's activity as resembling unprofessional prying or to enter into dialogue about the frustrations that seem to be associated with the participant observation. Paradoxically, despite the increased distance, the altered relationship, the changed position, and the at times harsh comments, the teachers simultaneously approached the researchers not as colleagues but as people who could and would evaluate their teaching and teaching competencies.

Thus, while the teachers did not like the idea of being observed, they consistently sought to be reassured about their teaching. The quest for evaluation was often expressed in spontaneous inquiries, as described in the following two field note excerpts:

> I left the classroom at the same time as the lecturer and decided to grab a cup of coffee in the teacher lounge. We had barely left the room before she turned to me and asked, "How do you think I did today?" (Field notes, Noer 2012)
>
> As we were coming back from the pig herd, leaving the bus, and saying goodbye to the students, the teacher immediately turned to me and said, "At first, I really thought a lot about you being there to observe . . . then I forgot about it. But it was okay, right?" (Field notes, Nielsen 2014)

Common to both teachers and students was the notion that the researcher should take a stance and share observations and reflections with them either in response to what they should do or to what they had already accomplished. It was always with the underlying premise that the participants knew that the researcher had in-depth knowledge of the field and, thus, they could not escape with reasons otherwise.

STUDENT PERSPECTIVES ON PROFESSION-ORIENTED EDUCATION

The relationships prompted by the fieldwork, which allowed the researchers to get close to the students, have provided valuable insights into the basic conditions and challenges of profession-oriented educational programs with an emphasis on student life as experienced and handled by students. A surprisingly important empirical finding was the hectic bustle of tasks that pervaded all educational contexts (university classrooms) and clinical practices (hospitals and pig herds). The buzzing bustle of clinical settings at hospitals and commercial pig farms did not come as a surprise to either the nurse ethnographer or the veterinary ethnographer.

The clinical practice contexts were demanding, and everything took place at a rapid pace. Tasks were multiple, diverse, and needed to be dealt with in a continuous flow. An urgent need for speed was included in the expectations of the fields of professional nurses and veterinarians. However, what stood out as a major empirical surprise in both projects was the fast pace and bustle at universities and in classrooms as well.

Such bustle can be a reflection of a strong constituent marker that is found across all learning contexts and a basic educational condition in much the same manner as the inherent alternation between learning contexts that are characteristic of profession-oriented education. The studies show how students in profession-oriented educational settings manage the underlying conditions and challenges of the curricula using both common and different strategies within and between different educational learning contexts (Nielsen, 2018; Noer, 2016).

The fieldwork showed how students developed and operationalized their own strategies. However, these strategies were not confined empirically to the handling of specific situations in classrooms or clinical practices; they were developed in a much broader sense and were oriented toward handling "life as a student" both as an individual and as part of a larger group of students. Consequently, this strengthens the empirical analytical potential of the concept of study strategies, showing that strategies as a whole are about handling "study life as lived."

Occupied with the inherent alternation between theoretical classrooms and clinical practice, the initial phases of the fieldwork paid special descriptive attention to the different traditional learning contexts with attempts to compare and contrast both physical settings and interactions among participants. The researchers engaged in contextual ethnographic mapping of the learning contexts, seeking to reveal specific contextual markers, cross-contextual markers, recurrent patterns, and/or deviations. Indeed, the observations confirmed the contrast between the classrooms with their traditional arrangement of tables and chairs suited to lecturing, rows of MacBooks, and the unmistakable smell of old sneakers combined with packages of warm lunch, on the one hand. On the other hand, clinical practical settings were filled with high-tech medical equipment, students wearing uniforms or disposable coveralls, dusty stable equipment, noisy animals, patient suffering, and odors ranging from the sharp smell of urine and feces to the clinical smell of disinfectant.

However, the students themselves seldom reflected upon the inherent alternation between the different learning contexts, the multiple shifts between them, and the sequence of stays in classrooms and clinical practice. The multiple shifts and alternations between the learning contexts were somehow silently embedded in the students' awareness that they were a part of a profession-oriented program. Conversely, the students expressed that being a student nurse or veterinarinary student was all about being capable of handling, organizing, and structuring a busy schedule and multiple tasks while coping with overloaded curricula and the constant pressure from a continuous flow of assessments and their own ambitions.

To the researchers, the bustle was noticeable and was felt in both classrooms, as well as at the hospitals and commercial pig herds, and it was reflected in a common study strategy among students: a "notch-on-the-list" strategy. This strategy had students focusing on solving tasks and assignments one by one and, as such, being more occupied with "getting things done" than with being susceptible, present, contemplative, and reflective. Although a common "notch-on-the-list" strategy was identified, the field studies also showed considerable differences between the strategies of nurse and veterinary students, respectively.

The fieldwork in nursing education showed how nurse students, in addition to attending to "another notch on the list," were eager to keep the scholastic learning context and the clinical practical learning context separated. The nurse students' development and operationalization of the study strategy of disassembling were reflected to a large extent by their expressed need to differentiate between being "just a student" at school and being "a professional" at work. The nurse students' study strategy of disassembling was in marked contrast to the study strategies that were revealed by the fieldwork in the veterinary learning environment.

Here, an important empirical point related to the recontextualization of the classroom in the commercial pig herds can be made. Observations in pig herds showed how the participants themselves developed and operationalized study strategies that in many ways resembled those that were developed and operationalized in the traditional university classroom. For the veterinary students, coping with the complex and unfamiliar context of commercial herds seemed to require strategies of returning to the familiar by reconstructing the known to cope with the unfamiliar and a need to assemble the learning contexts.

In seeking to identify the contrasts, similarities were also revealed through the comparative analyses. They related to students' choices of strategies developed to cope with the inherent conflicts between doing, being, and knowing, as well as the formative processes along the path of being a student to becoming a professional. Educational stories were mixed and woven into more personal and private ones as the students acknowledged how study strategies formed their educational trajectories.

The students' handling of basic conditions and the development and operationalization of their study strategies are of special interest to profession-oriented educational programs and the ongoing political educational discourse concerning the theory–practice gap and the efforts made to bridge this gap. However, the findings challenge the authors to reformulate the questions asked and to further reflect upon what needs to be bridged and what might instead need to be separated. Likewise, the findings point out the need to challenge the political efforts to produce professionals who match the market and health care systems, rather than supporting the formation of students "becoming agents of change" (Benner et al. 2010, 222) and being prepared for a lifelong professional career.

The findings and perspectives on students' study strategies and the possible consequences of these strategies for both "life as a student" and the process of professionalization were the results of the researchers' long-term fieldwork and the inherent development of close relationships with the students involved in both studies. However, becoming closer also implied challenges in terms of both balancing the newly established close relationships and handling the previously existing relationships with other participants who became more distant.

DISCUSSION OF FIELDWORK DILEMMAS

When discussing the role of the researcher among fellow qualitative researchers, negative connotations are often linked to doing fieldwork at home. The arguments are largely centered on the negative consequences of researchers' prior affiliations and existing knowledge of the field. In this respect, researchers who have conducted field research at home often risk having to argue their cases and claims in defensive terms. For both the researchers and the empirical results, this type of argumentation can be simultaneously inappropriate and distorting and all too often overstates the empirical results of the research. It may also mask an important developing dialogue related to the positive aspects that, in the view of the authors, are linked to conducting fieldwork at home.

> Fieldwork is possible because social actors can "take the role of the other." That is, it is a human capacity to be able to perceive the world not only from one's singular perspective, but also—however imperfectly—from the perspectives of others. (Atkinson 2015, 39)

Atkinson's quotation points to the very essence of fieldwork while emphasizing its possibilities and limitations. The human capacity to perceive from more perspectives can indeed be realized in fieldwork that is done at home.

The authors agree that their prior knowledge of and relationships to field sites have been an overall strength of the projects. To summarize the advantages, fieldwork at home allows the researcher quick and easy access. This is of particular importance for the quality of the documentary descriptions of the field settings, the possibilities of being able to focus more freely on the actors' actions and interactions, and the expansion of space/time for researchers to situate themselves in the field. The acceptance of the presence and endeavors of researchers is of tremendous significance in building the trust and confidence that allows them to come close to some participants while increasing their distance from others.

Due to its complexity, fieldwork cannot be prepared for by following manuals and writing protocols. Ethnography is lived and experienced at the time and rhythm of the field. Fieldwork is improvisational and full of important decisions, strategic considerations, and choices that must be made—often within seconds. Fieldwork that is conducted at home is a meeting with many unexpected and insistent appeals to researchers from several different perspectives. These appeals require researchers' prompt and sincere assistance or rejection. This chapter aims to make visible the value for new researchers conducting fieldwork at home and daring to be open and explicit about the embedded benefits of their relationships with the field, rather than excusing and pointing out limitations only. The authors suggest that researchers conducting fieldwork at home should engage openly and fully with their home fieldwork, put historicity at risk, and dare to present the fieldwork in its imperfect forms.

LEAVING THE HOME FIELD AND RETURNING HOME

Ethnographic fieldwork requires a high level of personal, emotional, and intellectual commitment. Hence, the researcher can neither eliminate him- or herself from the research endeavor nor suspend him- or herself for the duration of the fieldwork. The self is shaped by the relationships and interactions during the fieldwork, and over time, the role of the researcher becomes a part of the self. It is well known that the researcher influences the field and the actors in it, but it is equally important to understand that the field and actors influence the researcher as well.

Bearing this in mind, the researcher who leaves the field is not the same one who enters it. In many ways, returning home is reminiscent of the process of accessing and remaining in the field during the research. It is beyond the scope of this chapter to elaborate on the challenges that are associated with reentering the field. However, the point is that in all cases, the field researcher must be able to deal with the various challenges, conflicts, frustrations, and opportunities that are associated with being a field researcher in a familiar work setting. It can never be a matter of leaving the role but merely one of reconciling the past, present, and future of the researcher.

REFERENCES

Atkinson, Paul Anthony. 2015. *For Ethnography*. London: SAGE Publications Ltd.

Benner, Patricia, Molly Sutphen, Victoria Leonard, and Lisa Day. 2010. *Educating Nurses: A Call for Radical Transformation*, 1st edition. San Francisco, CA: Jossey-Bass.

Borgnakke, Karen. 1996a. *Pædagogisk Feltforskning Og Procesanalytisk Kortlægning - En Forskningsberetning. Procesanalytisk Teori Og Metode*, Vol. 1. København: Thesis & Akademisk Forlag A/S.

Borgnakke, Karen. 1996b. *Procesanalytisk Metodologi. Procesanalytisk Teori Og Metode*, Vol. 2. København: Thesis & Akademisk Forlag A/S.

Brinkmann, Svend. 2012. *Qualitative Inquiry in Everyday Life*. London: SAGE.

Hammersley, Martyn and Paul Atkinson. 2007. *Ethnography: Principles in Practice*, 3rd edition. London: Routledge.

Hastrup, Kirsten, ed. 2010. *Ind i Verden : En Grundbog i Antropologisk Metode*, 2nd edition. Kbh.: Hans Reitzel.

Lindblad, Sverker and Fritjof Sahlström. 2003. "Klasserumsforskning - En Oversigt Med Fokus På Interaktion Og Elever." In *Pædagogik - En Grundbog Til et Fag*, edited by J Bjerg, pp. 243–276. København: Hans Reitzel.

Marcus, George E. 1995. "Ethnography in/of the World System: The Emergence of Multi-Sited Ethnography." *Annual Review of Anthropology* 24, no. 1, 95–117. doi: 10.1146/annurev.an.24.100195.000523

Nielsen, Camilla Kirketerp. 2018. "Dyrlæge På Spil… Uddannelsesetnografiske Studier i Professionsorienteret Spilbaseret Læring På Den Danske Dyrlægeuddannelse." Københavns Universitet, Det Sundhedsvidenskabelige Fakultet.

Noer, Vibeke Røn. 2014. "Zooming in—Zooming out—Using IPad Video Diaries in Ethnographic Educational Research." In *Networked Together—Designing*

Particpatory Research in Online Ethnography, edited by P Landri, A Maccarini, and R De Rosa, pp. 85–96. Napoli, Italien: Istituto di Ricerche sulla popolazione e le politiche sociali. https://www.ucviden.dk/ws/portalfiles/portal/107145322/Zooming_in_zooming_out_Vibeke_R_n_Noer.pdf

Noer, Vibeke Røn. 2016. *"Rigtige Sygeplejersker." Uddannelsesetnografiske Studier Af Sygeplejestuderendes Studieliv Og Dannelsesprocesser.* Københavns Universitet, Det Humanistiske Fakultet.

Walford, Geoffrey, ed. 2008. *How to Do Educational Ethnography. Ethnography and Education.* London: Tufnell Press.

Chapter 2

Identity, Positionality, and Discovery

Researching Race in Local Context

Phillip Ryan and Mary Anne Poe

White faculty administrators researching race as lived experience among African American students is already an involved intercultural endeavor; conducting this research in their small, Christian, predominantly White university in the southern United States is a far more complex process. The authors of this chapter conducted an eighteen-month qualitative research project exploring the racial climate of their predominantly White institution (PWI) and the impact of this lack of diversity on members of the university's African American community. The aim was to illuminate how the construct of race manifests as a lived experience for African American students at this PWI and to apply the findings to the university's current diversity initiative.

As stakeholders in this university, the researchers' institutional positioning, racial identity, sociopolitical beliefs, and interdisciplinary thinking were undeniable factors in their research about race relations at this PWI. Through presenting the research and its findings, this chapter analyzes the impact of these four factors on the process. It also introduces a subsequent community-based, participatory project designed to continue raising awareness and expand the conversation about racial justice.

RESEARCH RATIONALE

The researchers embarked on this qualitative study to bolster their own work as professors and also as part of the university's race initiative which they co-lead. The following is an environmental scan that reveals race-based challenges for African Americans in U.S. universities in general as well as the racial challenges that African American students and those committed to racial justice face at this PWI in particular.

RACE AND HIGHER EDUCATION
IN THE UNITED STATES

Research on race in higher education consistently points to a range of commonalities, especially regarding race discrimination and exclusion at low-
diversity institutions. For example, PWIs often maintain a campus racial
culture that normalizes White, Eurocentric values, perspectives, and symbols
that contribute to the distress and marginalization of underrepresented groups
(Johnson et al., 2007). University faculty and staff in low-diversity institutions can be unaware of the subtle but persistent race discrimination and bias
that underrepresented groups encounter on their campuses. Campus racial cli-
mates that are not attentive to diversity concerns can result in feelings of marginalization, isolation, and distress for students of color. One's personal racial
identity development and life experiences prior to the college experience
influence race relations on campuses and how one perceives and engages the
campus racial climate (Chavous et al., 2018). Cross-racial interactions provide clear advantages for White students as well as underrepresented groups
(Chang, Denson, and Misa, 2006).

Moreover, research has established a link between campus racial climate
and a variety of student outcomes (Bowman, 2010). Development of a psy-
chosocial climate that attends to specific cultural stressors, such as social
isolation and microaggressions, enhances retention of African American
students until graduation (Hurtado and Alvarado, 2015). Positive diversity
experiences for college students are strongly associated with gains in cognitive outcomes (Bowman, 2010).

Despite these challenges, the college environment, in both classroom and
co-curricular opportunities, is ideal for promoting interracial encounters and
relationships that help to build awareness and respect for differences (Hurtado
and Ruiz, 2012). Many campuses, however, have not studied sufficiently the
problems or challenges that racial/ethnic groups face on their campus. This
reality underscores the importance of qualitative research by campus leaders
to understand the experiences of underrepresented groups whose voices may
not be heard through normal institutional processes of assessment (Hurtado
and Ruiz, 2012).

RACE IN THE UNIVERSITY CONTEXT

The main campus of this university is located in a city with a population of
approximately 60,000 residents, 55 percent of which is White, 42 percent is
African American, and 3 percent represents other ethnicities. The city has
a history of persistent racial segregation and discrimination evident in its

education, neighborhoods, economic distribution, and churches. The university was located near the city-center for most of its history and moved to a suburban location in the 1970s during the period of desegregation of public K–12 schools.

At the time of the study, the university's demographics reflected the persistent Whiteness that challenged this broader community. In 2017–2018, the university's traditional undergraduate student body included approximately 5 percent African American students. Only 1 percent of full-time faculty members were African American. Despite these low ratios, significantly higher numbers of custodial and food service staff were African American, creating a stark contrast of race and positioning among employees.

As a PWI, this university's White faculty, staff, and students do not have many diverse experiences and relationship opportunities. Thus, many are insulated from race-based stress that underrepresented minorities experience and are thus unaware of the stress those students experience. DiAngelo suggests that this protection actually creates White fragility, a "state in which even a minimum amount of racial stress becomes intolerable, triggering a range of defensive moves" (2011, 54). She concludes that it is critical that White people address their "fragility" by engaging in intercultural relationships and activities.

Within this university community, this fragility is often framed as "the bubble," referring to the insular nature of the institution's sociopolitical conservatism and its Whiteness. While both White and African American participants in this research recognized this insular bubble, one African American participant described life for her in the bubble the following way:

> I feel like the majority here is very conservative, which is okay because this is [a conservative region of the country] and they don't want to recognize it, and they want to stay in their little bubble. And to get by in this school, guess what? I don't pop their bubble. I let them believe whatever they want to believe, and I'll just shake my head, "yes," because that's what they want to hear. And that's how you get through, and that's how you stay on their good side. Because you don't want to ruffle any feathers at [this university].

The university's Christian denominational affiliation is also predominantly White. It has consistently held to its identity as a sociopolitically and theologically conservative regional institution. Despite a range of Christian denominations represented among this university's faculty, staff, and student body, for one African American research participant, the denominational association is problematic concerning race:

> There is nothing here that makes them feel at home or comfortable for those of different skin tones, religious affiliations, or cultural backgrounds. Not even

just African Americans. I'm not saying that it has to be all Black. I'm saying that there needs to be a place that they [others] feel comfortable to congregate. And that's not here.

The resurgence of White nationalism in the United States, as arguably captured in President Donald Trump's "Make America Great Again," reflects either the U.S. society's broader lack of understanding of White privilege and resulting racism or a comfort and acceptance of it. As a conservative campus, this institution has members who support conservative politics broadly. African American students and staff members who participated in the research cited national politics as a further dividing line for them as community members of color. For them, this political climate, which encourages some White nationalist and xenophobic rhetoric, made them feel out of place. One African American participant shared the following:

And the night of the election on Facebook was just unbelievable. The things that were being said. Just absolutely unbelievable. And I'm the president of [minority student organization]. And I'm having my friends contact me, saying, "Do you see this? Like can you believe this is what they're saying? Can you believe we go to this school? Like are you serious?" And I'm having to deal with that and trying to figure out as a student how to lead.

Another African American participant shared the following:

There was a lot of backlashing even with this year's election. There was a lot of hate. There was a lot of you know, bananas. There was a lot of chalk on the sidewalks with the election saying, "Go Trump. F—Hillary."

Currently, this university's administration is addressing the racial climate. The university has enhanced scholarship programs for African American students while a student organization provides support, educational opportunities, and resources for them. The university has also developed a significant relationship with the historically Black college in the city that includes faculty and student exchanges and a shared class.

In summer 2014, the university president appointed a task team to develop a strategic plan for addressing the racial climate. The authors of this chapter are part of the leadership team for this initiative that includes one other White faculty member and an African American faculty member. Strategic goals include: establish an ongoing advisory council that will serve this initiative; establish a campus location for the Center for Reconciliation and for the Minority Student Resource Center; increase the ethnic diversity of the student body, faculty, and staff; provide ongoing support for faculty and staff to enhance intercultural competence and to support racial justice and reconciliation efforts; and support and expand culturally diverse learning opportunities for the campus community.

The research in this chapter is an outgrowth of the strategic race initiative. While the primary focus of this research is the experiences of current and former undergraduate students who identify as African American on this particular PWI campus, researchers included not only the voices of this self-identified group but also those of African American faculty and staff. In addition, the researchers sought voices of White majority students through a qualitative research project conducted by an undergraduate class.

STAKEHOLDERS AS RESEARCHERS

Conducting research in one's own familiar workspace brings with it a range of researchers' identities and complex positionings that impact all aspects of the project. The researchers are White faculty administrators, each with over twenty years of service to this university; they are clearly integrated into the life of the university as well as outreach activities to the community. The researchers teach in and lead academic programs and university centers that afford them the opportunity to engage in curricular and co-curricular race matters. They co-lead the university's race initiative. They participate in cross-campus initiatives with a historically Black college in the same city. Both researchers intentionally integrate race into their courses and curricula and act as resources for students of color who seek them out as "safe spaces" to unpack their ongoing challenges and frustrations with navigating the dominant Whiteness at this university.

The researchers committed to a framework of context, subjectivity, and interpretation to ground their research. They recognized that their positioning (Harré, 1997) would be evident with this research approach throughout the process of gathering participants' stories, perceptions, and emotions about their experiences. Their positioning—relatively fluid and often complex— can be best framed in terms of in-group/out-group dynamics. Specifically, the researchers' prior experiences with students of color and race dynamics both in and out of the classroom clearly positioned them with a level of familiarity about race at this PWI. However, being established faculty with administrative responsibilities provided status that both legitimized the research and at times may have created greater distance between the researchers and the participants. While the researchers engaged with participants at a level of familiarity and rapport, their institutional alignment with the university was undeniable.

For participant recruitment, the researchers contacted students they knew, utilized friend-of-friend connections, and invited students whom they had not met to participate; to avoid coercion, they did not include students in their own programs. Researchers sent invitations to participate through email and made an appointment to discuss the research and its purposes. They provided all participants with an informed consent form approved by the university's institutional review board; participation was predicated on their signed consents. The researchers conducted hour-long interviews in their campus offices and ninety-minute focus groups in a small classroom. With participant consent, the researchers recorded the individual interviews.

In this project, the researchers represented the racial power majority while the research participants represented the minority. For example, coming from positions of White privilege, the researchers were at risk of being seen as objectifying and possibly exploitative. Also, the researchers' lack of cultural membership and familiarity with those they were researching may have limited their ability to understand the narratives of these students. With these challenges in mind, the researchers crafted a qualitative data approach that allowed them to take positions of learners in relation to the participants. They completed nineteen individual ethnographic interviews as the primary means of data collection for the project. They crafted a set of interview prompts based on their ongoing experiences as stakeholders in this context and research produced at other PWIs. Their intention was to provide participants with a range of entry points to share their narratives.

The interviews began with questions about the participants' backgrounds and experiences regarding race identity, including friendships, school and neighborhood characteristics, and parental guidance. Follow-up prompts often explored their developmental reflections and reasons for attending this university. The questions then addressed specific racial experiences at this institution and how they thought the university might resolve racial challenges. The researchers kept prompts open-ended. Participants had the opportunity to expound and even redirect the interviews. Thus, ethnographic interviews were spaces in which participants—in representing themselves and others through this process—transcended the researchers' limited expectations and the constraints of predetermined interview prompts.

In addition to ethnographic interviews, the researchers implemented focus groups: three African American students in one group and three African American staff in the other. Each focus group was intentionally less structured than the individual ethnographic interviews. The researchers sought spontaneity and experienced lively engagement among the participants. They pursued common themes and individual anecdotes with little structure imposed by the researchers. Their goal was to utilize camaraderie and shared experiences as a means of further understanding the complex nature of being Black at this university.

While the university is broadly sociopolitically conservative, the researchers are more sociopolitically progressive on a number of social issues. In addition, the researchers were perceived as sociopolitical outliers, and this contributed to their evolving work with African American students who see them as accessible and sympathetic to the challenges they face as a minority at this PWI. This aspect of the researchers' positioning contributed to their rapport-building and one-down stances in the interviews.

At the end of the data collection cycle, with interview transcripts and interview notes, the researchers then set out to code their transcribed data, looking not only for the themes the researchers saw emerge earlier in the process but also for any additional themes the researchers identified as viable. The researchers recognized the inherently subjective nature of identifying emergent themes. They framed a viable theme when it was robustly articulated by a participant (typically verbal paragraphing and back-and-forth engagement) as well when it was consistently discussed among participants.

The researchers chose to first code independently, simply annotating the transcriptions by marking key passages with denotations. Then, the researchers met and integrated their annotations. This process led to the following themes: (1) Participants portrayed starkly different racial realities based in part on their own developmental experiences with race prior to university; those who were critically reflective of race relations had navigated a range of racial contexts prior to coming to this university; (2) Participants exposed challenges with the university's image and its accessibility to minorities within the community; (3) Participants identified a scriptural imperative for racial justice and integration—recognized and understood within the broader ethos of this faith-based institution—that is in tension with the persistently White structural and cultural context of the university; and (4) While participants offered some ideas to address the lack of diversity, a comprehensive approach to changing university culture is as complex and systemically challenging as the problem itself.

As educators occupying different interdisciplinary spaces, neither researcher had an overarching disciplinary agenda for anchoring the research or analyzing the data. The researchers characterize the complex phenomenon of race as exhibiting a range of cause and effect variables, amorphous boundaries, multiple systems, and feedback loops (Klein, 1996). The result is a phenomenon that is chaotic, fluid, and beyond disciplinary theory and research. In addition, complex phenomena often have a range of disciplinary contributors that can speak to aspects of the phenomenon but fail to capture the complexities entirely.

For this complex topic, the researchers not only grounded their research approach within the qualitative domain, but they also integrated an interdisciplinary approach to their data analysis. Their intention with previously published research was not simply to build on existing disciplinary threads as in the traditional social sciences; their aim was to integrate existing theory and research into their findings to analyze more fully the narratives of their participants.

EMERGENT THEMES

While the researchers discovered a range of emergent themes in this project, one theme was more robust than the others: community stakeholders who describe growing up in racially and ethnically diverse contexts are keenly aware of the dominating and persistent Whiteness—and its seemingly irresolvable nature—at this particular institution; those who described growing up in broadly White social contexts generally did not have the same levels of racial awareness, regardless of how they self-identify racially. While this dominant theme addresses the personal narratives of participants, the remaining three themes address the institution and were less robust than the first in the research.

In the following analysis the researchers explore the primary theme of awareness. In addition, despite the range of racial awareness participants shared with us, in this analysis the researchers intentionally focus on data from their participants who were keenly aware of the racial imbalance in this institution.

AWARENESS: THE ROLE OF IDENTITY DEVELOPMENT

If they [African American students] come from a very diverse area, and they see color because they've had a very bad experience [with the White community] over and over and over again, they won't be interested [in this university]. Even if they offered them more money. Prior to university, unless the people, I think, unless a person comes from a background where they don't see color, they won't be interested in coming to an all-White school. (participant, August 4, 2017)

The researchers crafted questions of background as part of the interview prompts. Subsequently, this area of inquiry emerged significantly through the data collection process. Participants who grew up and studied in diverse—if not exclusively African American—contexts were more likely to see the racial divide and persistent Whiteness at the university as problematic. Those who were immersed in broadly White worlds seemed unaware or unconcerned about racial injustices at this university. In addition, the researchers have no evidence to the contrary; that is, the researchers have no data from their participants who came from diverse backgrounds choosing not to see racial imbalance at this university or any who awoke to racial imbalance at this university after having been in a broadly White world.

One of many examples the researchers have of participants who entered this university with a cultivated cross-cultural background who readily integrated racial injustices into their interview responses involves a racial aggression:

Participant: And there have been a number of problems that have been swept under the rug, which you know the researchers have talked about. I talked about my friend last time when she was just walking from the library and something happened to her, and that was not addressed. You know school-wide.

Researcher: And someone called out something to her?

Participant: mm-hm.

Researcher: They used a racial epithet toward her?

Participant: mm-hm and then threw an egg at her.

Researcher: Oh, the egg.

Participant: She internalizes all of that and goes through that, but then as a whole, that means something for all African Americans here. We're not safe. They don't really like us. They don't accept them here. I mean, if you allow this at a school and don't even tell them about it, or don't protect us, or say a statement this is not how you feel, you accept that. You're just like that.

This participant not only included this racial aggression as part of her own perception of the university, but she also saw a systemic problem in the university's failure to respond to her satisfactorily.

The researchers did not expect to find African American students who described growing up in broadly White contexts also articulating no real awareness of or concern for the lack of diversity and challenges that they face on their campus. These participants described operating in almost exclusively White networks prior to and in university, including White fraternity and sorority organizations and White roommates. These same participants identified little in the way of awareness or concern for the challenges of the African American minority on this campus. One even referenced his White friends often calling him "nigga" and had simply dismissed the racial epithet as friendly banter. Generally, when given the opportunity to share possible racial incidents other African American students experienced, these participants were at a loss given their lack of contact with other African Americans.

Given prior experiences with African American students and understanding White privilege, the researchers did not anticipate that some African American participants would not articulate any engagement with racial justice matters. The researchers turned to social network theory, the concept of the embodied self, and identity complexity theory as an analytical framework for better understanding the relationship between participants' developmental experiences and their subsequent levels of racial awareness.

First, social network theory (Milroy, 1997) provides an approach for researching individuals' networks and these networks' subsequent influences on these individuals' lives. Operating in what researchers describe as an individual's first-order zone, members of a network offer a range of influence on one's worldview, language, and identity. Networks range from dense to diffused. Dense networks allow for little-to-no variation or innovation; they are strict norm-maintaining structures. Diffused networks are far more varied and creative; they are occupied by individuals who co-create a broader and more fluid spectrum of worldviews, discourses, and identity constructions.

When analyzed for race, the degree of density and diffusion of participants' networks prior to coming to this university aligned with their perceptions of race at this university. Specifically, participants who grew up in more racially and ethnically diffused networks were typically more aware of race at this university. Participants who described coming from broadly White social networks, regardless of how they self-identify racially, tended to maintain networks of the same density of Whiteness at the university level.

In addition, for the participants who described a diffused network prior to coming to this university, their racial awareness at this university was acute. For example, the following African American participant, who would go on to describe racial challenges she faced at this university, described a remarkably diffused middle school network that would continue on through her secondary education:

> It seemed that [participant's middle school] was a predominantly Black middle school. But somehow I found all the White people, and one Asian, and we were just all friends. And it was in that time that I started to question my identity if that makes sense because it seemed as though I wasn't quite Black enough to fit in with the—well, they weren't really my friends—the cool Black kids who I wanted to hang out with, and I wasn't White enough to be exactly like my friends, so it was like this weird space that I was in, and it took a really long time to get out of it.

Another participant—with one parent whom he described as Black and the other Latina—entered this university with the understanding that he was "going to be a minority," regardless of the school; it was an accepted part of his post-secondary experience. By the end of his time at this university, he had attained a leadership position within the school for a multicultural organization, and he was mentoring first-year minority students with a long-range goal of transforming the racial climate of the campus.

Second, as an aspect of identity, the notion of the embodied self (Harré, 1997) is significant in understanding the complex nature of positioning for many of our participants. According to Harré, one's sense of self is "a sense of one's location, as a person. One's point of view, at any moment a location in space from which one perceives and acts upon the world, including the part that lies within one's own skin" (1997, 4). Repeatedly, participants who engaged with race questions at this university recognized the impact of not having a sizable cohort of students and faculty who "look like me," and there were clear implications for their sense of self in this context. Contrarily, African American participants who grew up in White social networks—as well as the White participants in this research—were less inclined to recognize the impact of underrepresentation of Black students at this PWI regardless of their embodied selves.

One participant who identified as African American and was deeply aware of racism at this university describes the reductive and dualistic categorization others placed on her as an African American who also had White friends:

> Because you can go to school and their friends can be like oh you're an oreo, you're Black on the outside, White on the inside. And for a while I accepted that. I quickly found out that that's not okay. Like, don't compare me to food, I'm just a person.

Another anecdote captures the culture shock one student faced in light of her positioning as a first-year student:

> Coming from a multi-ethnic place to a single-ethnic school, I didn't think that [attending this PWI] would affect me really, because I knew people that went there, so I was oh, it's going to be fine, but I guess like a month in, I started to freak out a little bit. I was like, I need to see someone different, and I was like constantly looking for people who were different. A part of me hates that I did that, but it happened. I was like, where is a Hispanic person? Oh, found one! It was like a game to me, how many people can I find that are different than me. And I always always looked for a Black person in my classes and it was either me or [fellow African American student].

While participants aware of race at this university valued having more community members who look like themselves, as a minority they also recognized the more negative aspects the White majority assigned to them, further complicating their positionings. One participant who recognized racism felt that skin color was an essentializing feature of her dormitory placement. Consider the following exchange:

Participant: Because I'm African American, they put me with a bunch of African Americans who I had nothing in common with, but just because I was African American, they put me with African Americans.
Researcher: So, what did you want?
Participant: I wanted my interests taken into account. It was just the fact that . . . .
Researcher: Based on interests taken, not on . . . .
Participant: Right.
Researcher: Race. Skin color?
Participant: Not on skin color.

Third, in addition to social network theory and the construct of the embodied self, identity complexity theory (Roccas and Brewer, 2002) contributes to the analysis of this theme by describing how individuals fluidly negotiate partially overlapping in-groups such as the border spaces students of color occupy at this university. Specifically, while African American students have varying degrees of in-group affiliation with the majority White community through shared faith, programs of study, and general educational goals, many also operated outside of these in-groups due in part to their avowed identities as Black students.

Identity complexity theory suggests that individuals negotiate overlapping spaces with four possible approaches: intersection, or the consolidation of multiple groups into one single in-group; dominance, the selecting of one particular group while subordinating others; compartmentalization, the accessing of in-groups based on particular contexts; or merger, in which an individual moves beyond in-group–out-group dynamics (Roccas and Brewer 2002, 89–91). With intersection, dominance, and compartmentalization, varying degrees of essentializing avowed identity exist. Merger is the most complex approach of the options and reflects a summation and integration of one's various group identifications.

Both African American and White participants who grew up in less culturally diffused networks tended to employ dominance, selecting White in-group membership when possible. Likewise, participants who grew up in more culturally diffused environments typically attempted some level of merger as part of their identities. One clear example of merger comes from an African American participant who described her ability in secondary school to move fluidly among a range of groups: "I also called myself a floater because I was friends with hippies, if, you know, they rocked the rebel flag, if you know, they loved the liberal arts department and drama. I was friends with everybody. I could get along with everybody, so I really could." Shocked at the reference to the rebel flag, a symbol of racism in America, the researcher pressed the issue: "Even with the rebel flag?" The participant confirmed the claim: "I could, I could get along."

While the participant describes merging with "hippies" or those "who rocked the rebel flag" at her secondary school, in other interview segments she maintains a deep awareness of the racial challenges she and other African American students face at this PWI. Negotiating and merging with the White community at this PWI is, in fact, more challenging. She signals that merger requires significant effort in order to integrate one's various group identifications.

IMPLICATIONS

For this research project conducted in their own community, the researchers' positioning played an undeniable part in the development, data collection, and analysis of the project. Given that qualitative research readily accepts and integrates the impact of the researcher on the process and product, these findings bear witness to the value of conducting qualitative research in one's own context: a move toward a perspective about a phenomenon that centralizes the undeniable role of context and positioning on meaning making.

This research contributes to a complex narrative: the story of African American student life at this PWI that provides insight necessary for the implementation of this university's strategic race initiative. As co-leaders of this initiative, the researchers utilized this data to continue to address diversity matters on this campus. They also included the research and its findings in their own course content when relevant.

As the university's administration advances its strategic efforts to create a racial climate that is more sensitive and hospitable, it must consider how to move beyond essentializing diversity as simply skin color and self-identification to include and support African American students, faculty, and staff who are culturally distinct. For example, understanding that African American students who come from more diverse backgrounds will have a heightened awareness of the racial challenges at this school, including feelings of isolation, marginalization, and even racial microaggressions, can better inform the university's student services as they develop support systems for students of color.

In fact, the researchers found that those African American participants who articulated awareness of this institution's dominating Whiteness and racial divide also pointed to the importance of mentorship for students and faculty of color for support as they navigate the Whiteness of the institution:

There needs to be a connection, somebody I can go to to learn the ins and the outs and who mentors me, helps me through . . . . You, you got to have that sense that there's a place where I can feel like I'm accepted for who I am and who will help me grow.

The researchers recognized that furthering this research would possibly cultivate not only these four themes but also the development of new ones. Continued research warranted greater representation among community members—not just for the participants but also for the researchers. To that end, based on principles and practices in Lassiter's *Chicago Guide to Collaborative Ethnography* (2005), the researchers are now continuing this line of inquiry with a coalition of university students and staff, many of whom identify as African American and all are demonstrably committed to racial justice.

The volunteer team collaborates as co-researchers, taking a participatory approach to the development and implementation of research on race at this PWI. The team met regularly for an academic year to explore the phenomenon, consider data collection and target population options, and craft and submit a plan to the university's institutional review board for approval. The team proceeded to collect data through qualitative interviews and met regularly to discuss the data collection process and to consider possible emergent themes during year 2.

Qualitative research in one's own "home" context can be conducted out of convenience or curiosity. It can also assist organizations and communities in fostering positive social change. This research began as an effort to understand the racial climate at this PWI in order to advance racial justice. With a participatory approach, the research process itself, and not just the data collected, is expanding understanding, dialogue, and action. It speaks to the value of conducting qualitative research in one's own familiar context.

REFERENCES

Bowman, Nicholas. 2010. "College Diversity Experiences and Cognitive Development: A Meta-Analysis." *Review of Educational Research* 80, no. 21, 4–33.

Chang, Mitchell, Nida Denson, Victor Sáenz, and Kimberly Misa. 2006. "The Educational Benefits of Sustaining Cross-Racial Interaction Among Undergraduates." *The Journal of Higher Education* 77, no. 3, 430–455.

Chavous, Tabbye, Bridget Richardson, Felecia Webb, Gloryvee Fonseca-Bolorin, and Seanna Leath. 2018. "Shifting Contexts and Shifting Identities: Campus Race-Related Experiences, Racial Identity, and Academic Motivation Among Black Students During Transition to College." *Race and Social Problems* 10, no. 1, 1–18.

DiAngelo, Robin. 2011. "White Fragility." *International Journal of Critical Pedagogy* 3, no. 3, 54–70. https://libjournal.uncg.edu/ijcp

Harré, Rom. 1997. *The Singular Self: An Introduction to the Psychology of Personhood.* London: Sage.

Hurtado, Sylvia and Adriana Ruiz Alvarado. 2015. "Discrimination and Bias, Underrepresentation, and Sense of Belonging on Campus." *Research Brief, Higher Education Research Institute* (October): Los Angeles, CA: Higher Education Research Institute. https://www.heri.ucla.edu/PDFs/Discriminination-and-Bias -Underrepresentation-and-Sense-of-Belonging-on-Campus.pdf

Hurtado, Sylvia and Adriana Ruiz. 2012. "The Climate for Underrepresented Groups and Diversity on Campus." *Research Brief, Higher Education Research Institute* (June): Los Angeles, CA: Higher Education Research Institute. https://www.her i.ucla.edu/PDFs/Discriminination-and-Bias-Underrepresentation-and-Sense-of-B elonging-on-Campus.pdf.

Johnson, Dawn R., Patty Alvarez, Susan Longerbeam, Matthew Soldner, Karen Kurotsuchi Inkelas, Jeannie Brown Leonard, and Heather Rowan-Kenyon. 2007. "Examining Sense of Belonging Among First-Year Undergraduates from Different Racial/Ethnic Groups." *Journal of College Student Development* 48, no. 5, 525–542.

Klein, Julie. 1996. *Crossing Boundaries: Knowledge, Disciplinarities, and Interdisciplinarities.* Charlottesville, Va: University Press of Virginia.

Lassiter, Doug. 2005. *The Chicago Guide to Collaborative Ethnography.* Chicago, IL: University of Chicago Press.

Milroy, Lesley. 1987. *Language and Social Networks.* Oxford: Wiley-Blackwell.

Roccas, Sonia and Marilynn B. Brewer. 2002. "Social Identity Complexity." *Personality and Social Psychology Review* 6, no. 2, 88–106.

Chapter 3

Can Basque be Protected in Multiethnic Environments?

Methodological Dilemmas in Basque School Ethnography

Elizabeth Pérez-Izaguirre

This chapter examines methodological dilemmas derived from conducting ethnography in a familiar setting. More precisely, it analyzes the intersection between being both an insider and an outsider in a Basque schooling community. The Basque Country extends through the Cantabric Sea border and comprises the northern region, or Iparralde, on the French side, and the southern region, or Hegoalde, on the Spanish side. In both Iparralde and Hegoalde, Basque is a minority language, while Spanish and French are the majority languages. Fieldwork took place in the Basque Autonomous Community (BAC), a region located in Hegoalde where schools promote Basque learning as a way to reinforce the language and promote educational inclusion.

The chapter refers to a group of immigrant students and their teachers who had to teach in Basque. This group of students refused to speak in Basque, and this worked to their detriment as a tool for inclusion was being rejected. The teachers positioned themselves in two distinct ways: whereas some showed a protective attitude toward Basque, others showed more flexibility and did not seek to address immigrant students' negative attitudes. Protective attitudes toward Basque created a tense environment, whereas flexible teacher discourses brought about smoother classroom interaction. Navigating between these discourses involved a strong dedication to the fieldwork that was being conducted.

Any ethnographic fieldwork necessitates long-term commitment to a research setting and its participants, as well as an investment of time and energy in each of the relationships built in the field. Such work has been complicated historically, as the ethnographer must immerse herself in the field, which is usually foreign and distant. Nowadays, it is more common to read work by ethnographers working in familiar settings, often in their own communities. A priori, the latter may be perceived as easier, as the ethnographer knows the context and most of its particularities. Indeed, many elements are easily recognizable for the ethnographer; patterns of relationships, rituals, or simple ways in which participants look at each other may be easily captured by the researcher because they are familiar to her.

Other elements also should be considered if the research is conducted in the ethnographer's own community. On the one hand, the ethnographer feels that she is an insider in the community that is being analyzed. On the other hand, she feels like an outsider, as an observer of her own community. Indeed, being both an insider and an outsider can be a strength and a limitation of conducting research in familiar contexts, and the ethnographer must navigate her own position toward the practices of the community she is a part of.

The classical dualistic approach to considering the boundaries between insider and outsider might be conceptualized as rigid. This is because the approach derives from the very simplistic idea that an ethnographer can be considered an insider and/or outsider, but it does not take into account the communication between these two positions. Following McNess, Arthur, and Crossley (2015), a concept that overcomes such dualism in the dialogue between insider and outsider categories is the Third Space. The Third Space remains fluid and enables communication between insideness and outsideness, while being internal to the ethnographer conducting the research. According to Gregory and Ruby (2011) and Vickers (2019), dialogue between the insider and the outsider enhances the researcher's awareness during data collection and analysis, and self-reflexivity becomes fundamental for the process of conducting ethnography in a familiar context.

Fieldwork was conducted between 2015 and 2016 in a Basque school. This school had a 37 percent proportion of immigrant students, compared to the 8.6 percent average in the region in 2016 (Rioja Andueza, 2016). Previous publications (Pérez-Izaguirre 2018, 2019) referring to this research have assessed the academic inequalities between locally born and immigrant students. Students with immigrant backgrounds in this school showed a tendency to refuse to learn Basque, though both Basque and Spanish language instruction were used. Inequalities as observed in this case are derived precisely because of this: while most local students accepted and complied with the rule that they must learn Basque as part of the Basque curriculum, immigrant students did not. This refusal to learn Basque became problematic, as they were not part of the Basque schooling community, where the main purpose is in fact to promote Basque (Pérez-Izaguirre 2018, 2019).

Indeed, the Basque language today represents community belonging for Basque people (Echeverria 2003, 2010). However, Basque did not always hold such a position in society. Indeed, speaking and teaching Basque was prohibited from the 1930s until the 1970s under the Franco dictatorship (Cenoz, 2009). Only since 1979 have both Spanish and Basque held official status in the BAC. In 1982, the Basque Government approved the Law for the Normalization of Basque. This law enabled inclusion of the study of Basque in the curriculum and its use as a language for instruction in the BAC. In 1992, both Spain and France signed the European Charter for Regional or Minority Languages, according to which protection of minority languages (Basque, in this case) and their private and public use must be guaranteed (Council of Europe, 1992).

In general, Basque is a matter of public discussion in the BAC, in part because some people perceive that it is not sufficiently promoted (Urla, 2012). Discussions appear in the media and public institutions, and thus also in schools. Indeed, Basque is subject to continuing analysis in schools, in terms of how should it be taught, how proficient students in each grade should be, and whether students speak enough Basque during recess. In line with these public discussions, the Basque administration encourages the use of Basque to strengthen its minority status (Basque Government, 2014). As Basque schools and most members of society in the region promote and advocate the learning of Basque, many younger generations in the BAC speak or understand Basque. However, such efforts meet resistance when, as in this study, immigrant students refuse to learn Basque. This chapter considers precisely how Basque teachers manage these attitudes and analyzes the position of the researcher observing them.

ETHNOGRAPHIC IMMERSION INTO
THE TEACHING PROCESS

The ethnographic process corresponding to this case study started in July 2015, when the ethnographer had an initial meeting with the head of the school in question. The school head agreed to the ethnographer's presence in the high school throughout the 2015–2016 academic year. In September 2015, the ethnographer began the process by conducting interviews with teachers. Following Marvasti (2010) and Woods (2012), the ethnographer took an interactive approach and focused on how relationships between teachers and students were built in relation to Basque. Most teachers at the school spoke Basque to each other on a daily basis and tried to teach Basque to all students, regardless of their proficiency in the language.

After conducting the first three interviews with teachers (out of sixteen total, as detailed below), the ethnographer began the participant observation, which enabled deeper exploration of these interactions in real time (Woods and Hammersley, 2017). The main issue noted was the attitude in one classroom with a majority of immigrant students who refused to learn Basque. This classroom was composed of nineteen students, fifteen of whom were immigrants, with the majority coming from Ecuador, and others from Bolivia, Colombia, Nicaragua, Peru, Portugal, and Bulgaria. There was also one student from another region in Spain, who will be described herein as a national immigrant; two local Roma; and one local student who self-identified as Basque. Except for the three local students, the rest vigorously opposed learning Basque, using phrases such as "I don't like learning Basque."

These reactions were observed from the first day of participant observation and remained prominent themes during subsequent interviews with teachers and students in the school. The difficulty of teaching such a resistant audience was obvious, and many teachers at some point ceased teaching in Basque, reverting to Spanish instead. However, some complained that while they could not teach in Basque to these students, they felt it was their duty to do so. Complaints were sometimes followed by expressions of frustration because the teachers were not able to fulfill one of their main tasks, that of protecting and promoting Basque.

In total, nine months of participant observation, twenty interviews with students, and sixteen interviews with teachers were conducted. The results of the observation and interviews indicating that Basque was a matter of conflict were triangulated via three focus groups conducted with groups of six to eight students. In these groups, immigrant students expressed their views about Basque, and in most cases, these views were negative.

During the months in which the fieldwork took place, two main teacher discourses were identified in relation to these students' lack of motivation to learn Basque. In the first discourse, teachers perceived Basque as a necessary tool of the education system and that it was their duty to protect this tool at all times. In the second, teachers understood that Basque was important but were not compelled by the same duty of protection. On the one hand, the defensive reactions of the teachers activated an automatic promotion of the minority language. However, these reactions also created tensions in the teachers' discourse, and relations with students who refused to learn Basque became acrimonious. On the other hand, avoidance of teaching in Basque promoted a more flexible teacher discourse and teaching environment. In the following section, examples of these two extremes are presented from six teachers and are complemented with data from field notes taken during the participant observation.

THE PROTECTION OF BASQUE AS
A MINORITY LANGUAGE

As mentioned above, the law and educational policies in the BAC promote the learning of Basque. Consequently, it was unsurprising that some teachers believed that their duty as Basque promoters was being undermined when immigrant students undervalued Basque. For example, one indication in this regard includes, "Why do I need to learn Basque?" Examples 1, 2, and 3 illustrate some of the discourses collected during interviews with teachers in relation to their classroom practice.

Example 1: Marianne Introducing the Students

This example was extracted from one of the first interviews conducted before participant observation started. The ethnographer and the teacher, referred to here as Marianne (all names are pseudonyms), did not know each other, and Marianne was trying to explain the characteristics of the group of immigrant students the ethnographer was going to observe. Marianne had previously explained that immigrant students in this classroom had acrimonious relationships with teachers and mentioned learning Basque as a source of conflict. When asked about the teaching of Basque, Marianne mentioned the following:

> These students don't feel the need to speak in Basque daily, right? Neither at home nor with friends or in town, unfortunately. . . . Consequently, they say, "Why do we have to learn this?" For them, learning Basque is annoying and they have a very negative view towards it. Last year, I also taught them and tried to teach them [some words] in Basque. I gave them notes and spoke to them in Basque, but they asked, "Why do you talk to me in Basque?" They don't want to listen to it, and I tell them: "You have come here; we have two languages, so. . . ."

Marianne clearly explained why the immigrant students did not want to learn Basque. Marianne highlighted the minority status of Basque in mentioning that students did not speak any Basque with their friends or in town. Indeed, in many areas of the BAC, Basque is not used in the public sphere. Marianne indicated that she found this regretful via her use of the term "unfortunately."

In line with the Basque revitalization efforts, Marianne mentioned that she had tried to teach some words and give notes to students in Basque, but the responses she obtained were discouraging. These were corroborated by the ethnographic observations, as recorded in the field notes; in most observations of Marianne's class, she tried to teach some words in Basque to students. When she received negative responses, she often commented that in the BAC there are two languages and that all students should comply with the rule that they must learn Basque.

Example 2: John's Explanation of Students' Refusal to Learn Basque

The next example is an extract from an interview that was conducted with another teacher, John, once participant observation had started. Initially, this teacher tried to speak to students in Basque, but he encountered the same reactions as Marianne. In the interview, he mentioned that some immigrant students did not comply with the rule that they must learn Basque:

> When I spoke in Basque, some students [asked] me why they had to learn Basque if they could speak Spanish. [I told them,] "Well, you have to learn Basque because the law obliges you to. You are in a Basque environment and there are two official languages and you have to learn both." Well, they refused . . . , they said it was not useful and mentioned that in the street they spoke in Spanish. . . . If they don't speak Basque at home or are not motivated to use it . . . they can't value it.

John expressed similar views to those of Marianne in the above excerpt, although his position regarding the revitalization of Basque was more radical. In fact, when he referred to the law his tone was adamant, implying that the protection of Basque should be respected in all cases. However, his comments also indicated that he understood that the linguistic environment of these students did not motivate them to learn Basque. According to the field notes, after unsuccessfully trying to teach in Basque to these students during initial sessions, John was typically obliged to switch to Spanish in order to teach his subject.

Example 3: Iñaki's Confusion When Teaching Students

This example is extracted from an interview with Iñaki, who had to teach in Basque. The interview was conducted at the end of the fieldwork period. This teacher had to teach precisely in the language that students most opposed, and this is why his interview discourse was probably the most defensive. Iñaki mentioned the following when asked directly about his duty as a teacher of Basque:

> I asked these students how long they had been in the BAC, and most of them answered [somewhere between five and seven] years. Of course, I told them they hardly spoke Basque and asked them if they [had] been [here for] five years

... [and] some even . . . born here . . . why did they show such an opposing view towards Basque? . . . If they had been [here] for eight years . . . well, they can understand some Basque, more than they claim they do. But they are [very] unmotivated.

In the above excerpt, Iñaki detailed a time when he highlighted students' lack of proficiency in Basque. The need to acknowledge this situation probably derived from the many efforts Iñaki had made as well as the negative responses he received from his students. His defensive and protective attitude is evident from the extract, and Marianne and John also detailed negative responses like those encountered by Iñaki. The discourse and tone used by Iñaki also indicated frustration, as he was unable to advance the class according to the syllabus. His duty was to teach in Basque, but classroom interaction was often defined by a series of problems derived from the negative view students held about Basque.

In terms of the dialogue between insider versus outsider discourse, all of the above student resistance to learn Basque detailed by teachers undoubtedly led to a protective response. The discourses by Marianne, John, and Iñaki revealed their identities as Basque promoters, which is obviously characteristic of linguistic and cultural insiders. From the ethnographer's perspective as a similar allied insider, reacting defensively against negative reactions toward Basque seems like a reasonable response. However, from an outsider perspective—that of a researcher of teaching and learning—it was clear that such tense discourse worked to the detriment of these teachers and their classroom interactions. Specifically, the teaching of Basque encountered negative responses from the immigrant students, which led to a clash of values between the two groups.

INCREASING OR REDUCING THE EMPHASIS ON LEARNING BASQUE?

The legal and pedagogical framework for the Curriculum in Basic Education in the BAC that was in force during the 2015–2016 school year established that valuing Basque culture and language should be the basis for creating inclusive student identities in multiethnic environments. However, according to this framework, other reference cultures and languages relevant to students should also be respected and valued[1] (Basque Government 2007, 26,047). In educational practice during the months of the participant observation, Basque was the main tool for inclusion in the academic community. Curricular and extra-curricular activities were preferably conducted in Basque, which implies that in order for students to be part of the academic community, Basque had to be spoken.

Inclusive education can be defined as the idea that every child and young learner take part in the teaching, learning, community, and culture of schools from a democratic point of view (Whitman and Plows, 2017, 9). However, Ainscow and César (2006) acknowledged that "the field (of inclusive education) remains confused as to what actions need to be taken in order to move policy and practice forward" (231). Indeed, the idea of inclusion is often ambiguous; that is, how inclusion should be promoted in each educational setting is not always clear. In the case presented, the tool intended to promote inclusion—speaking Basque—led to conflict as the immigrant students refused to use it.

Some of the teachers in this school understood that inclusion through Basque was not going to be possible and did not show defensive attitudes regarding the protection of Basque. These teachers were aware that students were unmotivated to learn Basque, and thus they applied other teaching strategies. Examples 4, 5, and 6 present discourses revealing these attitudes and are complemented by notes from observation of their practice.

Example 4: Paul on His Use of Spanish

In the middle of the fieldwork period, Paul taught a foreign language, and when he needed to clarify a term he provided translations using Spanish instead of Basque. In the interview, he mentioned the following:

> Yes, I have heard some students say Basque is not useful . . . [Hence], when I have to make translations, I use Spanish. . . . Students think this way because they believe they are temporarily in the BAC, they are going to go back to their home countries and Basque will not be useful for them.

In the above example, Paul showed a less protective position compared to Marianne, John, and Iñaki. His tone and discourse showed flexibility toward the immigrant students. In fact, he acknowledged that these students understood that they were in the BAC only temporarily, and hence, he believed that they would not need Basque in the future. According to the field notes, Paul showed an understanding attitude and his classroom interaction was relatively free of conflict. Indeed, students in his class did not complain about learning Basque since they were not required to learn it.

Example 5: Students' Expectations According to Mark

This example was extracted from an interview conducted once participant observation had started. Mark explained that he was not very demanding of his students. He believed that if he were strict, he was not going to get a good response from students. He mentioned the following:

> If I am very strict to these students, if I behave like a dictator, these students are going to say "I'm going to do nothing at all!" . . . And if you want them to work in class you have to try to be [flexible].

Later on, Mark explained why he thought students in his classroom showed negative attitudes toward Basque:

> I believe this studentship is here temporarily and their expectations do not include the Basque Country, many of them see their future in their home countries. So what they want is to get a Certificate of Basic Education, and Basque for them is not necessary. They don't have a positive attitude towards Basque. They say many things, such as, "Basque is shitty" or "I don't want to study Basque." Sometimes it is very negative, as they hate it, or they simply do not care about it. And I believe that they aren't going to use Basque in the future, that's why they don't want to learn it. Even if they are staying here . . . their mind is outside of the BAC.

Mark's description is similar to the one provided by Paul. In this case, Mark clearly explained why students' expectations did not include learning Basque. His tone was calm, and his discourse showed his flexibility, which corresponded with his interactions in class. He was not observed using Basque in his explanations, and classroom interactions were smooth, as were the sessions conducted by Paul.

Example 6: When Tony Explained Student Diversity

Example 6 was extracted from an interview conducted with Tony, again once participant observation had started. This teacher was quite adamant in his claims, and soon after starting the interview, he acknowledged the difficulty of addressing diversity in his classroom. More precisely, he mentioned:

> This group of students is quite diverse, right? Academically, their behavior and the situation of each family are very heterogeneous. Hence, it is very difficult to teach all of them.

When this teacher was asked about his classes, which were conducted entirely in Spanish, he mentioned the following:

I don't believe that everyone should speak Basque, I don't believe in such an idea . . . I think that we have to be aware of the place Basque occupies in our future, as well as the place [the Basque Country] holds. I would say that it should be understood as a puzzle, and in this puzzle there are going to be some Basque [speakers], and some others are never going to be Basque [speakers].

Tony acted similarly to Paul and Mark, as he did not use Basque when teaching immigrant students. However, his discourse varied from those previously mentioned. In fact, he conveyed a belief that in Basque society not everyone will speak Basque. Although his claim did not specifically refer to a need to reduce revitalization efforts, his discourse implied that if he did not teach Basque to his students, some would never learn it. Hence, Basque would not be promoted.

From an insider point of view, or that of a member of the Basque community, Basque as a minority language was not being sufficiently promoted in the school; however, the attitudes of the students did not give teachers much power to do so. In addition, Tony openly claimed that Basque could not be promoted at all times and thought that Basque should be relegated to the sidelines on some occasions. From an outsider point of view or that of an external observer, the discourse of Paul, Mark, and Tony did not correspond with the Basque revitalization efforts. However, in the role of external observer the ethnographer also appreciated the merit of ensuring a smooth functioning of classroom interaction via teaching that took place in Spanish, which enabled more active participation by students.

METHODOLOGICAL DILEMMAS IN NAVIGATING BOTH DISCOURSES

Conducting ethnography in familiar settings is a complex task that involves the positioning and repositioning of the ethnographer during the research process. This process is even more complex in multiethnic settings, as the ethnographer must study her own local context while simultaneously taking the viewpoint of an outsider. In the present case, the conflict between playing the role of both insider and outsider exposes the controversies of conducting ethnography at home. The insider view that Basque should be protected and defended as a minority language in the Basque Country—a reasonable position for a local—clashed with an appreciation for the need to put this language aside in order to overcome the problems faced by teachers. The latter point was derived from an outsider perspective, as an external observer analyzing multiethnic academic interaction and teacher discourse.

All in all, the simultaneous promotion of inclusion and of learning Basque as a minority language was impossible. Indeed, the fact that the immigrant students refused to learn Basque made it almost impossible for teachers to use the minority language to ensure the inclusion of these students. The two kinds of positions teachers took in this respect are designated here as "protective" and "less protective" of Basque, where the former created a tense teacher discourse, and the latter generated smoother classroom functioning. The ethnographic process was defined by these views and required the researcher's constant positioning and repositioning as an insider and outsider. Following McNess, Arthur, and Crossley (2015), such a state can be designated as the Third Space. The Third Space, as a consequence of the communication between "insideness" and "outsideness," enabled the ethnographer to experience and understand the dialogue between both.

In fact, the dialogue between both positions and discourses enabled greater awareness of the research process via the ethnographer as a member of the Basque community and the perspectives of teachers making sense of immigrant students' actions and discourses toward the Basque language. Self-reflexivity and a clear awareness of the self and the other were present at two levels. From the perspective of an observer in a familiar context, the ethnography required navigating between the self, or observation of the ethnographer's own community, while dealing with the other, or teacher discourses. However, it also required dealing with a second other, represented by the immigrant students who refused to learn Basque.

ETHNOGRAPHER'S POSITIONALITY
IN THIS CONTEXT

This chapter has analyzed the position of the ethnographer when dealing with two kinds of teacher discourses referring to their interactions with immigrant students who refuse to learn Basque. More precisely, it focused on a Basque school attended by an ethnically diverse studentship and in classrooms composed of primarily immigrants. Basque schools are thought to be the main tool for the promotion of Basque—a principle that teachers adapt into their practice. Another important principle of Basque education is inclusion or the fact that all students, regardless of their ethnic or social backgrounds, abilities, or previous experiences at school, should receive a fair, democratic education.

However, in this case study, Basque could not be taught because students refused to learn it. Teachers had two kinds of reactions to this fact: either they expressed a defensive reaction and expected students to change their attitudes, while acknowledging the reasons students had for not engaging in learning Basque, or they showed a more understanding attitude and did not make strong efforts to teach Basque. While the first attitude led to tense discourse and teaching practice, the second resulted in greater flexibility and smoother classroom interactions.

The ethnographic practice of recording these kinds of discourses was complicated by the fact that the study was conducted in the researcher's own community. Hence, controversial ideas about the need to protect Basque in a resistant environment and the necessity to promote inclusion outside of learning Basque arose. The ethnographer had to navigate between the discourse of the insider promoting Basque, and the outsider seeking other strategies that would facilitate less acrimonious interactions, but would avoid the use of Basque.

This chapter contributes to literature that analyzes the ethnographer's position in a familiar context. More precisely, it examines the ethnographic stance in connection to the discourses of teachers' experiences with negative attitudes of immigrant students learning Basque. Navigation between the positions of insider versus outsider enabled the researcher to conclude that reflexivity is a fundamental element of the observation and interpretation processes.

Reflection on the actions of local teachers and immigrant students was fundamental to understanding the controversies derived from having to promote inclusion through the teaching of Basque in a resistant environment. This chapter also provides insights to education practitioners teaching a multiethnic audience, as it reveals that enforcing teaching and discourses that do not focus on the obligatory learning of Basque provide better classroom interactions than do protective discourses pertaining to Basque. In the former case, Basque remained unlearned, but similarly, in the latter case, Basque was not practiced extensively, since resistant discourses rose above the rule that it be practiced in the school setting. Further research should focus on the elements that facilitate the use and teaching of Basque that promote the inclusion of immigrant students.

NOTE

1. In 2014 and 2016, the Basque government approved new pedagogic and legal frameworks, which were officially enforced in the 2016/2017 school year. In these documents, designated as Heziberri 2020 (literally "New Education 2020") and the Decree 235/2015 Education for the Basic Education Curriculum in the BAC, the relationship between Basque promotion and inclusion was made more explicit than it had been previously (Basque Government 2014, 2016).

REFERENCES

Ainscow, Mel, and Margarida César. 2006. "Inclusive Education Ten Years after Salamanca: Setting the Agenda." *European Journal of Psychology of Education* 21, no. 3, 231–238.

Basque Government. 1982. *10/1982 Basic Law for the Normalization of the Use of Basque.* Vitoria/Gasteiz: Official Gazette of the Basque Country. https://www.boe.es/eli/es-pv/l/1982/11/24/10/con

Basque Government. 2007. *Decree 175/2007, Curriculum for Basic Education in the Basque Autonomous Community.* Vitoria/Gasteiz: Official Gazette of the Basque Country. http://www.euskadi.eus/gobierno-vasco/contenidos/decreto/bopv2007 06182/es_def/index.shtml

Basque Government. 2014. *Heziberri 2020. Pedagogical Framework in Education.* Vitoria/Gasteiz: Basque Government. http://www.euskadi.eus/contenidos/inform acion/heziberri_2020/es_heziberr/adjuntos/Heziberri_2020_c.pdf

Basque Government. 2016. *Decree 235/2015, Education for the Basic Curriculum in the Basque Autonomous Community.* Vitoria/Gasteiz: Official Gazette of the Basque Country. http://www.euskadi.eus/eli/es-pv/d/2015/12/22/236/dof/spa/html /web01–ejeduki/es/

Cenoz, Jasone. 2009. *Towards Multilingual Education: Basque Educational Research from an International Perspective.* Bristol: Multilingual Matters.

Council of Europe. 1992. *European Charter for Regional or Minority Languages.* Strasbourg: European Treaty Series. https://www.coe.int/en/web/conventions/full -list/-/conventions/rms/0900001680695175

Echeverria, Begoña. 2003. "Schooling, Language and Ethnic Identity in the Basque Autonomous Community." *Anthropology & Education Quarterly* 34, no. 4, 351–362.

Echeverria, Begoña. 2010. "For Whom does Language Death Toll? Cautionary Notes From the Basque Case." *Linguistics and Education* 21, 197–209. doi: 10.1016/j. linged.2009.10.001

Gregory, Eve, and Mahera Ruby. 2011. "The 'Insider/Outsider' Dilemma of Ethnography: Working With Young Children and Their Families in Cross-cultural Contexts." *Journal of Early Childhood Research* 9, no. 2, 162–174. doi: 10.1177/1476718X10387899

Marvasti, Amir Barzegar. 2010. *Interviews and Interviewing.* London: Elsevier Science.

McNess, Elizabeth, Lore Arthur, and Michael Crossley. 2015. "'Ethnographic Dazzle' and the Construction of the 'Other': Revisiting Dimensions of Insider and Outsider Research for International and Comparative Education." *Compare: A Journal of Comparative and International Education* 45, no. 2, 295–316. doi: 10.1080/03057925.2013.854616

Pérez-Izaguirre, Elizabeth. 2018. "'No, I Don't Like the Basque Language.' Considering the Role of Cultural Capital Within Boundary-work in Basque Education." *Social Sciences* 7, no. 15, 1–20.

Pérez-Izaguirre, Elizabeth. 2019. "Educational Inequalities, Teacher Authority and Student Autonomy in Multi-ethnic Basque Secondary Education." *Issues in Educational Research* 29, no. 2, 519–536.

Rioja Andueza, Iker. 2016. "Escuelas de Dos Velocidades." *El Mundo Education Section, Basque Country Edition*. January 31, 2016. https://www.elmundo.es/pais -vasco/2016/01/31/56add7f9e2704e40788b458f.html

Urla, Jacqueline. 2012. *Reclaiming Basque: Language, Nation, and Cultural Activism*. Reno: University of Nevada Press.

Vickers, David Andrew. 2019. "At-home Ethnography: A Method for Practitioners." *Qualitative Research in Organizations and Management: An International Journal* 14, no. 1, 10–26. doi: 10.1108/QROM-02–2017–1492

Whitburn, Ben, and Vicky Plows. 2017. "Making Sense of Everyday Practice: By Whom, for Whom, for What?" In *Inclusive Education: Making sense of Everyday Practice*, edited by Ben Whitburn and Vicky Plows, pp. 3–12. Rotterdam: Sense.

Woods, Peter. 2012. *Sociology and the School: An Interactionist Viewpoint*. London: Routledge.

Woods, Peter and Martyn Hammersley. 2017. *School Experience. Explorations in the Sociology of Education*. New York: Routledge.

Chapter 4

Navigating Insiderness in a Study of Newcomers' Construction of Citizen Identities

Tricia Gray

Ethnographic inquiry is well suited to contexts like Washington River, a Midwestern U.S. community of 26,000 residents. The dramatic growth in the number of Spanish-speaking residents who began arriving in the 1990s in the mostly White, monolingual English-speaking community seeking work in the community's meatpacking plants cultivated a complicated sociopolitical context. The controversial 2007 city ordinance to ban offering housing, employment, or sanctuary to undocumented residents instantiated the growing pains of demographic change.

Schools located in communities throughout the "New Latino Diaspora" (NLD) have struggled to adapt to their changing demographics (Wortham, Murillo, and Hamann, 2002). The resulting changes in the social fabric of NLD communities are evident in the public high school in Washington River. The school's work of responding to the needs of a changing social and linguistic demographic is compounded by the effects of the political animosity surrounding the ordinance and a general anti-immigrant sentiment in the country (Gray, 2017).

A history of relationships in the school and community after teaching at Washington River High School for four years provided the researcher insight and "insiderness" about the culture in both productive and challenging ways in subsequent ethnographic work there. However, it also fostered a deep understanding of the sociopolitical context of the community. This chapter describes how familiarity with the school and community complicated the research as well as the strategies employed to navigate the challenges this familiarity posed.

Research within a community resistant to demographic change informs policy and practice in schools and classrooms like those in Washington River. This study explored questions about how students in Washington River High School (WRHS) construct citizen identities. Ladson-Billings (2004) acknowledges that Whiteness has historically been a criterion for U.S. citizenship. "Citizen" is used here to refer to *all* people who, by virtue of their humanity, are guaranteed equal protection of rights and responsibilities under the Constitution of the United States *regardless of legal status* (Levinson, 2012). *Citizen* identity is distinct from *civic* identity in that it implies a broader sociocultural identity beyond discussions of politics and voting (Rubin, 2007).

This research was framed by two questions: How do high school newcomer students construct citizen identities in social studies class? Who are the key individuals who influence the construction of citizenship and how do they influence them? A third question emerged through ongoing data analysis: Given the institutional nature of schooling, how do newcomers transform the school and how does the school transform them? These questions were explored in Mrs. Durham's English Learning American History class at WRHS with her newcomer students (Anyelín, Caterín Michelle, Saraí, Alexis, Alejandro, and Mateo), and the para-educator, Mrs. Sánchez.

These research questions positioned the students as "creators and holders of knowledge" to inform schools and communities responding to their changing demographics (Delgado Bernal 2002, 105). As is common in ethnographic research, the questions were shaped by observations in the classroom. Thus, having entered the research with a preconceived cultural and contextual understanding of citizenship, deferring to participants' language and actions was essential to understanding the conditions in which newcomer students constructed citizen identities.

EXPLORING POSITIONALITY

Qualitative research requires that the researcher—as the primary research tool—explicitly describes the position from which she observes, participates, and writes, as well as represents herself and the intent of the study truthfully to the participants and readers. All knowledge is value-laden and is filtered through the political values of the researcher (Hatch, 2002). A brief discussion of the commitments, experiences, and identities of the researcher follows.

Living in Washington River for the past twelve years offered the researcher insights into the unspoken norms, culture, and relationships in the community. Having grown up in a small, rural Nebraska community provided a deep understanding of the "Midwestern" way of life that is prevalent in Washington River. As a formally educated, bilingual White woman who grew up with married parents and shared family dinners around the table, the privileges that come with those identities in the United States (i.e., Whiteness) were also brought to bear.

Having been an educator for over twenty years in a variety of contexts informed observations and insights about the study for the researcher. The sting of gang violence and overcrowded classrooms staffed by almost all White teachers in a diverse urban high school prompted concerns about social stratification and race-based power dynamics. Leveraging Whiteness to amplify marginalized voices came from teaching Spanish in a public school located on Ojibwe tribal lands in northern Minnesota. As a bilingual teacher in Washington River prior to this research work, the researcher's Spanish proficiency fostered opportunities for intercultural interaction and to act as a linguistic and cultural translator for Latinx families inside and outside school.

These experiences and identities extended to the researcher's family members as they were placed in a position to be different from many of their friends at school within a very conservative community. They often expressed conflicting emotions about befriending someone who called all Spanish speakers "Mexicans" or about a vote for Barack Obama in 2008 when their friends told them that "Obama wanted to kill babies" before they were born. Indeed, parenting young people to value human rights and fight for social justice for *all* people was (and still is) difficult in this context. The lens of motherhood thus informs the work in important ways.

Partners' identities matter, too. The researcher's husband's position as the executive editor of the local newspaper revealed the underground discourse of the community. Evening discussions at home often involved commiserating about the racist and hateful letters to the editor to whom community members wrote shameless nativist manifestos. This familial relationship in connection to local newspaper work also limited activism in the community lest residents question the objectivity of the newspaper.

However, conducting research that interrogated the public discourse perpetuating racialized identities of immigrants and nativist portrayals of who counts as American was a way for the researcher to take action. Citizen, mother, partner, and educator roles all undergird this work. The idea that one's freedom depends on the freedom of others, regardless of their immigration status or other identities, was central to the study (Freire, 1970; Levinson, 2012). Mother, partner, and educator identities implored action to counter injustice. As an educator, the young newcomers represented many former students whose hopes, courage, and perseverance were and are transformational and inspiring.

COMPLICATIONS OF "INSIDERNESS"

The researcher's prior teaching experience at Washington River High School was not without contention, and this influenced future research work there. Creating and later teaching a Spanish class designed to more equitably serve the needs of the already Spanish-fluent students working toward college entrance requirements was a subversive endeavor. It required staying under the anti-immigrant radar of surveillance of the small but shrill conservative body politic. Coordinating the implementation of professional learning communities in the school and requiring more collaboration and interaction among colleagues were met with resistance. Sports teams' coaches were required to attend these meetings, and this requirement was not happily accepted by colleagues who were also coaches.

The web of relationships that were built and navigated during those first four years influenced access to the school for ethnographic research later. The original research design aimed to compare how students constructed citizenship in different social studies courses (i.e., general education and English Learning). However, none of the general education social studies teachers—most of whom were coaches—would consent to research in their classroom; thus, the research design changed to focus only on the English Learning (EL) classroom's social studies class.

NAVIGATING INSIDERNESS THROUGH ETHNOGRAPHIC INQUIRY

Ethnographic inquiry provided an approach through which one understands the culture from the perspective and in the words of the people who live it (Agar, 1996). Ethnography offered two key affordances in relation to the study in a local context and the Critical Race Theory (CRT) that framed it (Delgado and Stefancic, 2012). Regarding the participants and the context with "epistemological humility" was a reminder that the researcher's interpretations were tentative and evolving. Deference to the participants' interpretations was essential to learning from those being studied (Spradley, 1979). Documenting observations with "thick description" resonated with CRT's concern with disrupting dominant epistemologies. "Thick description" required intensive time in the field (three days each week from September through December of 2016) and detailed field notes to tell a full story (Geertz, 1973).

"School ethnography" aims to make sense of a school culture by acknowledging the macro- and micro-influences on the work of school, which likewise requires the ethnographer to be situated in the context.

Moreover, ethnographers are obligated "to portray the actors in the situation as humans. . . . Maybe not nice or good or wise people but human people" (Erickson 1984, 61). This sensitivity to the everyday work of schools and the people who work and learn in them was helpful in interrogating the institutional structures that influenced them, especially having had previous relationships with most of the people in Washington River High School.

LEVERAGING FAMILIARITY AND AIMING FOR SCIENTIFIC RIGOR

Familiarity with the school and district policies, people, and culture required "fighting familiarity" in data collection and ongoing analysis (Delamont and Atkinson, 1995). However, purposefully *leveraging* this familiarity maintained scientific rigor in the study. Because culture is encoded in language and action, data was collected through participant observation, interviews, and artifacts that people in the culture use (Spradley, 1979).

Data Collection

The "ethnographic record" for this study consisted of 28 sets of field notes generated from almost 600 pages of "jottings," 9 interview transcriptions, and 24 documents (Emerson, Fretz, and Shaw, 2011). This extensive set of data documented observations but also included thoughts and memories of the researcher's past experiences in the school. "Jottings" are "a brief written record of events and impressions captured in keywords and phrases" and were recorded in a field notebook during each visit to the school (Emerson, Fretz, and Shaw 2011, 29). The jottings were more fully developed into "descriptive field notes" as soon as possible after leaving the school.

The researcher's prior experiences sharing a classroom with the teacher in the study also influenced the researcher's observations. Writing asides in jottings and field notes was a helpful strategy for illuminating preconceived ideas about the teacher and her classroom. These asides were explored more fully in writing up extended field notes and memos. These details are important in all ethnographic research, but especially so in local contexts.

Semi-structured interviews provided opportunities to ask questions about observations or to clarify something heard or seen, which helped the researcher delve into meanings of language and action. Interviews were transcribed, and asides and commentaries were added to the transcriptions during the process when the discussion prompted a memory of the researcher's experiences in the school. Documents provided meaningful background information and included pages of the textbook, copies of test review guides, slides of student notes, and the school handbook. These documents were helpful in triangulating data among multiple sources.

Data Analysis

Writing jottings, field notes, and memos was a reflexive activity in the study. Data analysis began at the onset of the study and included asides and commentaries in jottings and field notes; these consisted of "brief questions, ideas, or reactions" (Emerson, Fretz, and Shaw 2011, 80). Writing up field notes was an onerous and time-consuming process, but capturing sensory details and reactions to things that happened became data and also the first level of analysis.

Asides in the field notes were generally an interjected thought or question, such as, "She used to do that with Miguel, too" (in reference to a student the researcher had known at the school) which was set off in italics in the full field notes. Commentaries were more extensive notes on the background or issues relevant to the day's events and were also set off in italics in the full field notes. For example, the following extensive commentary on the day after President Trump's 2016 election reflected the ways in which his history of loathsome behavior and speech had been amplified and encouraged by his election and helped frame the context of the research.

> The ugliness of the Trump campaign—the misogynist, sexist, racist, nationalist, and nativist bigotry so blatantly on display—was divisive, to say the least. His personal and professional history seemed, at several passes in the past two years, to preclude and disqualify him from holding the highest office in the nation. (See, for example, Keith Olbermann recount the list of "176 Reasons Donald Trump Shouldn't Be President Using Trump's Own Words." His incisive indictment of Trump's offenses goes on for nearly 18 minutes.) While it's impossible to identify the most egregious offenses, certainly many thought he would not be able to remain a legitimate candidate after the release of a recording in which Trump boasts of his ability to sexually assault women with no repercussions, which he later dismissed as "locker room talk." (Fahrenthold, 2016)
>
> The groups Trump offended in just a little over a year span the spectrum of all identity descriptors. However, perhaps most outrageous was Trump's campaign promise to build a wall on the southern border the United States shares with Mexico. His assault on Mexicans—which became code for "immigrants"—began in his June 16, 2015, campaign announcement speech during which he stated: "When Mexico sends it people, they're not sending their best. . . .

They're sending people that have lots of problems, and they're bringing those problems with us *(sic)*." (Kopan, 2016)

These comments became the foundation of Trump's foreign policy platform—to instill fear of the Other. He would continue to layer insults (e.g., describing "bad hombres" from Mexico during the final Presidential debate October 19, 2016), and those insults covered even natural-born U.S. citizens who were of Mexican descent—as in the case of Judge Gonzalo Curiel, who Trump said could not be objective in hearing a case involving Trump University because of his Mexican heritage. (Kendall, 2016) (Field notes, November 9, 2016)

The field notes commentary attempted to capture and contextualize the dystopic fog much of America (and the world) experienced that day and in the days that followed—and alas, still today. Reading and re-reading the completed field notes served to zoom out and search for story lines and subplots, which later emerged as themes. Brief "in-process memos" that included observations of patterns and interesting episodes and dialogue guided future fieldwork and were especially helpful early in the study (Emerson, Fretz, and Shaw 2011, 124).

Methodological Validity

A number of data validation techniques lent authenticity to the study. The variety of data collection methods (i.e., interviews, observations, documents) ensured "internal validity" of the study through "triangulation" (Merriam, 2009). "Member checks" were opportunities to seek validation of initial findings from the participants (Merriam 2009, 229). Intensive engagement in the field was evident in the over 100 hours in the classroom, observing and talking with students and teachers. Regular discussions about the research between the researcher and a mentor proved to be productive in understanding the themes that emerged (Carspecken, 1996).

FINDINGS

Data analysis revealed that the researcher's preconceptions of citizenship were unrecognizable in this space. Instead, drawing on Levine's (2007) and Abu El-Haj's (2009) reminder that citizenship practices are situated within the routine of everyday life, the relational, emotional, and cultural expressions of citizenship within Mrs. Durham's classroom were illuminated. The school's commitment to integrating newcomers into the school and by extension into the community was dubious. In acts both subtle and overt, newcomer students' experiences of school lacked aspirational guidance and instead focused on meeting newcomers' (many) immediate needs. Newcomers' marginalized positions narrowed their biographies *and* their aspirations for their futures.

Three themes emerged from the study that speaks to the experiences of newcomers in Washington River High School and the growing pains the school experienced as it attempted to respond to its new students. First, schooling structures were durable and a "mismatch" with newcomer students' dual realities (Deschenes, Cuban, and Tyack, 2001). Second, the ways in which different people in this classroom—the teacher, the para-educator, and the students—manifested *care* held different implications for the aims of schooling and of citizenship for newcomer students. Third, even with the best of intentions, there were missed opportunities to connect school to students' lives and to integrate students into the school community in meaningful and justice-oriented ways.

Challenges of Mismatch

The newcomer students in Washington River High School experienced duality in their everyday realities. They were at once adolescents and adults, being teenagers starting at a new school and also dealing with the stress of acculturation that bespoke their very adult lives of caring for themselves, often without adult assistance. Students who held jobs faced the duality of being a worker and a student, often working under an assumed name that literally marked this duality. Students negotiated the duality of being a human and being an immigrant in the United States—a criminalized identity that racialized and dehumanized them and equated their rights to their legal status (Santa Ana, 2002). The newcomer students' home language(s) were marginalized at school as they became "English Learners," framing a duality between linguistic and cultural *pro*ficiency and *de*ficiency.

The extant policies and operational procedures of school did not acknowledge or accommodate these dual realities. Students traversed school by breaking rules and navigating the margins to work around the mismatches. The school managed newcomers as a problem, and the structure of their classes communicated to them that learning English was their most important goal in school.

Students at Washington River High School had to contend with rules that limited what they could do at school and, therefore, how they could function in their adult roles. Students learned either to hide or to overtly break the rules in order to do what they needed to do. For Mateo, the "no cell phone" policy meant that if he wanted to help his father by mediating the phone call between him and his immigration attorney, he needed to frantically gain permission to break the rule or suffer the consequence of having his phone confiscated and withheld from him for the rest of the day.

> Mateo's phone buzzes and he looks at Mrs. Sánchez pleadingly as he holds up his phone to her. He walks to the back of the room to answer the call without having gotten her permission. Mrs. Durham yells, "What the heck, Mateo?!?" Mrs. Sánchez is quick to calm her, "It's his father." This is a game-changer; Mrs. Durham nods and walks back to the front. Mateo's father's attorney had called him—in school—to discuss his father's immigration case. Looks like students multitask too. He is at once a youth and an adult. (Field notes, November 7, 2016)

Mateo's cell phone use—even though it was not during instruction—was policed, and he was forced to break the rule or risk missing the opportunity to speak with his father's attorney. It seemed absurd for Mateo to have to apologetically take a phone call to help his father. The "no cell phone" policy and other rules of school were not sensitive to the students who handled adult situations like Mateo did.

Students were also policed as they searched for help. EL students who were enrolled in a general education class often came to Mrs. Durham's classroom for assistance on their assignments and exams for these classes. Since their general education classes (i.e., art, American Literature, physical education, etc.) were conducted in English, they often sought help in understanding the content. Alexis, a more advanced student from an American Literature class, demonstrated how students searched for help and when they were denied help how they went to the next stop on their underground map of safe spaces. They were policed, however, as they scurried from one stop to the next.

> Alexis comes into the classroom to take a final exam and Mrs. Durham tells him that she needs to find out what she is able to do to help. She leaves to go talk with the teacher, and Alexis rolls his eyes dramatically. A few minutes later, Mrs. Durham returns and says to him, "I can't read 'cold reads' but I can read and translate questions." The student's shoulders fall, and then he asks, "Can I go to the TAC room?" *This is a room where all students can get assistance with any of their classes.* Mrs. Durham shoots back, "They aren't going to help you any more than I am," and she turns away. She mumbles, "Let me go somewhere else to see if I can manipulate," and her voice trails off. *She is acting out what she believes he is really saying. It must get to her to have to police this kind of thing.*
>
> The student leaves and Mrs. Sánchez, the para-educator, goes to the TAC room to tell the para-educators there about the limitations of the help he can

receive on the work he has to do. Mrs. Sánchez returns a few minutes later and reports that Alexis was already getting help from the bilingual para-educator in the TAC room. They roll their eyes in mutual frustration. (Field notes, October 10, 2016)

In this case, Alexis was able to get to the TAC room before Mrs. Sánchez arrived to communicate with the para-educators there about the help he could receive. This routine of policing seemed more focused on catching students in the act of "manipulating" the system than on critiquing the system that Alexis felt the need to manipulate. Certainly, rules have a necessary place in school, but it would be wise to reconsider the rules in response to newcomer students' realities.

The Aims of Care

The students in this study described the classroom and their teachers (including the para-educator) as "helpful" and "caring"—qualities they attributed to "good people." Mrs. Durham and Mrs. Sánchez both mentioned on several occasions how much they cared about their students; however, their words and actions expressed care very differently. Different people demonstrated care in ways that conveyed important implications for the purposes of schooling and citizenship for newcomer students.

Mrs. Sánchez demonstrated care in the person of a "warm demander," one who held students to high expectations and employed "tough love" to promote students' persistence and perseverance in school (Ware, 2006). Her work was thus oriented toward preparing students for full participation in a democratic society. Mrs. Durham, on the other hand, was motivated by good intentions to help students navigate their new realities, but she reminded them frequently just how much she did for them. Regardless of intentions, she discouraged them from discussing politics and insisted that they come to her for help, this care was aimed toward helping students find "their place" in a stratified society.

The care that teachers demonstrate for their students is much more widely explored in research than the care manifested by students toward each other (Watson, Sealey-Ruiz, and Jackson, 2016). Students in this classroom demonstrated care for each other by helping new students learn the ropes of their new school. They drew upon and built their "cultural community wealth"—encompassing "aspirational, linguistic, familial, social, and navigational capital"—to help each other navigate their new realities and to imagine futures for themselves (Yosso 2005, 78).

New students enrolled in Washington River High School with dizzying frequency. The students in Mrs. Durham's classroom served as guides for the new students, helping them navigate their new school. Anyelín explains, "We help [the new students], and the teachers tell them how to learn and what they have to do" (December 3, 2016). As ambassadors, the students helped new students open their lockers, showed them how to navigate the lunch line, and invited them to join their table in the cafeteria. As the students helped each other to navigate the school in a way that allowed them to "play the game" of the institution, they mapped the safe spaces within the school while also remaining unnoticed.

Missed Opportunities

The arrival of newcomer students to a school most certainly prompts some growing pains. However, Washington River High School's response to newcomer students was more focused on fitting students into the existing structure of the school than on transforming itself to welcome and integrate newcomers. What this researcher viewed as opportunities were regarded by the school as problems or were sometimes overlooked altogether. The school did not leverage their linguistic "funds of knowledge" unless these skills could be deployed to assist in translation (Moll, Amanti, Neff, and Gonzalez, 1992). There were also missed opportunities to integrate newcomers into U.S. history and the national narrative. Missed opportunities to integrate civic education into the history curriculum erased valuable lessons in the pursuit of equal rights throughout American history.

Isabel's experience in an introductory Spanish class was illustrative of how students' linguistic funds of knowledge were neglected. Having attended school regularly in El Salvador, her Spanish literacy skills were well developed. However, she was placed in a Spanish 1 course, during which she "learned" introductory vocabulary (words and phrases that were most likely among her first words as a toddler) and simple grammatical structures. She explained, "Pues, hago lo mismo que los güeros, repito todo (*Well, I do the same as the White kids, I repeat everything*)" (Isabel, December 13, 2016).

Her teacher treated her with the same expectations as the non-Spanish-dominant learners in the class. This placement in an introductory Spanish class completely disregarded her Spanish proficiency and literacy. Moreover, the school's erasure of the Spanish class for proficient speakers (which this researcher had developed and taught as a teacher in the school) took away the opportunity for her enrollment in Spanish to further develop her Spanish literacy skills.

Missed opportunities to integrate newcomers into U.S. history and the national narrative were glaring. In some instances, students seemed dumbfounded by the willful ignorance of how the course material related to their lives. In the following example, students were learning about the immigration of people from Northern Europe to the United States during the mid-1800s. Mrs. Durham referenced a chart from the textbook that depicted Ireland and Germany as the two main "sources of immigration" between 1820 and 1860 (Duran, Gusman, and Shefelbine 2005, 132).

> Mrs. Durham, sitting at her desk, finishes the passage in the textbook about U.S. immigration in the 1820s and when Mrs. Sánchez finishes translating it, she asks, "So, who are immigrants?" There is laughter from all the students. She smiles, "I know we have a roomful" and Alejandro suggests, "Nosotros." She nods, and rephrasing her question, asks, "Which two countries had the most immigrants?" Someone shouts, "Guatemala!" and they all laugh again because clearly, he was right. The room was full of Guatemalan immigrants. Mrs. Durham clarifies with a playful roll of her eyes, "in 1820?" and someone mumbles, "Ireland and England." Mrs. Durham praises their answer (Field notes, November 11, 2016).

The passage in the textbook most certainly resonated with the students in the room, especially references to immigrants coming to the United States "in search of jobs and freedom" and to "escape huge problems" in their home countries (Duran, Gusman, and Shefelbine 2005, 132) However, the connections to current immigrants searching for jobs and an escape from the "problems" in their home countries were willfully ignored. The opportunity to connect historical factors in immigration to their own reasons for immigrating was lost as immigrants of the mid-1800s were isolated in time.

Even though Mrs. Durham taught history class, there were missed opportunities to integrate civic education into the course. Students learned symbolic gestures of American citizenship, such as standing and reciting the Pledge of Allegiance each day. However, amid an impactful historical moment, students grappled with learning to do life in America and to do life in America under Trump. Trump's election added to the stresses that students already experienced. As Caterín Michelle explains, she felt "at the same time nervous, fear, surprised" when faced with living in the United States during a Trump presidency (December 13, 2016).

Students questioned the politicization of their bodies in the United States asking, "Why doesn't Trump like Hispanics?" (Field notes, November 11, 2016). The historical moment was ripe for discussion of civil rights and civic participation. Students, however, were discouraged from participating in political dialogue. Mrs. Durham advised them in a serious tone as she introduced a short unit about elections in the two weeks prior to the general election of 2016, "Politics are a taboo in society" (Field notes, October 26, 2016). She explained that discussion of politics damages relationships.

This was contradictory to what they had learned earlier in the semester about freedom of speech. The First Amendment, it seemed, guaranteed freedom of speech and expression *unless* the speech was political. By discouraging political dialogue and action, Mrs. Durham encouraged students to remain hidden in the margins of society. However, the tension between teaching to amplify students' voices and acknowledging the dangerous reality of an anti-immigrant political context was a real dilemma with which Mrs. Durham grappled.

The school as a whole segregated and distanced newcomer students and their families in a number of ways. Newcomers were regarded as problems—with deficiencies in schooling and in English—and the school managed the problems by labeling them as English Learners and isolating them from the rest of the school community. Newcomer students rarely left the hallway in which the EL classrooms were located, and when they did, they seldom did so alone. This physical segregation from the rest of the school distanced students from the daily life of the school and literally relegated them to the margins, as their hallway was located in a lonely corner of the school.

DISCUSSION

The researcher's preexisting notions of citizenship, even though framed by the construct of "cultural citizenship" (Rosaldo, 1994), were interpreted through a lens of Whiteness. However, by exploring the context ethnographically, it was imperative to attend to the shared understandings for constructing, describing, and navigating the social world. The students' experiences illuminated how "being different"—embodying a reality of Brownness—had very real implications for the public space in which to construct citizen identities (Rosaldo, 1994). The quotidian relational, cultural, and social practices in this classroom and school narrowed newcomers' access to the public space in which they could see and be seen and hear and be heard.

WRHS was a "mismatch" for newcomer students, and they largely operated underground and in the margins of the school (Deschenes, Cuban, and Tyack, 2001). This location of citizenship construction negates opportunities for newcomers to experience the full realm of public space and to enter into the public consciousness. Newcomers and long-standing residents must deliberately cultivate opportunities for interaction and dialogue (e.g., bilingual social studies classes) if they are to regard one another in "political friendship" (Allen, 2004). For this to become a reality, schools must transform themselves in response to newcomers rather than justifying segregated arrangements based solely on newcomers' deficits in English.

CONCLUSION

In communities like Washington River, ethnographic inquiry allows for a range of ways with which to understand how culture is shaped and transformed by people. In the case of Washington River, demographic change catalyzed the Trump-fueled anti-immigrant sentiment. Any number of questions could be explored in a context like this. Working in the school and living in the community in which this research was situated meant that the researcher had been *among* and *with* the people of the cultural site for an extended period of time.

The people, culture, and policies of the school were familiar, or at least *had been* familiar at one time. Given this familiarity, exploring reflexivity as a researcher became even more consequential. Purposefully taking steps to interrogate "the known" about the school, community, and the people in it was a productive way to leverage prior knowledge and experience and to juxtapose them with new understandings. Leveraging past experiences by juxtaposing them with new observations enriched the fieldwork. Employing purposeful strategies maintained the scientific rigor of the study. These strategies can support future ethnographic work in local contexts by encouraging ethnographers to leverage, rather than ignore, their own local experiences without making the work auto-ethnographic.

REFERENCES

Abu El-Haj, Thea. 2009. Becoming Citizens in an Era of Globalization and Transnational Migration: Re-imagining Citizenship as Critical Practice. *Theory into Practice* 48, no. 1, 274–282.

Agar, Michael. 1996. *The Professional Stranger: An Informal Introduction to Ethnography*, 2nd edition. San Diego, CA: Academic Press.

Allen, Danielle. 2004. *Talking to Strangers: Anxieties of Citizenship Since* Brown v. Board of Education. Chicago, IL: University of Chicago Press.

Carspecken, Phil. 1996. *Critical Ethnography in Educational Research: A Theoretical and Practical Guide*. New York, NY: Routledge.

Delamont, Sara and Paul Atkinson. 1995. *Fighting Familiarity: Essays on Education and Ethnography*. New York: Hampton Press.

Delgado Bernal, Dolores. 2002. "Critical Race Theory, Latino Critical Theory, and Critical Raced-Gendered Epistemologies: Recognizing Students of Color as Holders and Creators of Knowledge." *Qualitative Inquiry* 8, no. 1, 105–126.

Delgado, Richard and Jean Stefancic. 2012. *Critical Race Theory: An Introduction*, 2nd edition. New York, NY: New York University Press.

Deschenes, Sarah, Larry Cuban, L., and David Tyack. 2001. "Mismatch: Historical Perspectives on Schools and Students Who Don't Fit Them." *Teachers College Record* 103, no. 4, 525–547.

Duran, Elva, Jo Gusman, and John Shefelbine. 2005. *Access American History: Building Literacy Through Learning*. Wilmington, MA: Great Source Education Group.

Emerson, Robert, Rachel Fretz, and Linda Shaw. 2011. *Writing Ethnographic Fieldnotes*, 2nd edition. Chicago, IL: University of Chicago Press.

Erickson, Fredrick. 1984. "What Makes School Ethnography 'Ethnographic'?" *Anthropology & Education Quarterly* 15, no. 1, 51–66.

Fahrenthold, D. A. (2016, October 8). "Trump Recorded Having Extremely Lewd Conversation About Women in 2005." *The Washington Post*. October 8, 2016. https://www.washingtonpost.com/politics/trump-recorded-having-extremely-lewd -conversation-about-women-in 2005/2016/10/07/3b9ce776-8cb4-11e6-bf8a-3d268 47eeed4_story.html?utm_term=.e7251fa0806c

Freire, Paulo. 1970. *Pedagogy of the Oppressed*. London: Penguin Books.

Geertz, Clifford. 1973. "Thick Description: Toward an Interpretive Theory of Culture." In *The Interpretation of Culture: Selected Essays*, pp. 3–30. New York, NY: Basic Books.

Gray, Tricia. 2017. "'Hear Us, See Us': Constructing Citizenship in the Margins." Doctoral dissertation, University of Nebraska-Lincoln.

Hatch, J. Amos. 2002. *Doing Qualitative Research in Educational Settings*. Albany, NY: SUNY Press.

Kendall, Brent. "Trump Says Judge's Mexican Heritage Presents 'Absolute Conflict'." *The Wall Street Journal*. June 3, 2016. https://www.wsj.com/articles/donald-trump -keeps-up-attacks-on-judge-gonzalo-curiel-1464911442

Kopan, Tal. "What Donald Trump Has Said About Mexico and Vice Versa." *CNN Politics*. August 31, 2016. http://www.cnn.com/2016/08/31/politics/donald-trump -mexico-statements/

Levine, Peter. 2007. *The Future of Democracy: Developing the Next Generation of American Citizens*. Lebanon, NH: University Press of New England.

Levinson, Meira. 2012. *No Citizen Left Behind*. Cambridge, MA: Harvard University Press.

Merriam, Sharon. 2009. *Qualitative Research: A Guide to Design and Implementation*. San Francisco, CA: Jossey-Bass.

Moll, Luis, Cathy Amanti, Deborah Neff, and Norma Gonzalez. 1992. "Funds of Knowledge for Reaching: Using a Qualitative Approach to Connect Homes and Classrooms." *Theory into Practice* 31, no. 2, 132–141.

Rosaldo, Renato. 1994. "Cultural Citizenship and Educational Democracy." *Cultural Anthropology* 9, no. 3, 402–411.

Rubin, Beth. 2007. "'There's Still Not Justice': Youth Civic Identity Development Amid Distinct School and Community Contexts." *Teachers College Record* 109, no. 2, 449–481.

Santa Ana, Otto. 2002. *Brown Tide Rising: Metaphors of Latinos in Contemporary American Public Discourse*. Austin: University of Texas Press.

Spradley, James. 1979. *The Ethnographic Interview*. New York, NY: Holt, Rinehart and Winston.

Ware, Franita. 2006. "Warm Demander Pedagogy: Culturally Responsive Teaching that Supports a Culture of Achievement for African American Students." *Urban Education* 41, 427–456.

Watson, Wanda, Yolanda Sealey-Ruiz, and Iesha Jackson. 2016. "Daring to Care: The Role of Culturally Relevant Care in Mentoring Black and Latino Male High School Students." *Race, Ethnicity and Education* 19, no. 5, 980–1002.

Wortham, Stanton, Jr., Enrique Murillo, and Edmund Hamann, eds. 2002. *Education in the New Latino Diaspora: Policy and the Politics of Identity*. Westport, CT: Ablex Publishing.

Yosso, Tara. 2005. "Whose Culture Has Capital? A Critical Race Theory Discussion of Community Cultural Wealth." *Race, Ethnicity, and Education* 8, no. 1, 69–91.

Chapter 5

"You Pulled the Chair from Right Under Me!"

How a Black Young Man Disappears from a High School Reading Class

Loukia K. Sarroub

Relational identities in the classroom shape teachers and their students as well as the researchers who study them for the long term. Researchers whose fieldwork is located at "home" simultaneously embody with research participants the past, present, and future interactions on a shared continuum of experience. The collaborative enterprise of fieldwork is relived, retold, remade, and it is always present.

In this chapter, the shared, embodied experience that infused the ethnographic space in situ transformed one's understanding of young people, their teacher, and the researcher. The study was focused on better understanding students' experiences with literacy in high school. Within the context of ethnography and education, it is important to examine carefully teacher and student interaction relationally in connection to the reproduction of social class tropes and gendered identities as well as discourse norms.

Of particular interest was the exploration of literacy learning within the contexts of multiple texts, such as assigned novels and newspapers, standardized tests, school district Reading Graduation Demonstration Exam (RGDE), and students' reading and writing interests. Questions that informed fieldwork included what does "a reading class" mean in high school? What practices constitute such a class, and how do students resist these practices? And, how do relational activities around texts and also between teacher and students create a sense of belonging in connection to reading as an academic home in the classroom?

Adolescents' literacy practices, interaction with teachers and with texts are in part influenced by both their self-perceived and imposed identities (Beach and O'Brien, 2007). Male students, in particular, sometimes become less engaged with literacy as time passes in high school reading classes. How can reading play a more central role in young men's lives such that it engages them rather than alienates them? The dynamics around literacy presented here, especially for young men, whether from the school or home literacy context, seem to defy the notion of a possible commonality.

Three central ideas inform the research in this chapter: how discourse affects students' abilities to be perceived as "literate," the challenge of separating academic accomplishments from personal experience, and the relational interactions that mediate the success of boys in such classrooms. Through the ethnographic study of Reading Ideas, a high school reading intervention class aimed at students who read at grade levels 4–5 was observed during several months. The researcher and the teacher noticed how the young people in the class constructed their identities and managed literal space, and, by analogy, the figurative space of "good student" in a reading class fraught with tension for teenagers who are lumped together because they are perceived to be struggling with reading.

Within a sociocultural perspective in literacy, *literacy identity* is interpreted as a process of socialization and acculturation of particular conventions that recreate and interact with texts from a particular discourse in community. That learners are "becoming literate means more than apprenticeship with texts—it means apprenticeship in particular ways of being" (Kern 2000, 35). When students bring to classrooms their literacy practices as acquired strategies and ways of being literate, alternate and competing discourses encountered in classrooms problematize the "literacy identity" previously practiced and valued.

SHAPING LITERACY IDENTITIES

Hall (2012) identifies a form of identity that summarizes the multiple identities of youth but also characterizes their literacy as "reading identity." Reading identity, Hall (2012) explains, "refers to how capable individuals believe they are in comprehending texts, values they place on reading, and their understandings of what it means to be a particular type of reader within a given context" (369). She argues that students' reading identities are created over time based on their experiences in school and understandings of different identities available.

Furthermore, Heath and McLaughlin (1993) claim that adolescents' identities are not limited to how they view themselves; they are influenced by how adults, media, and school systems have represented them. How adolescents view themselves or are viewed by adults both shape adolescent identities in general and reading identities in particular. Identities stemming from culturally constructed and socially imposed worlds (Holland, Lachicotte Jr., Skinner, and Cain, 2001) thus become a main factor guiding adolescents' interactions with teachers and text in classrooms.

One benefit of ethnographic study lies in the rapport researchers develop with research participants, leading to better understanding them as unique individuals in relational, non-static contexts. For example, students help shape the classroom experience, and Dante, the focus student in this chapter, was a flirtatious, outgoing, rapping Black sophomore whose gregarious personality was always evident in the classroom. He read books to which he could relate, such as *Forged by Fire* by Sharon M. Draper (1997), and always wanted to read aloud, egging others to let him have another reading turn. Dante was removed from class before the semester ended because of his unmanageable behavior and altercations with Ms. Day, his reading teacher. He was earning a C in the class but did not pass the district RGDE.

Ms. Day, a teacher of European ancestry with eight years of experience teaching reading intervention classes and thirty-five years teaching both English and reading classes, worked hard at relating the curriculum to students' lives. Even when students found the RGDE newspaper pieces boring and confusing, Ms. Day helped link the articles to their lives through activities and discussion questions. Ms. Day also seemed open to trying new ideas, adjusting the curriculum when possible to fit students' interests. Clipping out newspaper articles in which students appeared, encouraging students to research books and subjects of their interest, and giving pointers on personal writing done on their initiative were all ways of showing her support. As a result, students seemed to generally respect and like Ms. Day.

Over time, Ms. Day was not only a research participant but also a colleague, engaging in many informal conversations about the reading classes. She and the researcher consulted each other in class and had lively conversations about classroom events, the texts students produced, student interactions, and students who were in trouble academically. They also shared information about Ms. Day's knitting club, Ms. Day's partner's work with community youth, or the antics of family members. Ms. Day was generous with her time, allowing the researcher's university graduate students to observe her reading classes and to learn how to write field notes there, and she also sponsored the school's LGBTQ club after school hours. Outside class, they would sometimes see each other at the grocery store and exchange quick greetings and chats.

THE CLASSROOM CONTEXT

Student and teacher interactions and engagement with literacies in their typical classroom situation were observed, capturing a detailed day-to-day picture of literacy practices and surrounding events, verbalized thoughts, and activities (Emerson, Fretz, and Shaw, 1995). Ms. Day and her students interacted within the literacy curriculum, allowing the researcher to understand students' interactions with reading, other students, and the teacher, and to see how these interactions affected their perceptions of their world and literacy itself. Because Ms. Day often talked informally about classroom activities and interactions, this allowed the researcher to have an immediate insider perspective of the teacher's perceptions, and it was included in daily field notes.

Site and Participants

The class chosen was an inner-city, reading intervention, Reading Ideas, with twenty-one students—seven Black, seven White, and seven Latinos. Of those, seven were male students. There were two English language learners in the class from Iraq and Sudan. All students participated in the free or reduced lunch program. In this high school, 40 percent of all students were on free and/or reduced lunch; 97 percent of those students were in reading classes (Sarroub, 2007). Indeed, this was a high percentage of low-SES students.

An important aspect of this study was that the students had been identified as needing extra instruction in reading according to standardized and placement tests or teacher observations, resulting in placement in that classroom. If they passed Reading Ideas but not the standardized RGDE, they would be placed in the same or a similar reading class again the following semester. Although the class label may have been the same, there were different curricular materials each semester on a four-semester cycle. Over half of the students had been in a similar reading class at least once in previous semesters.

Data Collection

The larger study included several years of ethnographic fieldwork. However, in this reading intervention classroom, field observations occurred during the fall semester and took place approximately three times a week. Video recordings were made one out of every three periods (total of fifteen), and collecting artifacts also occurred simultaneously during this period. Field observation was conducted 47 times with over 400 pages of field notes of the interactions among students, teachers, and curriculum. Artifacts included daily bulletins, worksheets, seating charts, or other classroom materials.

Informal interviews and friendly conversations with the teacher concerning classroom interactions took place throughout the semester. Some examples of student work for grades such as journals and completed worksheets were also collected, along with one student's creative work (poetry, not class related but composed during class). Standardized test results and samples of practice tests along with grade reports were gathered and shed light on how students' works translated to passing class and high-stakes tests determining their academic success or failure.

Upon completion of observations and field notes, catalogs of the interactions observed on the videotapes were developed to identify key teaching and learning moments, and then occurrences were transcribed and micro-analyzed. Field notes were coded with open and focused coding, and a list was generated of almost 450 emerging codes occurring a total of 8,752 times. Those codes were subsequently collapsed into a more compact and manageable list. Not surprisingly, the codes Teacher Telling, Questioning, and Answering, and Student Answering and Questioning occurred most frequently, showing the typical classroom use of the Initiate/Response/Evaluation (Mehan, 1979).

THE CASE OF DANTE

Competing to Read Aloud

Students' desire to read books of their own choosing occurred when they had "reading debates," especially when they read as a class *Forged by Fire* by Sharon M. Draper (1997), a problem novel about a teenage boy who overcomes tragic circumstances of living in poverty and child abuse. Students would argue over who would get to read the book aloud and try to one-up one another by saying things like, "You can't read!" (Dante, field notes, September 30) One example of a reading debate is highlighted in field notes given below (September 16).

"This side don't want to read," Lakeisha said when Ms. Day asked if there is a volunteer on the left side of the room.

"I want to read," Anastasia said.

"Everyone try to prove they can read when they know they *can't*," Dante said.

Ms. Day decided that Samantha should read.

"Maybe we should start at the top of the page," Ms. Day said, then she proceeded to remind students what had been happening in the story up to this point by asking review questions. "What did Gerald [the main character] think when his mom asked him to come live with her?" Ms. Day asks.

"He choked on his food," Dante said.

"Why?" Ms. Day asked.

"He doesn't know her," Samantha said.

"What page we on?" Dante asked, and someone answered him.

"Who says Dante should read?" Dante questioned the class. Tyler, Tamika, and most of the people on the right side and those at the back table raised their hands. Ms. Day tried to calm them down.

"Ms. Day, come on man," Dante pleaded.

"You know what you should do, you should let everyone read," Anastasia said.

"I just want to get through chapter six!" Ms. Day whimpered in a mock crying voice.

Samantha started to read quietly, but Dante continued to interrupt, so she stopped reading. After a few more moments of loud debate among students seated on the right side of the classroom, including Dante, Anastasia noted, "You know, I'm just gonna read," and she started reading at the top of her voice while the others continued arguing. The right side of the room grew quiet almost immediately, and Anastasia stopped reading. Samantha read the first paragraph again, and the room was silent. Maria and Gabriela also read paragraphs. It was Dante's turn to read. "You know I'm just gonna read the rest of the chapter," Dante said. "Yeah, you can split it between you and Anastasia," Ms. Day said firmly.

The central two people arguing for a turn to read were Anastasia, a ninth grade English language learner from Ukraine, and Dante, but several other students expressed interest in reading as well. Dante started to use one-upmanship to jockey for position as reader over Anastasia. Ms. Day selected Samantha rather than either Anastasia or Dante. After Ms. Day asked some comprehension questions, Dante initiated a voting process in order to override Ms. Day's decision.

Dante's next tactic was to plead while Anastasia tried to persuade Ms. Day to allow everyone to read. After Samantha attempted to take control by reading, Dante took the floor by talking over her. Strangely enough, when Anastasia took back the floor, the arguments stopped, and Anastasia seemed surprised. After several students had the opportunity to read, Dante took the floor again, announcing that he would read the rest of the time.

Ms. Day's reaction to this argument suggests some frustration and eventual concession to Dante and Anastasia, the most vocal of the students requesting to read. Through those actions and the multiple ways in which the students attempted to one-up each other, it is apparent that the desire to read this particular book was quite high. It was frustrating to the teacher who struggled to rein in their excitement.

Ms. Day, in revisiting this excerpt of data with the researcher, commented frankly, "But to me this exchange seems like a personal power struggle and a way to take the focus off the task at hand, delaying the reading as well as drawing attention to oneself." Ms. Day was replying to the suggestion that students seemed engaged with reading aloud, which was surprising to see in a high school reading intervention class. It was clear that most students read above the grade level of the intervention meant for students who read at grades four to six. Ms. Day was comfortable disagreeing collegially and perceptively with the researcher. Both agreed that this event suggested that the students were comfortable in carrying out the argument and had a strong sense of belonging in this reading class.

Ms. Day also noted that some of the students were involved in Special Education services, and certain conditions, particularly behavior disorders, influenced their interactions with one another and texts. This was an important reminder that classroom interaction is always mediated by intersecting contexts, some of which are not immediately discernable to researchers. Power struggle or no, students were genuinely engaged with the book and demanded turns to read. Ms. Day and the researcher collaboratively engaged in conversations together to better understand what was meaningful to students in the reading class such that Ms. Day could promote further engagement.

"GETTIN' ALL RACIAL"

Race was a factor in how students perceived power figures in the school. For example, Dante was upset to find that the protagonist is White rather than Black in the book *Mississippi Trial, 1955* by Chris Crowe (2003).

> At 9:30, Dante said, "So, Ms. Day, this is a White boy speakin' in the book."
> "What?" Ms. Day asked, genuinely surprised.
> "His grandpa had the cotton field. Why can't it be about a Black boy?"
> "Good question," Ms. Day said.
> "Thought the way you described it was 'bout a Black boy," Dante said almost accusingly.
> "I did too," Ms. Day noted. "I think the important thing is for people to get it. Maybe that is why the author had the narrator be a White boy."
> "Now you gettin' all racial," Dante said.
> "No, that just might be why the author wrote it that way. I have others if you want a different one," Ms. Day offered.
> "Nah," Dante said.

For Dante, the book had less appeal because the protagonist's race was not what he believed it to be, and his taking offense that it was not about a Black boy shows that he probably chose it because he thought he identified racially with the protagonist. Ms. Day admitted that she had thought the book's protagonist was Black, and her response suggests that it is important to figure out who is speaking. Ultimately, Ms. Day let Dante decide if he would rather read a book with a Black boy protagonist.

Interestingly, students perceived a race gap between themselves and Ms. Day as exemplified in Dante's talk. Dante grew excited and began to talk quickly in Black vernacular speech and also used slang in this next field note excerpt:

> "What do you think selling shoes would be like?" Ms. Day asked.
> "Boring," Marissa said.
> "Fun, cuz you know you're getting people kicks they like. . . " Dante talked quickly until Mia interrupted him.
> "I don't think she understands you, Dante—she's White," Mia said dryly.

Ms. Day was aware that the students were interested in protagonists and resources related to their social, cultural, racial, and ethnic identities. For example, on October 17, Ms. Day shared a newspaper written in Spanish for which Marissa's mother wrote, and on October 21, she shared many new books, seven out of ten of which, she observed, "have minorities as protagonists." Ms. Day attempted to bridge the gap between students and school discourse, actively trying to create a home space wherein race relations was also the topic of conversation in this classroom because of students' strong identification with it.

Although the ratio of boys to girls was originally only one to two at the beginning of the semester, that ratio dwindled to one to six by the end of the semester. Boys often absent from the classroom left largely because of behavior problems or due to excessive voluntary skipping of class. By the end of the semester, only two boys actually took the semester final, Juan and Gerald. There were five boys who gradually left the class.

Leaving school occurred despite the fact that at least two of the boys showed genuine interest in reading material of their own choosing. Ms. Day remarked that "skipping seems addictive." Many students began to skip after the first semester. "As the work piles up from days missed and grades go down, students give up and stop coming all together," she said. She and the researcher shared looks of disappointment each time they discovered that students skipped class. Dante argued many times about reading aloud a book he liked, and Tyler independently researched the background of the books he read. In contrast, only two girls left the class, one because her family moved away and the other for unknown reasons.

HOW DANTE STOPPED READING IN CLASS

One day in class in late October, Ms. Day jokingly stood behind Dante's chair as he was about to sit and pulled it from under him. He fell backward to the floor, hitting the floor hard on his bottom. There was a moment of utter silence as Ms. Day looked aghast, her eyes wide as she remembered the video recording and said that she never expected him to fall down. She said she thought he had seen her pull the chair back and that it was a joke.

Then, as she looked at Dante, he jumped up and accused her of purposefully making fun of him by pulling his chair from under him because he was Black. *You pulled the chair from right under me!* he yelled. His pride was hurt, and his trust in Ms. Day plummeted at a critical moment for him as a "struggling reader" in her class. The researcher remembers not being able to look their way because she was paralyzed by the embarrassment Dante felt at being bested by his teacher, thus becoming the butt of her joke. She could not make eye contact with Ms. Day because she could also feel Ms. Day's consternation in having made such public mistake with all students watching.

Dante returned to class one more time after this incident and then disappeared altogether. Ms. Day often commented afterward at school that she regretted her innocent joke because she had developed a real connection with Dante even though he was difficult in class. The researcher was never sure how to respond other than to agree with a supportive nod. In the grocery store or in the community, this moment was etched in the minds of both the researcher and the teacher and was relived every time they saw each other. Ms. Day did not talk about it outside school, yet this interaction continued to be pivotal in understanding how young people, especially young men, lose their sense of belonging in classes such as these and how well-meaning teachers inadvertently foster alienation.

DANTE AS THE PROTAGONIST IN
THE RESEARCH STUDY

A key finding in this study that linked the teacher and researcher across years in their home spaces in the field was that of the protagonist and identification with the protagonist (the agent in the story, the agent in one's own story) as being key to engaging students and changing their "reading identities." Students mostly identified with protagonists like themselves as they engaged with reading. Dante, when the chair was pulled from under him, became the protagonist of his own classroom story of the Black boy who is inadvertently treated in an unjust way by his teacher's humorous intent.

Students' identification with protagonists of their ethnicity, race, socioeconomic status, age, and gender affected their ability to accept the literacy curriculum, which they resisted when there was a discrepancy. The deeply embarrassing moment that Dante experienced as a Black youth and as reader in the intervention class led him to believe that his teacher was the antagonist in his story, someone who violated what Noddings (1984) has characterized as a caring ethic "rooted in receptivity, relatedness, and responsiveness" (2). The students' resistance to the curriculum and the teacher often had a negative impact on the students' success in the class and on their ability to remain in the classroom.

A recurring question remains regarding why boys are unable to adapt as well as girls in school to reading classes. Rowan, Knobel, Bigum, and Lankshear (2002) explore the fact that while gender affects success in schools, other aspects such as low socioeconomic status and previous success combine together to create "a network of disadvantage" for boys (24). For example, the boys did not see themselves as being positioned by the teacher or the texts in the curriculum as legitimate students. Furthermore, social class and its constitutive discourses emphasize differences in schools and are perpetuated by continuously linking "struggling reader" with low socioeconomic background, boys with low literacy achievement, and lack of connection with well-intended teachers.

While reminiscing some years after Dante's chair was pulled from under him, Ms. Day noted one day in the school hallway, "Higher level students have a classroom persona that they turn on and you don't get to know those students as well. The students [low socioeconomic status students] wear their emotions more at the surface and can't turn that off. For kids in poverty, it's all about relationships." This shared insight demonstrates how "home" is reinvented between the researcher and the research participants with every new "ah ha," thus informing the relational understandings founded in educational ethnography that lead to a sense of belonging in the field.

REFERENCES

Beach, Rick and David O'Brien. 2007. "Adopting Reader and Writer Stances in Understanding and Producing Texts." In *Secondary School Literacy: What Research Reveals for Classroom Practice*, edited by Leslie S. Rush, Jonathan A. Eakle, and Allen, Berger, pp. 217–242. Urbana, IL: NCTE.

Crow, Chris. 2003. *Mississippi Trial, 1955.* Speak Press.

Draper, Sharon. 1997. *Forged by Fire.* New York, NY: Atheneum Books.

Emerson, Robert M., Rachel Fretz, and Linda L. Shaw. 2011. *Writing Ethnographic Field Notes, 2nd Edition.* Chicago, IL: The University of Chicago Press.

Hall, Leigh. 2012. "Rewriting Identities: Creating Spaces for Students and Teachers to Challenge the Norms of What It Means to be a Reader in School." *Journal of Adolescent & Adult Literacy* 55, no. 5, 368–373.

Heath, Shirley Brice and Milbrey W. McLaughlin. 1993. *Identity and Inner-City Youth: Beyond Ethnicity and Gender.* New York, NY: Teachers College Press.

Kern, Richard. 2000. *Literacy and Language Teaching.* Oxford, UK: Oxford University Press.

Mehan, Hugh. 1979. *Learning Lessons: Social Organization in the Classroom.* Cambridge, MA: Harvard University Press.

Noddings, Nell. 1984. *Caring: A Feminine Approach to Ethics and Moral Education.* Berkeley, CA: University of California Press.

Rowan, Leonie, Michele Knobel, Chris Bigum, and Colin Lankshear. 2001. *Boys, Literacies and Schooling: The Dangerous Territories of Gender-based Literacy Reform.* Buckingham, PA: Open University Press.

Sarroub, Loukia K. 2007. "Seeking Refuge in Literacy from a Scorpion Bite." *Ethnography and Education 2*, no. 3, 365–380.

Chapter 6

Gaining Access to Students' Informal Conversations with Peers

An Explorative Approach on Educational Research and Staging of Recording Devices

Charlotta Rönn

During a lesson, it can be that you sit together and talk to a peer about just anything. Then you see the teacher approaching and you swap and start to talk about the task instead. Just to show the teacher that you are involved. (Alexandra, interview, last year of compulsory school, 2018)

Fifteen-year-old Alexandra recounts how she and her peers, in order to please and impress their teachers, deliberately changed the topic of their conversations when the teacher was within earshot. Their intention was to provide the teachers a touched-up version of their doings in order to give a better impression of their interactions to the teacher. Hence, what a teacher, or researcher, in a classroom overhears may differ significantly from the students' more authentic conversations when talking with friends.

This chapter describes a research design embracing fieldwork with four months of participant observation of students at a Swedish junior high school, followed by two weeks of explorative audiovisual recordings during lessons, and, lastly, interviews with eighteen students. As Illeris (2008) and Packer and Goicoechea (2000) highlight in their study, one of the many unspoken standards at school to which students adapt is that it is better to remain silent, instead of asking questions directed at the classroom teacher when they do not understand. The data collection focused on student-teacher interaction, and also allowed access to the students' informal talk when dealing with lesson-related tasks with peers. This particular interactional behavior motivated research on how to gain access to students' informal interactions with their friends and their collaborative coping strategies when doing schoolwork in a local context.

AN OUTLINE OF THE ETHNOGRAPHIC METHODOLOGY

In ethnographic research in the social sciences, participant observation is one of the most central methods, where the researcher aims to study people's everyday lives by participating with them. In the field of education, there is extensive classroom research about teachers and teacher-student interactions, such as spoken discourse in the classroom context. These discourses are mainly part of formal, public discourses, which may be heard by others in the classroom.

Traditionally, as Heath (1986) describes, the teacher's talking time in the classroom follows the structure of initiation–response–evaluation or initiation–response–feedback, where the teacher with his/her power engages with students through steering and prompting spoken responses and defining what is regarded as correct. Contrary to this, the students' talk with friends in the classroom is often quieter and not meant for everyone to hear, nor do they usually know the answers to lesson-related issues beforehand. Due to the inherent limits of overhearing the students' quiet, informal talk during lessons, little is known about how students informally communicate and respond to their assignments.

There is little educational research on students' discourse from the student-participant perspective, including work that captures the natural flow of students' informal conversations with peers. Therefore the purpose of the study was twofold: to explore how to approach *accessing* students' informal communications and learning-related informal dialogues in the classroom, and also to demonstrate examples of the structure and content of the students' informal conversations. In doing so, there were three objectives: first, to minimize the researcher's interference with the students' familiar context of peer-to-peer conversations; second, to prevent the researcher from falling into a familiar teacher's role in a shared context; and, third, to explore a research design that gained access to the students' quiet interactions with peers.

Gaining Access to the Students' Informal Conversations

It is not possible to conduct participant observations without, to some extent, intervening in the development of processes. The metaphor that the researcher should try to be "a fly on the wall" is often used to describe an *ideal* research observation, where the researcher has no, or little, impact on the research participants, and the participants are unaware of being observed. The research participants' awareness of being recorded can be regarded in relation to the Hawthorne effect, which generally means that being aware that one is being observed alters behavior. Heath, Hindmarsh, and Luff (2010) argue that being recorded with audiovisual equipment may change the participants' behaviors to some extent.

Classroom research is traditionally teacher-focused. However, if audiovisual recordings focus on the teacher-student interaction, there is in general but one person talking at a time, usually following the initiation–response–evaluation or initiation–response–feedback, and the teacher regulates the spoken word and defines what is correct (Heath, 1986). These louder dialogues are easy to record. In such teacher-student turn taking, Macbeth (1994) notes that all the students are aware that the teacher knows the answer to the posted question and the correct response is already "in the room" (317).

In student-focused audiovisual research, a small group of students is often the focus and placed apart from classmates to decrease disrupting background sounds. This facilitates recording one topic at a time but hinders the students' spontaneous flow of the topics they have chosen for themselves. Tie-clip microphones are sometimes used and attached to a few selected students inside the classroom. With these staging designs, it might be difficult for individuals to be oblivious of the attached recording gear, which may alter the students' spontaneous talk with peers. Some students might interact more with those wearing tie-clip microphones while others might avoid talking to them.

The Classroom as a Familiar Space and Students' "Backstage"

The Swedish school context is considered a familiar context for the students in the class, as well as for the researcher. The explorative research design was implemented among students (fourteen-year-olds) at a Swedish municipal junior high school in an eighth-grade class. The school's merit rating was approximately 10 percent below the national average. During the introduction of the research to the class, the students learned the researcher was Swedish, grew up in Sweden, and studied at Swedish schools and universities. Moreover, they learned that she had lived in Morocco for approximately a decade and had worked there as a teacher. The students were told that if adults knew more about how students talked and helped their peers informally, it might provide important knowledge on how to improve the teachers' teaching in the future, thus making it easier for students to learn at school.

The local school context in general and the classroom in particular are regarded as familiar contexts for a variety of reasons. First, carrying out the study in an eighth-grade class implied that many students had been in class together for several years and had time to develop cultural patterns, such as adapting strategies in doing schoolwork. Second, the students had been in the same classroom as their "home" classroom for most of their school subjects in eighth and ninth grades when the interviews were conducted. Third, the researcher's former teaching experiences with similar age-groups and classrooms fostered familiarity in the research setting.

The research design and, in particular, the staging of the recording devices aimed at getting close to the students' informal spaces and social relations. The more informal context with which students are familiar in the classroom could be compared to Goffman's ([1959] 1990) dramaturgical approach to people's interactions and "face-work." In the theater metaphor, people's behaviors are considered as either enacted on the "frontstage" or the "backstage" of social life. Social interaction corresponds to performing as actors on a stage for an audience while also watching as if part of an audience. The metaphor lends itself to the ordinary classroom context during lessons.

Applying Goffman's metaphor to the classroom setting and the often loud and formal school discourse developed and maintained around a teacher, who traditionally engages in lecturing, could be regarded as the "frontstage." Teachers and students share this stage. However, the students' quiet social interactions with peers can be regarded as the "backstage," where they learn the "line" for the frontstage, prepare their performances, and then prevent the teacher from catching glimpses of them. Thus, though the formal classroom space was familiar to the students and the researcher, it is less familiar for the researcher to cross over into the informal backstage spaces of the classroom, spaces which are created by discursive registers or speech genres used in quiet peer-to-peer interactions.

Concerning the researcher's positionality related to field (home) work, two conscious decisions were made to hinder the researcher from falling into a familiar teacher role inside the classroom. She distanced herself from her habitual teacher's role and simultaneously ensured that students would not regard her as a representative of "teachers" in the formal frontstage classroom setting. During the participant observations, she was seated behind the students. Second, she did not answer the students' lesson-related questions. Being seated behind the students and not responding to their questions was awkward for someone with previous teaching experience, and it was a constant reminder to distance herself from her usual role during the field (home) work.

There were several reasons for not responding to the students' questions. Answering questions would have taken the focus from observing and writing field notes, and it would have restrained the researcher from trying to be "a fly on the wall." Moreover, answering the questions would have encouraged students to turn to the researcher for help at the expense of the students' conversations with peers, which was the research topic. It might have competed with and caused friction between the teachers and the researcher. In hindsight, deviating from the teacher's role proved to be a winning strategy, though it slowly but surely became apparent that the students almost never turned to their teachers after having turned, in vain, to the researcher for help. The reluctance to turn to the teachers could have gone unnoticed if the researcher had not restrained from stepping into the familiar teacher role and responded to the students' questions.

Ethical Aspects of the Research Design and the Access to the Site

Getting access to the students' quiet, backstage social interactions would not have been possible without recording devices, and, in accordance with the Swedish Research Councils' principles, informed written consent was requested from the students and their guardians. The researcher chose not to stand behind the camcorders with a headset, even though listening to the students' backstage conversations in real time would have rendered it possible to pose follow-up questions regarding their conversations on the same day. The rationale for not doing so was that during the initial participant observations, a fragment of an informal conversation between peers had been overheard by the researcher, but when she tried to ask a student follow-up questions, the student had instantly denied what had been said. The researcher concluded that when the students became familiar with having the researcher and recording devices in the classroom, they would be oblivious to them. However, her interpretation was that the students thought it was permissible for her to listen to their quiet, informal conversations as long as she did not know what they discussed during her stay at their school.

The students were regularly reminded that, of the recorded informal conversations, it was only the ones related to schoolwork and learning that would be in the focus of the research and analysis and not talk concerning leisure time and private life. During the transcription phase, it turned out that some recorded parts were private and personal, such as when some boys talked about when to get married, or when some girls talked about their dislike for a teacher, which generated a feeling of peeping into a keyhole. Listening to these conversations in real time would have created a massive power imbalance in the researcher's everyday encounters with the students. Thus, the researcher had to be oblivious of the activities backstage for as long as the fieldwork lasted.

The Regional Ethical Review Board (in Umeå, Sweden) reviewed the study and approved the informed consent form. No one withdrew their consent. The following year, when the interviews were conducted, the students in the class had turned fifteen years of age and were allowed to give their own written informed consent, even though some students checked with their guardians before they signed the forms.

The Classroom Context and the Staging of the Recording Devices

In a goal-and-result oriented school context such as the one in Sweden, students regulate themselves (Carlgren, 2015) and whole class teaching becomes less frequent. Self-regulated learning increases when students work independently on tasks and plan their efforts and time management. In the Swedish school context, therefore, the teachers' roles are less authoritarian compared to those of other countries, such as France and Morocco. The students in the study often turned to peers and were very helpful to each other, and also often moved around in the classroom and talked to peers sitting farther away—unless it was the teacher who led the lessons. This emerged in the participant observations, and the audiovisual recordings revealed a complex flow of the students' informal schoolwork-related conversations in mathematics, science, social studies, Swedish, and English as a foreign language.

The research design—in particular, its explorative staging of the recording devices—allowed access to students' informal, quiet conversations. Moreover, the intention was to reduce the students' awareness of being recorded and explore the natural flow of all students' whereabouts in the classroom. Consequently, the staging rendered it possible to reveal the knowledge of the students' coping with schoolwork, comprising *how* they communicated, *with whom* they talked, and also *what* they discussed with friends during lessons.

During the participant observations and the *initial* audiovisual recordings, the activities in the whole classroom were in focus. The classroom was covered with discreetly positioned recording devices. Recording all of the students' quiet conversations in the entire, noisy environment of the classroom through quality sound recordings was challenging, and several arrangements were attempted and modified prior to finding the optimal placement of the recording devices.

An explorative research design was applied, focusing on one rear part of the classroom where all of the students occasionally went. The students were not aware that the *final* audiovisual recordings only covered the rear corner. To reinforce the impression that activities in the *whole* classroom were in focus, there were discrete recording apparatuses in the window section of the classroom, as well, but these were considered by the researcher as a mock recording. Had the students been aware of the focus on the corner, it might have altered their movements and the topics of their conversations.

Eight students had their seats in this quieter rear corner, and all but two students sometimes went there, so the front camcorder was adjusted to include the two students who did not go to the rear corner. Discreet placement of the recording devices facilitated access to the natural flows of interaction between friends and their quieter and informal conversations. Afterward, it was revealed that the students seated in this corner had passing grades in all school subjects, which could explain why almost all students occasionally went there.

The front main camcorder and the rear window camcorder were placed in the window corners. They seemed to cover all desks but were, in fact, zoomed out to comprise only the activities in the rear corner. When the four students in the front row turned around to classmates behind them, or students walked to the corner facing their friends, their faces were recorded by the rear window camcorder. Four external microphones connected to the main recording devices were suspended from the ceiling between the pair of students in the two rear rows. The wires were passed through the ceiling and were kept out of sight.

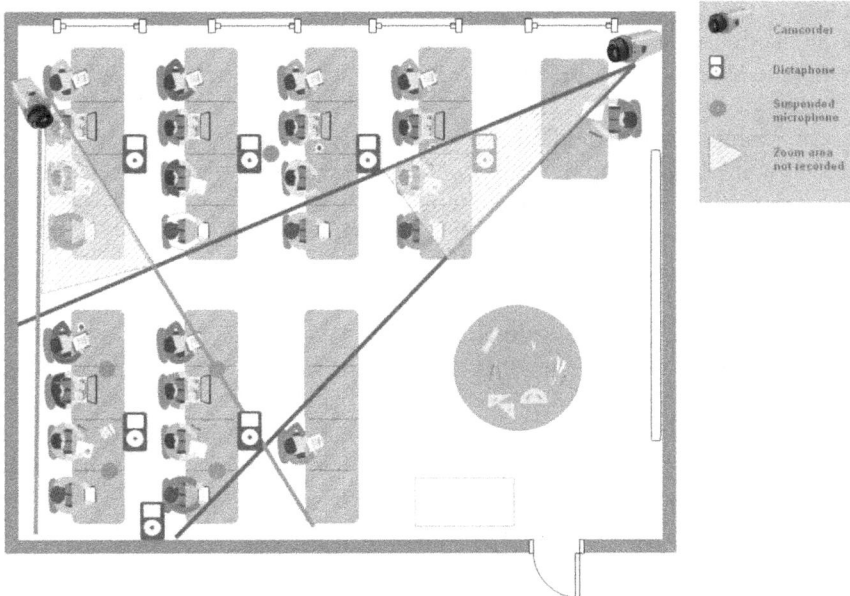

Figure 6.1   The Passive Staging of Recording Devices with a Main Focus on the Rear Corner of the Classroom with Two Camcorders, Seven Dictaphones, as well as Five External Microphones Suspended from the Ceiling. *Source*: Charlotta Rönn.

Several Dictaphones were used and taped on the edges of the students' desks as a reinforced backup for recording. This kept the desk surfaces clear of recording equipment. All of the devices were close to the students but out of their direct sight and not attached to their clothing, which preserved the classroom's familiar "home" environment. In addition, a small GoPro camera was attached to the ceiling to capture the desks from above, including where the students were in their books and gestures that otherwise could be hidden behind peers.

The passive staging with no one standing behind the camcorders prevented the researcher from actively zooming in and out, changing angles, or listening to the students' conversations in real time, which, to some extent, was a disadvantage. However, it kept the researcher out of sight and made the camcorders less conspicuous. The researcher mainly sat out of sight in the middle of the rear part of the classroom. From the students' perspectives, not having the researcher or the recording devices in sight facilitated them being able to ignore that they were recorded.

The Students' Informal Conversations with Classmates

A wide variety of task-related topics emerged from the collected data of the students' quiet communication with friends. They made suggestions for how to proceed with a given task, posed questions, and searched for affirmation of the procedures. The students sometimes corrected peers' written tasks in Swedish or English and occasionally wrote assignments for their classmates in, for example, social studies. They sometimes professed uncertainty about how to write down the correct answer for particular exercises, made counting errors in mathematics, and dictated to peers the answers to assigned questions in English. The students occasionally struggled to formulate problems (e.g., from the course book) and to identify the correct responses to the questions and problems.

In some of these conversations, some of the students did not know how to proceed, but they reasoned together and sometimes arrived at a solution. Even though students did turn to teachers for help with various matters and took for granted that the teachers knew the answers to questions or procedures, all three data collection methods disclosed that students were reluctant to ask teachers for help and preferred to turn to peers instead. However, one disadvantage for students when turning to peers for help seemed to be the uncertainty of whether the one to whom they turned actually knew how to proceed and could help.

In this study, the use of audiovisual devices helped to illuminate one complex collaborative strategy the students had developed for mathematics when working on tasks to which they did not have the answer key. During a lesson in mathematics, where the students were expected to work independently in their books, Madeleine started to calculate an exercise on her own but was uncertain whether she had correctly understood the problem: "With how many percent has the price increased if it increased from 150 SEK to 300 SEK?" Madeleine turned to Mona, who was sitting next to her, for help. Mona had not yet completed the task herself but tried to help. She counted, used the calculator, and reached a result of "1," and then tried to explain the answer. However, a moment of uncertainty followed wherein the girls doubted whether the answer was correct. Madeleine said, "Or, should I ask . . ." and looked up at the teacher who was few meters away, but chose not to address him. Mona continued trying to help, searching to apply another strategy to solve the problem and got the same result: "1." Madeleine was not convinced it was correct.

Instead of suggesting that they ask the teacher, Mona directed Madeleine to another girl: "Or, you can check it with Nour and see what she has done." Madeleine turned to Nour, who, like Mona, had not yet done the exercise, but they discussed it, tried to solve it together, and arrived at the same answer as Mona reached twice. Then, they realized that "1" was equal to 100 percent. It was not until this point that Madeleine turned to the teacher and got his attention as he approached her. The following louder conversation regarding the same exercise took place:

"Patrick, in this one (pause) are you to take the difference," Madeleine said. (Pause)

"Uh-uh," Patrick answered.

"The difference is 150; divided in 150," Madeleine continued.

"Uh-uh," Patrick responded.

"And that is equal to 1—which is 100 percent," Madeleine stated.

"YES!" Patrick said.

Thus, after three supportive interactions from two classmates, Madeleine eventually turned to the teacher, but rather than asking him for help, she *told* him not only how to proceed but also how to interpret the answer. The teacher answered affirmatively to the strategy as well as the numbers. Madeleine showed the teacher that she knew how to proceed, demonstrating her ability to do so without his help. The analysis of the recorded data indicated that Madeleine actually used her peers as teachers when she did not understand. Contrary to this, she did not turn to the teacher for help when she struggled but turned to him only when she understood how to do the problem and explained it to him.

The example illustrates that the audiovisual recordings made it possible to follow the students' natural flow of interaction, including to whom they turned and *what* they talked about. A picture emerges showing that several peers could be involved, in turn, in the same student's problem-solving rather than ask the teacher and show a lack of understanding. Thus, one finding is that the students developed complex social and intellectual practices in acquiring and providing support and also eagerly showing their knowledge to the teacher after talking with their classmates. The teacher and researcher were unaware that Madeleine had already attempted the same task several times in quiet, backstage conversations with several friends before she addressed the teacher in the formal frontstage and louder conversation.

One reason the students avoided turning to the teachers for help, according to the interviews, was the embarrassment that ensued when everyone in the class knew that they had not understood the math, which was revealed by the teachers' compelling loud explanations. Madeleine emphasizes this when she says, "[The teachers] don't think about it as we do. They think that they are there to help us. But, we think it's embarrassing that others will hear that you haven't understood how to do [the exercise]." Implicit in the comment is that students turn to their friends in class because the conversations are quiet and not embarrassing. Drawing on Goffman ([1959] 1990), the teacher's position in the classroom's public frontstage kept the pupils from showing they had not understood. In the example from the lesson in mathematics, Madeleine literally learned "the lines" backstage with her friends before she showed the teacher in the frontstage that she *had* understood.

The students' helpfulness toward peers, their unwillingness to turn to the teacher, and their systematic and complex social and intellectual practices, prevented them from exposing their uncertainty or lack of ability to the teacher. Using Goffman's theater metaphor, one can demonstrate that the girls' quiet conversations could be regarded as the classroom's backstage, wherein Madeleine, Mona, and Nour united in complex social practices to prepare performances for the classroom's public space, such as the formal questioning communication with the teacher. Alexandra's introductory comment to the chapter also illustrates that the students have a second familiar context that they solely share with peers but not with the teachers. Implementing audiovisual research facilitated access to their otherwise secret conversations.

There was an unspoken agreement among the three girls not to involve the teacher. Illeris (2008) and Packer and Goicoechea (2000) had similar findings in their studies when they discovered that students adapt to unspoken standards at school, such as not asking teachers questions when they do not understand the assigned material. However, instead of remaining silent, they turn to friends. If the described interaction among the girls had been observed solely by a participating researcher and/or a teacher and had not been recorded, it would have seemed as though Madeleine merely checked with the teacher that she was right. The recording allowed for the complex backstage strategies involving the efforts of a set of friends to be observed. Thus, the audiovisual recordings uncovered the students' more private and quieter "home" space in the classroom.

SUMMARY

The essence of ethnographic research can be described as devoting a long time in the research site and striving to get access to research participants' perspectives, often through multiple data collection methods. The explorative staging of the recording devices in the classroom was one main factor in obtaining access to the flow of nearly all students' quiet and informal conversations. Goffman's theater metaphor allows a better understanding of students' informal conversations, which could be regarded as the backstage. They prepared "the lines" for the frontstage, such as the formal and loud conversations with the teachers. The findings show that the interactions with which teachers might engage with the students, and also overhear, were often different from the students' perspectives of the same interactions.

The access to the students' backstage revealed a profound reluctance to turn to the teacher for help. Students did prepare their "lines" for the encounters with the teachers' frontstage, as Madeleine, Mona, and Nour did in resolving the mathematics problem or as Alexandra's vignette suggests at the beginning of the chapter. What the students proved to the teacher was an *individual*'s mastery of the exercise. Turning to the teacher was a third choice and one they used only when they knew how to calculate the answer. Hence, the teacher's frontstage perspective during the interaction with the students could lead to misconstruing the students' abilities and understandings, seeing the products of the students' achievements rather than their processes of getting there. Consequently, the teacher might not be able to provide the necessary support.

Overall, the research design for this study could be adapted and applied to other classroom research sites. If permission for carrying out video recording cannot be approved, the audiovisual recordings might be limited to audio recordings only. As observation is a hub in ethnographic research and in accessing research participants' perspectives, audiovisual recordings can be used as an effective tool when doing fieldwork at "home".

REFERENCES

Carlgren, Ingrid. 2015. *Kunskapsstrukturer och undervisningspraktiker.* Gothenburg: Daidalos.

Goffman, Erving. (1959) 1990. *The Presentation of Self in Everyday Life.* London: Penguin.

Hammersley, Martyn and Paul Atkinson. (1983) 1993. *Ethnography —Principles in Practice.* London: Routledge.

Heath, Cristian, Jon Hindmarsh, and Paul Luff. 2010. *Video in Qualitative Research— Analysing Social Interaction in Everyday Life.* London: SAGE Publications Ltd.

Heath, Shirley B. 1986. "What No Bedtime Story Means: Narrative Skills at Home and School." In *Language Socialization across Cultures*, edited by B. Schieffelin and E. Ochs, pp. 97–124. Cambridge: Cambridge University Press.

Illeris, Knud. 2008. *How We Learn—Learning and Non-learning in School and Beyond.* New York, NY: Routledge.

Macbeth, Douglas. 1994. "Classroom Encounters with the Unspeakable: 'Do You See, Danelle?'" *Discourse Processes,* 17, no. 2, 311–335.

Packer, Martin J. and Jessie Goicoechea. 2007. "Sociocultural and Constructivist Theories of Learning: Ontology, Not Just Epistemology." *Educational Psychologist,* 35, no. 4, 227–241.

Swedish Research Council. 2017. *Good Research Practice.* Stockholm: Vetenskapsrådet.

Chapter 7

Home and Away

Crafting an Engaged Ethnography of Textile and Entrepreneurship Training

Claire Nicholas and Surin Kim

This chapter centers on a co-designed crafts and entrepreneurship workshop series, as well as an ethnographic and qualitative study of the series that was initiated by the authors and community partners in their "home" context. The workshop series emerged from a partnership between two university-based researchers (the chapter authors), several local community organizations, and multiple campus-based units, that provided both space and staff time to assist with the workshop development and implementation. The project strove to develop a framework informed by participatory action research models in the sense that workshop concept, curricular content, and methods of studying and reflecting on the pedagogy and workshop experiences were undertaken in concert with local partners with varying degrees and forms of involvement (Greenwood, Whyte, and Harkavy, 1993; Hemment, 2007; Low and Merry, 2010; Ortner, 2019).

In what follows, the authors consider how this type of engaged educational research project presents methodological and ethical advantages as well as dilemmas in terms of proximity and familiarity along with distance and difference in relation to the identities and roles of researchers, partners, and workshop participants. Ultimately, the project was both enhanced and complicated by individual and institutional identities and positions, thus troubling the conventional binary distinction between "home" or "foreign" research settings with regard to researcher positionality.

The workshop series, referred to here as "Artisan Entrepreneurs" (a pseudonym), began with the following objective in mind: to foster cross-cultural exchange and social and economic connections between immigrant and refugee communities as well as long-term residents of the American Midwestern university town where the researchers are based. The programming was designed to foster these connections via the collaborative making of textile-related crafts. The project also sought to provide training in entrepreneurship and to spark relationships and ideas that would ultimately contribute to the "micro-ecology" of entrepreneurship for local immigrant and refugee communities.

The program was structured as a two-phased workshop series. It began with three crafts-based sessions during which participants worked together with mentors to create textile projects that took advantage of existing participant skillsets. The projects were also designed to allow for maximum personalization that would generate objects amenable to the development of products like those sold on marketplaces such as Etsy (an online DIY and craft marketplace). The second phase of the three entrepreneurship workshops extended the products, skills, and relationships created during the first phase in sessions aimed at launching viable microenterprises using the framework of human-centered design. Objects created in the workshops were later presented in a public exhibit in collaboration with key partners and a local museum.

Alongside the training program itself, the researchers sought to gauge the outcomes of the workshop series through pre- and post-workshop surveys, two post-workshop group interviews, field notes, electronic communication among researchers and partners, and a post-project "debrief" conversation between the two researchers. Pre- and post-workshop questionnaires captured snapshots of participants' skill level, educational background, demographic information, attitudes and perception toward different cultural groups, and hopes and fears for the project (Bradburn et al., 2004). Post-workshop group interviews sought both individual and collective reflections on workshop experiences and plans for future projects or business ideas. Interviews also provided evidence of the extent to which new relationships across cultural contexts were formed.

Field notes and electronic communication were mostly useful in reconstructing and documenting the day-to-day aspects of organizing and running the workshops. They included some discussion of the expected roles of various project partners. Taken as a whole, the analysis of these data enabled revision and publication of a facilitator's handbook to enable replication and expansion of the program beyond the pilot workshop site.

BEGINNINGS: PROXIMITY, RESEARCH DESIGN, AND ACCESS

This section focuses on the ways in which the authors' own multiplex identities and positionalities both facilitated and hindered the research process.

Some educational and personal background information is useful to situate the discussion. One researcher, a White American cisgender woman, who was married and visibly pregnant during the time of the workshops, was trained in cultural anthropology and had previously conducted research on artisanal handicrafts in Morocco. Her academic appointment was in the Department of Textiles, Merchandising, and Fashion Design, with a focus on teaching and mentoring students in material culture, textile, and quilt studies.

The other researcher, a South Korean unmarried cisgender woman and permanent U.S. resident with no children at the time of writing, had completed an MBA at a prestigious Ivy League institution in the area of entrepreneurial management. She had worked in a private tech company context before beginning her position at the university. Her institutional location and position description involved university extension (a particularity of U.S. land-grant institutions) working with and for underserved minorities and women in the state.

The objective in recounting these demographic dimensions of the researchers' identities is to highlight what Kirin Narayan's (1993) oft-cited work on "native anthropologists" also stresses, namely that "a person may have many strands of identification available, strands that may be tucked into the open or stuffed out of sight" (673). These "strands" of identity are of course tucked, stuffed, knotted, or unraveled—to push the textile metaphor further—in the context of relationships unfolding in real time and over time. In the case of the development of this project, these multi-strand identities were activated in the process of forming the partnerships that were integral to the development and implementation of the workshops, along with the ongoing work of building rapport with workshop participants.

At the outset of the project development, both university-based researchers leveraged personal and professional networks to reach out to potential community and institutional partners. The cultural anthropologist, who currently teaches in a material culture and quilt studies program, was able to explore possible partnerships for the workshop series because of previous collaborations and professional or personal relationships with staff of a university-affiliated museum. The museum also permitted participant recruitment for the workshops among museum volunteers (with a very active membership of about eighty) and facilitated contact with the president of a local quilt guild, who later served as a craft mentor. In other words, this professional familiarity constituted by a shared interest and background in craft and textiles was critical in cementing the partnership with both the museum and the local quilt guild, and it proved important in gaining access to potential workshop participants.

Similarly, the entrepreneurship researcher relied upon existing professional and personal networks to connect with a community organization that serves the members of the local immigrant and refugee population. This organization later became the project's key partner in terms of communicating with and recruiting potential workshop participants. In this particular case, existing relationships with members of the community organization's advisory board were instrumental in helping the university researchers connect with and present the kernel of the project idea to the leadership of this extremely busy nonprofit organization. Like the entrepreneurship researcher, board members were colleagues and immigrants (though not from Korea) whose academic work dealt with underserved minority and immigrant communities across the region.

For both researchers, then, the fact of being situated in a familiar context allowed them to rely on previously established relationships to gain access more easily to potential partners and research participants. This can be contrasted to the disciplinary paradigm wherein a foreign anthropologist arrives in a relatively unknown setting where trust-building requires more effort up front. Reliance on established relationships in the "home" context also mitigated the potential of this kind of endeavor (both the workshop and the associated research project) to be treated as "foreign." As discussed later in the chapter, this created some false assumptions of understanding and proximity.

BUILDING RAPPORT: IDENTITIES ASCRIBED AND ACHIEVED

In a different way, the researchers' multi-strand identities and the differences between the university researchers colored the complicated nature of rapport-building in the everyday interactions of the workshops themselves. The sociological notions of ascribed and achieved identity or status are relevant here, in the sense that both were at play in the interactions between researchers, partners, and workshop participants, though certainly not in a static or always anticipated manner. The vignette that follows highlights how familiarity or affinity related to language abilities, previous cultural knowledge and experience, or even national origin characterized the research encounters.

On the first day of the workshop series, the researchers arrived at the community partner's office after driving two twelve-passenger vans in order to transport the workshop participants to a makerspace-style studio on the university campus. Both women were uncertain of how many participants would actually show up, whether they would be on time, and what the cultural composition of the group would be, though considerable effort had been made by the community partner and the researchers to confirm commitments to participate in the workshop and send periodic reminders of the approaching dates and times. When they arrived at the community partner's location, a small group of four to five Chinese women were seated on a couch and chairs near the entrance. One of the organization's staff members introduced the women to the two researchers, directing her introduction to the Korean researcher in particular. She then reassured the five women, "She's from Korea, talk to her. She's safe."

In the remaining workshops, where participants were mostly working independently or in small groups, whenever a question arose, they would seek out the Korean researcher. In a later conversation between the university researchers, the Korean scholar reflected on this dynamic. She explained,

> The whole Korean culture, also known as K-culture, like media, music, and television drama, is huge in China. Whenever I meet Chinese people, the instant message is, "I love that K-drama; I love that K-pop music; I love that K-fashion; I love that K-beauty product." So, it's very friendly; I get these friendly reactions just by saying my nationality. And actually, some of the participants talked to me about a Korean drama series, which I'm not quite following.

She later noted with some irony that in conversations with a colleague, it was assumed that part of the reason why she would be engaging in the project had to do with a presumed sympathy or identification with the workshop participants, as a "fellow immigrant" from East Asia, rather than the fact that it was part of her job description. In unpacking that assumption with her fellow researcher, she examined the various ways that this was both true and not true.

For example, the South Korean researcher had come to the United States in pursuit of an MBA at a renowned Ivy League school and subsequently worked in a large West Coast tech company. Both institutions were located in very diverse urban environments where immigrants and individuals from minority ethnic or racial communities interacted "naturally" in the workplace or university settings. She contrasted this to the "home" context of the researchers and workshop participants:

> In [name of home city], most of the immigrant communities are either from refugee communities or student communities. There are not enough working professionals where you interact naturally with one another, in a work setting. I realized there is a segregation here and a stigma around immigrants.

In other words, while she appeared to have much in common with the immigrants with whom she was working in the community center, they actually shared few common experiences.

Anthropologists of immigration and immigrants in school settings (Lukose, 2007; Ogbu and Simons, 1998; Ong, 1996) have similarly drawn distinctions between voluntary migrants such as the Korean researcher and those who have been forced to leave their home countries for fear of violence, persecution, or extreme poverty. These diverse push-and-pull factors differentiate how individuals are positioned in host countries in terms of social, cultural, linguistic, economic, and educational capital. Ong (1996) and Lukose (2007) also highlight internal differences within such categories as "Asian American" or other diasporic groups and their often-unequal relationships with the host country state. So, while the Korean researcher acknowledged that there was a certain proximity due to the closeness of China and South Korea geographically and to a certain degree culturally, she also noted that other aspects of her identity and experiences as a voluntary immigrant distanced her from workshop participants and their situation.

To return to the issue of rapport-building, as much as the Korean researcher came to occupy the identity ascribed to her by participants and staff, although she did not always feel this was a perfect "fit," the American researcher experienced a similar process of "being positioned" by participants and staff based on a mixture of achieved and ascribed identity strands. As an ethnographer of artisanal textile production in Morocco, she was able to bring to bear linguistic capital and knowledge of somewhat analogous cultural and religious contexts to this "home" setting.

At preliminary visits to the sewing circles organized by the local community organization, where the university-based researchers presented the workshop concept and logistics to potential participants, the ability to use colloquial Arabic to engage in small talk greatly facilitated relationship and trust-building. Still, the researcher's Moroccan Arabic dialect (*derija*) differed substantially from the Sudanese, Egyptian, and other Middle Eastern Arabic dialects, so conversation topics were quite limited. It was possible to explain that the researcher had studied traditional weaving and embroidery in Morocco and had lived there for more than a year.

This was a pleasant surprise to members of the predominantly Middle Eastern sewing circles, who greeted the researcher with warmth in later encounters. In the end, these communicative acts were less about conveying volumes of nuanced information and more about establishing familiarity between potential participants and researchers. They demonstrated some basis for knowledge of cultural and religious backgrounds of the participants.

Indeed, throughout the workshop series, women of Middle Eastern background and those who were exclusively Arabic speakers showed a preference for riding in the twelve-passenger van driven by the American researcher. If a question arose in the course of the workshops, they caught her attention or called her to them to see their work. Likewise, the researcher felt more comfortable engaging with these participants socially during "breaks," and she quite enjoyed the ability to converse in Arabic. To a certain extent, these participants reminded her of the women with whom she had lived in Morocco. Admittedly, there was a certain nostalgia at play, perhaps leading to a false sense of familiarity.

This knowledge from previous ethnographic research also facilitated the planning of various aspects of the workshop logistics. It was especially helpful in thinking through dietary restrictions and the importance of providing *halal* food options, which was challenging in combination with addressing the dietary preferences of other participants such as the Chinese women or other non-Muslim participants. Familiarity with similar cultural and faith traditions in Morocco also played a role in understanding and accommodating the importance of hospitality and the exchange of food throughout the life of the workshops. For example, at the outset of the series, the university-based researchers and local community organization discussed that one key to making the workshops a success would be the provision of meals for every session.

In addition to the social interactions and empathy-building that were fostered by the researchers via shared meals, which are supported by scholarship on commensality in the anthropology of food and beyond, this was considered by the partners to be an expected dimension of the programming—in part because of the cultural background of participants, but also because of their structural and socioeconomic positions. Workshop participants already had an established way of interfacing with programming provided by the community partner, and this almost always involved some form of incentive or gift. This set up a similar expectation for the craft and entrepreneurship workshop. Researchers and community partners also wanted to offset the potential burden of the time required for the workshops (five-hour blocks of time spread across six weeks) plus transport to and from the community partner's site.

However, by the second and third sessions, some participants insisted on returning the "gift," so to speak. One participant from Iran began to prepare two varieties of spiced tea to share with fellow participants and workshop organizers. She also brought along dates and other sweet accompaniments. Introductions to the tea and its ingredients and flavors became the focal point of numerous lighthearted interactions over breaks from the normal workshop activities, bringing together the university researchers, mostly White craft mentors, participants from the Middle East and China, and the community partner's Middle Eastern staff member who was serving as an interpreter.

One of the participants from the long-term resident and local crafter community commented on the multiple ways food, or conversations about food, presented opportunities for connection:

In the first one [workshop] when we were sharing our object and telling stories, I was at the table with three Egyptian women and at some point we started talking about food. So that didn't make it into the crafts but it did make it into our diets in later weeks. And I enjoyed that, I felt like they were sharing their culture with us, they really wanted to do that and we all enjoyed it. So, in terms of making it into the [craft] project I don't know, but in this case it was something that was valuable apart from the [craft] project. It's part of the environment and the context of relating to one another and finding things that we could share that I think set a good tone for us working together on projects.

These gestures of reciprocation and connection were familiar to the researchers through both personal and professional knowledge of the importance of Middle Eastern and East Asian traditions of hospitality as well as the pride invested in culinary expertise and acts of generosity. They also align with anthropological insights about cultural values of honor and shame, or face-saving practices, where the ability to return a gift establishes some measure of social parity and reduces the debt or obligation created by the initial act of gift-giving (Bourdieu, 1966; Mauss, 1990; Meneley, 1996).

On a final note, one unanticipated "strand" of the American researcher's identity also played a significant role in rapport-building throughout the workshops, namely an increasingly visible pregnancy and her status as a mother. Pregnancy is already a time in a woman's life when certain norms surrounding social interactions are disregarded. These include initiating conversations about personal matters like family status or touching or referencing one's body explicitly through talk. This proved to be the case in the American researcher's exchanges with workshop participants, especially with those from the Middle East.

Motherhood confers a relatively high status on a woman in the Middle East, and, in addition to being married, it marks a woman as an adult member of society. In her previous fieldwork in Morocco, for example, the American researcher's mostly female interlocutors were constantly asking about when she and her husband (then fiancé) would have children and how many children they wanted. They even teased her about whether she knew how to "make babies," comments which were accompanied by gestures illustrating the process.

The pregnancy provided just one more strand of shared identity and familiarity with many of the participants in the community center who were themselves mothers. It also created a sense of empathy between the American researcher and the community organization interpreter and liaison, whose daughter was also pregnant at the time. In the post-workshop "debrief" conversation between the Korean and the American researchers, the Korean scholar noted that as an unmarried woman without a child, at times she felt less approachable in the eyes of the Middle Eastern participants. A linguistic distance was therefore amplified by this social and physiological difference.

Diverging fieldwork experiences akin to those faced by the university-based researchers related to marital and motherhood status feature prominently in accounts of team-based research projects like that related by Janet Theophano and Karen Curtis (1996) in their joint study of Italian American food culture experiences. In their case, differing treatment by interlocutors led to extremely productive insights about the research questions themselves. More generally, feminist anthropologists have written extensively about the importance of acknowledging how research encounters and researcher positionality are shaped by these dimensions of personal identity.

DEFAMILIARIZING HOME: MISCONCEPTIONS AND ACCOUNTABILITY

In this section, the discussion returns to the core theme of the volume, the benefits and challenges of conducting ethnography of teaching and learning in familiar contexts. The aim is to tease out the various ways that even at "home," assumptions of shared knowledge and experiences deserve to be re-examined. Indeed, in this particular workshop series, there were numerous ways that the research context and participants were in fact quite unfamiliar to one another.

First, the workshop was explicitly designed to bring together individuals from different cultural backgrounds, some of whom were friends, but many of whom were strangers to one another. That unfamiliarity was in a sense baked into the research project itself. In addition, the educational framework and pedagogical approach was experimental: a blend of craft and project-based learning and entrepreneurship education guided by human-centered design principles. Furthermore, the physical workshop settings were new to some or all of the participants at various points in time. They included the university-based museum, where participants from the refugee and immigrant communities were exposed for the first time to textiles as art objects (and had to be reminded not to touch the textiles), and the university makerspace and innovation studio, whose very concept was new to most of the participants and had not been used by the researchers previously as a teaching or research space.

Some of these dimensions of unfamiliarity were known, while others emerged only through moments of misunderstandings or confusion. One notable example occurred when the researchers assumed a homogeneity and camaraderie among the Middle Eastern participants that did not, in fact, exist. After the first workshop, a staff member at the community organization brought to the researchers' attention an issue that had caused tension among the participants. Some participants had apparently aggravated one

another through behavior considered by "some," who were never identified clearly, to be unseemly. This included certain participants' insistence
on "sacralizing" the workshops through frequent references to Allah and
sometimes heated discussions about religious issues. And, on the other hand,
some participants engaged in singing secular songs and making merry while
in transit. These tensions marked distinct attitudes toward participation in
the workshops.

It was at this point that some of the religious differences between Middle
Eastern workshop participants came into view, not only with regard to sect
(i.e., Shi'a or Sunni traditions) but also vis-à-vis the general orientation
toward piety and the role of religion in daily life and interactions. The community partner offered a solution—the adoption of a communication etiquette
pledge they used frequently in their own programming. One of its main rules
involved avoiding sensitive cultural and religious topics.

Similarly, after the location of the second workshop created parking
difficulties when participants missed the van shuttles departing from the
community partner's office, some of the participants asked about getting
an individual parking pass for campus. The American researcher suggested
that perhaps a number of the participants could organize a carpool. Fawn
(pseudonym) dismissed the idea immediately, "We don't do that. If there's
an accident . . . in our community it's just turned into a mess." Upon further
explanation, Fawn indicated the problem was at least partly related to liability
issues. Her response seemed to point to a perfectly normal consideration of
potentially complicated legal and insurance issues. It also indexed a tension
among different local immigrant and refugee communities represented by the
workshop participants, and perhaps a past incident that brought this tension
into view.

In a familiar context, then, it may be too easy to assume a shared
understanding of the "rules" of interaction and relationship management.
Ethnography at home can give one a false sense of security regarding the
nature of the research encounter and those present in the encounter. Likewise,
these assumptions have implications for the nature of engaged anthropology
and collaborations with partners. The assumption of shared undestanding
emerged as an issue in one moment of the project in particular.

As part of the documentation of the workshops, and in anticipation of a
subsequent public exhibition related to the crafted objects and the participants'
stories, the university researchers used some of their grant funding to com-
mission the creation of a student-led short video. The video included footage
of the workshop activities as they unfolded and short interviews with select
workshop participants. Because of funding limitations, the undergraduate
journalism students who created this video were constrained as to how much
footage was collected, amounting to approximately two hours of filming.

The researchers did not give much guidance to the students, other than to direct them to capture the participant diversity (one to two interviews with Middle Eastern participants, one interview with a Chinese participant, and one interview with a White long-term resident participant) and the more dynamic aspects of "making stuff."

Later the university researchers discovered that they should have included a brief overview of the workshop series, so they recorded thirty-second clips of one another introducing the basic workshop concepts related to craft and entrepreneurship. All partners were recognized in credits at the end of the five-minute video. Still, the researchers did not fully account for how project partners viewed the purpose of this video clip, nor the afterlife of the video as one of the most powerful and distributable outputs of the workshops. As such, though initially conceived as something to show in conjunction with physical objects in a public exhibition, the video gained importance as a potentially useful promotional tool for all partners involved, especially the local nonprofit organization.

However, the nonprofit organization did not perceive that the credit at the end of the film, or interviews with members of the communities that it also served, adequately recognized its integral role in the project. Several e-mail messages and a face-to-face meeting were required to address the situation and figure out how to repair the relationship to the satisfaction of the organization and the researchers. The university researchers ultimately organized the shooting of additional footage of the three main local partners, including two representatives of other partner organizations who were likewise not part of the original clip, and re-edited the video.

For the researchers, the result was a better understanding of the pressures experienced by organizations operating in the nonprofit sector, especially those heavily funded by grants, public money, and donations, to justify and make their activities visible to the larger public. The researchers ultimately understood that they had conflated representation of diverse workshop participants as representation of the main community partner serving most of those participants. In the end, the steps taken to repair the relationship translated into a rich and mutually beneficial future partnership for the exhibition that took place a year later at a local museum.

This event and its aftermath further demonstrate one key aspect of research "at home." Namely, the issue of accountability toward individuals and organizations in the field site. This is especially critical for engaged ethnography in familiar contexts, contexts in which one might hope to perform future research with the same partners. This approach to research accountability also raises the question of whom the research should serve. In addition to producing knowledge about cross-cultural empathy-building through project-based and collaborative learning and advancing the careers of two early-career faculty, the outcomes should benefit those with whom and for whom the educational programming was developed.

REFERENCES

Bradburn, Norman, Seymour Sudman, and Brian Wansink. 2004. *Asking Questions: The Definitive Guide to Questionnaire Design-For Market Research, Political Polls, and Social and Health Questionnaires.* Rev. ed. San Francisco: Wiley & Sons.

Bourdieu, Pierre. 1966. "The Sentiment of Honor in Kabyle Society." In *Honour and Shame: The Values of Mediterranean Society*, edited by Jean G. Peristiany, pp. 191–241. Chicago: University of Chicago Press.

Greenwood, Davydd J., William F. Whyte, and Ira Harkavy. 1993. "Participatory Action Research as a Process and as a Goal." *Human Relations* 46, no. 2, 175–192.

Hemment, Julie. 2007. "Public Anthropology and the Paradoxes of Participation: Participatory Action Research and Critical Ethnography in Provincial Russia." *Human Organization* 66, no. 3, 301–314.

Low, Setha M. and Sally Engle Merry. 2010. "Engaged Anthropology: Diversity and Dilemmas: An Introduction to Supplement 2." *Current Anthropology* 51, no. S1, S203–S226.

Lukose, Ritty A. 2007. "The Difference that Diaspora Makes: Thinking through the Anthropology of Immigrant Education in the United States." *Anthropology & Education Quarterly* 38, no. 4, 405–418.

Mauss, Marcel. 1990. *The Gift: The Form and Reason for Exchange in Archaic Societies.* Translated by W.D. Halls. New York: W.W. Norton.

Meneley, Anne. 1996. *Tournaments of Value: Sociability and Hierarchy in a Yemeni Town.* Toronto: University of Toronto Press.

Narayan, Kirin. 1993. "How Native is a 'Native' Anthropologist?" *American Anthropologist* 95, 671–686.

Ogbu, John U. and Herbert D. Simons. 1998. "Voluntary and Involuntary Minorities: A Cultural-Ecological Theory of School Performance with Some Implications for Education." *Anthropology & Education Quarterly* 29, no. 2, 155–188.

Ong, Aihwa. 1996. "Cultural Citizenship as Subject-Making: Immigrants Negotiate Racial and Cultural Boundaries in the United States." *Current Anthropology* 37, no. 5, 737–751.

Ortner, Sherry B. 2019. "Practicing Engaged Anthropology." *Anthropology of this Century* 25 (May): http://aotcpress.com/articles/practicing-engaged-anthropology/

Theophano, Janet and Karen Curtis. 1996. "Reflections on a Tale Told Twice." In *Journeys through Ethnography: Realistic Accounts of Fieldwork*, edited by Annette Lareau and Jeffrey J. Schultz, pp. 151–176. Boulder: Westview Press.

Chapter 8

Collaborative Intersectionality in Researcher-Participant Relations at a Hispanic Serving Institution

Jen Stacy

The mantra to "make the familiar strange and the strange familiar" becomes innate to the anthropologist as she navigates all social contexts that are either new (strange), common (familiar), or somewhere in-between. This became clear to Jen Stacy when she began her job as an assistant professor in the College of Education at Rancho State University* (RSU) (*pseudonym) as a freshly minted Ph.D.

RSU is a Hispanic Serving Institution (HSI) in the greater Los Angeles area whose mission is to make higher education accessible and transformative. Undergraduates are mostly Latinx (71.1 percent), Black (10 percent), or Asian (4.7 percent), and female (NCES, 2018). Most are the first in their families to attend college, and a good proportion (40 percent) are categorized as "adult students" who are over the age of twenty-five. In line with RSU's institutional data, the majority utilize state and federal financial aid (92 percent), and a large portion receive PELL grants (NCES, 2018), indicating financial need.

As an educator and an ethnographer, Jen had worked with Latinx populations in myriad capacities, including living in Monterrey, Mexico for four years while teaching and studying for her master's degree. Her philosophy aligned with RSU's commitment to justice in and through education for minoritized populations and in disinvested communities. Jen naturally drew on her ethnographic skills to better understand the culture of her new home institution and to pinpoint opportunities for enacting culturally sustaining practices. It became clear that conducting quality ethnographic research in this increasingly familiar context required grappling with a new nexus of identities, including social identities such as researcher and assistant professor.

The in-between space of familiar and strange occupied by the researcher offered a rich vantage point to consider the complexities of conducting ethnographic research at home. Asking questions of a new institution with a distinct student population permitted her to depict and question taken-for-granted aspects of institutions, thus providing new angles for reflection (Erickson, 1984). Conducting ethnographic research at her home institution illuminated her identities in a new way. Jen shared many attributes with her students: she identified as a bilingual (in English and Spanish) woman in her early thirties. Other attributes set her apart: she was White, of middle-class socioeconomic status, from the Midwest, and was an assistant professor.

As social beings who enter cultural spaces, ethnographers bring with them their social identities, past experiences, and biases. Thus, ethnographers must always be aware of their "presentation of self" (Agar, 1996). How they present themselves while conducting research must be informed by and reflexive of how they are perceived by their participants. Ethnographers must always be cognizant of how cultural background, status, and biases are in play and must identify how this amalgamation manifests in data collection, analysis, and findings (Agar, 1996). The comfort of a familiar context may not offer such a contrastive cultural experience that the ethnographer might encounter elsewhere, complicating this process.

This chapter explores how the author negotiated the process of presenting oneself during ethnographic research about undergraduate student-parents in the teacher education program at RSU. Plump and Geist-Martin's (2013) concept of collaborative intersectionality offers insight into how the research process is informed by the ethnographer's and the informants' identities while also being complicated by power, privilege, and positionality. Explicitly integrating a collaborative intersectional lens while conducting an ethnography in a local context strengthens the integrity through which data is collected, analyzed, presented, and understood.

RESEARCH CONTEXT

During her first year at RSU, Jen noted that her colleagues, students, and other stakeholders emphasized that the university's teacher education program must reflect "who our students are." Succinctly put, the program should take into account students' identities, including first-generation status, socioeconomic status, and lifestyles in general. Teaching and supporting "who our students are" was an invitation to enact humanizing (Bartolomé, 1994) and culturally sustaining (Alim and Paris, 2017) practices in teacher education. An ethnographic understanding of how students construct, enact, and maintain cultural practices would be necessary to authentically uphold practices that reflected and sustained culture, as opposed to trivializing student demographics into contrived methods and initiatives.

In order to teach "who students are," it would be essential to first ascertain—not assume—their unique cultural practices. While looking closely at students' identities and unique characteristics, one particular sub-population began to stand out: those who were parents. Undergraduate student-parents were a group of students that shared some social identities with others at RSU (e.g., ethnicity, language, economic status) but whose identities as parents were not highlighted in the typical discussions about responsive teaching and learning.

Many students shared their parent identities with the author during or outside class. While the student-parent identity came with rich resources and insights into teaching, it also reconfigured how the students approached schooling. It was common practice for all faculty to be sensitive and flexible regarding student-parents' needs and respond to issues as they arose. At best, this approach did not fully integrate student-parents' identities into teaching and learning; at worst, it viewed their parenting status through a deficit lens: as a problem impeding success.

THEORETICAL FRAMEWORK

Recent research has unveiled the unique needs of first-generation college students and has called for institutions to be more responsive to this group (Castillo-Montoya, 2017; Longwell-Grice, 2016). Attwell and Lavin (2012) argue that the term *non-traditional college student* is becoming obsolete, as the "traditional" notion of a full-time student who lives on campus, devotes at least forty hours a week to schooling, and graduates in four years, is waning across four-year universities. This is seen in the current and projected increase of part-time enrollment across the nation (NCES, 2019). At RSU, about a quarter of students are enrolled part time (NCES, 2018). Embracing a more diverse undergraduate population requires institutions to learn more about the nuances that contribute to students' lives, such as parenting.

Studies have highlighted how college students' parenting responsibilities interact with their schooling experiences (Muser, 2017) and advocate for equitable services (Lovell, 2014). However, much of this research centers on student-parent retention rates, university-based supports, and psychological attributes. A recent review of research literature did not result in any ethnographic studies about the cultural practices of undergraduate pre-service teachers who parent.

Distinctive from the essentialized understanding of culture as merely heritage artifacts and traditions, the phrase cultural practices captures how people construct culture every day through multiple identities, within and across social relationships, and in social contexts (Nieto, 2010). For example, understanding the norms of social media, like knowing which posts will get the most "likes," indicates cultural fluency in a space that is not connected with one's heritage or ethnicity (Scollons, Scollons, and Jones, 2012). Missing in the literature are textured insights regarding student-parents' cultural practices, how those practices are influenced and perceived by the institution, and how that perception interacts with learning.

Learning about student-parents' cultural practices can also illuminate their community cultural wealth, or "the knowledge, skills, abilities and contacts possessed and utilized by Communities of Color to [survive and resist] oppression" (Yosso, 2005, p. 77). Once authentic cultural practices are known, educators can enact culturally sustaining pedagogies (Alim and Paris, 2017) that affirm, reflect, and promote students' cultural practices instead of attempting to change them. When institutions view parents' unique knowledges, skills, and responsibilities from an additive (as opposed to deficit) perspective, learning is enhanced (Auerbach, 1995; Baquedano-Lopez et al., 2013).

Kimberlé Crenshaw raised the concept of intersectionality in 1989 to suggest that discrimination cannot be fully understood if analyzed from a single axis. She argued that the multidimensional experiences of Black women are distorted when only looked at through the lens of gender or that of race. Instead, Black women's experiences must be understood through the intersections of their identities and how those identities are situated within structures of power (Crenshaw, 1989). Crenshaw's work has been extended to include multiple social identities (race, gender, class, sexual orientation, religion, etc.) and unique experiences of oppression or privilege regarding these identities (Collins 1993, 2015).

Ethnographers and their participants move fluidly through their intersectional identities during the research process (Plump and Geist-Martine, 2013). As they enter into a relationship with one another, they negotiate these identities, influencing the research process. Recognizing that people navigate their social worlds with and through intersectional identities, it follows that ethnography, a methodology that unveils cultural practices as they are mediated through semiotic structures and experiences, should illuminate those experiences.

Ethnographers, then, must always be aware of how they are presenting themselves, how their participants perceive them, and how all of this is present in data collection, analysis, and reporting (Agar, 1993). The ethnographer brings her intersectional identity to the research site where it merges with the intersectional identity of her participants, complicated by power structures. Dissecting the process of the ethnographer's presentation of self as a critical component of research is necessary to uphold the quality and accuracy of ethnography.

RESEARCH DESIGN

In 2018, Jen began a multiyear ethnographic study of undergraduate student-parents in the RSU teacher education program in an effort to answer questions such as what are the cultural realities of undergraduate student-parents studying to be teachers? And, how can teacher education programs be more responsive to student-parents' cultural practices? To recruit participants, a gender-encompassing call was sent out to all undergraduate students in the teacher preparation program by email. The author and her assistants also announced the research in classes and reached out to students who had disclosed their parenting status. Several of the participants also informed their friends about the study.

Eleven students were identified as focal participants for this study. While the call for participants was explicitly gender encompassing, ten participants identified as female mothers and one as a male father. All were students of color: seven self-identified as Mexican American, three as Black, and one as Japanese. Most students ($n=9$) were first-generation college students; the others either had one parent who attended university in California ($n=1$) or both parents who attended university in Mexico ($n=1$). The average age of the participants was thirty-two-years-old. Nine parented with a partner at home; the other two were single mothers.

Ethnographic methods included observations, open-ended interviews, and artifact collection. At the time of writing, data collection and analysis for this project were ongoing. Field notes and artifacts were analyzed through open and focused coding (Emerson, Fretz, and Shaw, 2011), and interviews were probed via domain analysis (Spradley, 1979). Codes were constantly triangulated across data to generate common cultural themes. In-process memos were written to provide insight and direction for the ongoing fieldwork, while analytical memos offered ongoing theoretical analysis, such as the prominent role of intersectionality.

FINDINGS

Early findings from this study highlighted the critical process of the presentation of self (Agar, 1996) at the beginning and throughout the study. It was clear at the onset of the study that social identities (e.g., gender, age, ethnicity, language, and profession) became integral to how the students viewed the researcher and participated in the study. Taking time with informants to analyze the process of gaining entry illuminated the role intersectionality played in the ethnographic research process, particularly with regard to the shift in the author's role from professor to researcher. The researcher's and participants' intertwined identities were embedded in power structures and recognizing this early on informed how the research unfolded.

What follows is the analysis of two vignettes detailing the negotiation process of the author's presentation of self during initial fieldwork. Evident in each vignette is the nexus of collaborative intersectionality as it happened in the field: the participants' perceptions of the researcher were informed by how their intersectional identities came into play with those of the researcher and vice versa. Power structures between researcher and participants also mediated the scenario. Critical analysis of this process illuminated intersectionality as an important emerging theme in this research and suggested the need for innovative ethnographic research methods.

Coco: Mexican Connections

Coco arrived at Jen's office (the location she selected) for our interview. She sat down and immediately popped back up, looking closely at Jen's master's degree from La Universidad de Monterrey in Monterrey, Nuevo León, México. The degree distinctly includes a black and white photo of Jen, similar to those used in official government documents such as passports and visas.

"It's you, Jen?" she asked.
Jen smiled. "It is."
"¿Lo hiciste en español? ¿La maestría? [Did you do it in Spanish? The master's degree?]" Coco asked, mouth agape.
"Pues, sí. [Why, yes.]" Jen responded, smiling sheepishly.
Coco continued. "Do you think you'll get your doctorate?"
"I have it." Jen responded, pointing to the degree above her desk.
Coco stammered. "Really? You're a doctor?"

They continued discussing Jen's background and how her time in Monterrey influenced her doctoral studies. They translanguaged, moving back and forth between Spanish and English, discussing the differences in schooling in México and the United States. Though she traced her heritage to México, Coco had never been to the country.

By the time Coco volunteered to be a research participant, she was finishing her bachelor's degree and had taken three classes with the researcher. They had an established professor-student relationship: Coco visited the author's office frequently for academic and other supports. She was eager to participate in the student-parent study, and this vignette marked the beginning of her participation.

Four years older than the ethnographer, Coco was a Mexican American, first-generation college student. She graduated from an alternative high school in central Los Angeles, married, had children, and overcame struggles with addiction before enrolling in university. Both women's experiences with Mexico and Spanish fluency fostered some shared cultural knowledge, as did their identities as first-generation college students and women in their mid-thirties. The above vignette, however, illustrates the intersectional interactions between these identities as the two entered into ethnographic study.

How Coco and the author arrived at their different social identities, and how these identities influenced their research relationship was embedded in differentiated power dynamics. Jen's foray into Mexican/Latinx cultural practices had been largely academic through academic and professional endeavors. In addition to formally studying Spanish and Latin American studies in school, she worked as a teacher in bilingual schools and as a researcher in Mexican and Latinx communities. These experiences and her middle-class background contributed to securing her position as a professor and mediated her navigation of campus life.

Shared interest in Mexico with Coco was an important topic for exploring commonalities. However, the ethnographer's Mexican master's degree (now a research artifact) symbolized elements of social and academic capital that was embedded in her relationship with Coco. The authority that Jen previously held over Coco as her instructor would not disappear just because the focus of their meetings had shifted away from teaching-learning to research. From Coco's perspective, Jen continued to have a higher status which was inadvertently connected to commonalities she shared with Coco. Still, this status was complicated by the researcher's age, as indicated when Coco responded with surprise regarding the doctorate degree.

Intersecting identities are not static, allowing people to move fluidly between and within them while conducting research (Plump and Geist-Martin, 2013). These intersecting identities permit assumed hierarchies to be questioned and evolve in unexpected ways (Plump and Geist-Martin, 2013). Jen and Coco's discussion was one of several that supported them in redefining their relationship from that of professor-student to that of researcher-participant. Considering the power differential that was connected to the ethnographer's identities (White, middle class, bilingual, highly educated) was essential as she continued the interview.

While she answered Coco's questions genuinely, the ethnographer began asking open-ended questions about Coco's experiences with Mexican heritage in Los Angeles to shift the control of the cultural content to the participant. While the remainder of the interview focused on Coco's experience as a parent, later data analysis shed light on how Jen's authority as a professor in the College of Education influenced the information Coco and other informants were willing to share; for example, a clear theme emerging from interview data showed "contentment without critique" with their teacher preparation major.

Student-parents, including Coco, pointed to their enthusiastic, caring, and organized professors as key to facilitating their learning when asked to describe their experiences within the major. However, participants also shared being stressed and overwhelmed during their studies at RSU. When asked to elaborate, student-parents were reluctant to share critiques about the program, assignments, or instructors even though they had earlier mentioned that these things were stress-inducing. Even when they did, they did so vaguely. One informant even whispered a name of a staff member under her breath in connection to a negative experience and then immediately countered her comment with praise for the program writ large.

While it may be the case that the student-parents genuinely did not attribute their feelings of stress to their program and instructors, it could also be that the author's status as a professor still overshadowed how (if) the students viewed her as a researcher. The quintessential structure of the interview positions the interviewer in control and, by default, the interviewee in a subordinate role (Briggs, 1997). In this study, the structural hierarchy of the interview was compounded by the researcher and participant's former relationship as professor-student and by the aforementioned social identities. Some overlapping identities facilitated Coco's discussion of certain topics with the researcher (like spousal support) but others (student-professor) may have made her hesitant to share honestly.

Self-reflexivity regarding the ethnographer's identities and how they were intersecting with those of the participants during fieldwork became even more important during data analysis. Early thematic coding pointed to the emergence of intersectionality as a theme both generated from data and influencing the data. While it was natural for Jen's status and privilege to be a part of ethnographic research (as this is how she operates at RSU), building a newfound trust while being aware of how she was negotiating her intersectional presentation of self would be essential in authentically capturing her participants' lived realities.

Early analytical memos pointed to the need for more innovative ethnographic methods to dissipate the assumed hierarchy between researcher and participants. The researcher secured student research assistants whose identities were more overlapping with the participants (undergraduates, Latinx, female, mothers, and "adult students"). Not only were the student assistants trained in ethnographic methods, they also were consulted in brainstorming ways of reconfiguring the perceived hierarchy between the author and the student-parents and participating in data analysis.

In the following semester, all participants were asked to keep journals and to write about "stressful" or "overwhelming" moments. These were times where the demands of their courses interacted with their parenting or vice versa. The participants would document what happened, who was involved, what they were doing for school (class schedule, assignments, practicum, etc.), and how/if such moments were resolved. The hope was that the journal would foster some distance between the researcher and the participants, support them in capturing moments in real time, as well as serve as cathartic devices.

Enrique: Let me buy you a coffee

Jen arrived at Starbucks, the place Enrique selected for his interview, a few minutes early. She waited outside so that Enrique would see her when he arrived. Within seconds, Enrique appeared. "Hey Jen," he said as he leaned in awkwardly for an unexpected hug. Jen responded with a sideways, half-hug and asked how he was doing and how his summer was going. Enrique explained that he was so nervous for the interview that he had arrived 20 minutes early and had been waiting in his car, watching carefully for her arrival. To ease the moment, Jen laughed and explained that this should be the easiest interview he would ever do: he would only need to talk about his life. Jen suggested that they go inside and grab a coffee. Enrique responded, "Oh yeah! Let me buy you a coffee." Jen smiled. "No way. Coffee's on me. You're helping me with my project, after all." Enrique laughed nervously, looked around, and paced as they waited for their order. Jen made small talk about summer plans.

Enrique had volunteered to participate in the ethnographic research during the summer after he took a course with the author. Like Coco, their relationship had been that of professor-student but one that was recently established. Enrique had shared openly that he intentionally did not get involved in school activities during his first semester at RSU but was now trying new things. Participating in the student-parent ethnography project was a result of this initiative.

Enrique was also a first-generation college student who identified as Mexican American. A few years younger than Jen, he had a career in the U.S. Army before pursuing his studies in elementary education at RSU. From the beginning, Enrique articulated that his gender identity was an important factor. When he indicated his interest in the research study, he stated that he felt it was important that fathers' experiences be included in addition to that of mothers. At the time of writing, he was the only male participant.

Enrique was a confident student in class, constantly volunteering and generating small talk with the author and his classmates. The shift in Enrique's confidence as he and Jen reconfigured their relationship to researcher-participant was notable. As a researcher, she offered to meet Enrique in a place that he felt most comfortable, and it was obvious that the publicness of their meeting heightened the differences in their intersecting identities. Enrique was not sure how to act at a Starbucks with a woman within a few years of his age, who was also his former professor, while being tasked with doing something somewhat school related.

Sensing that Enrique's discomfort might influence his willingness to do the interview, Jen suggested that they sit outdoors on the sparsely populated patio. As with Coco, she began asking general open-ended questions about Enrique's summer vacation to shift the focus to his experiences. While Enrique's discomfort seemed to ease through this process, gender and status concerns were ever-present throughout the interview. An intriguing theme unique to Enrique's interview was how his responses about his experiences as a student-parent were juxtaposed between two attributes: his wife's professional identity and his desire to answer interview questions correctly.

Enrique constantly mentioned that his decision to go to school full time while caring for his daughters both facilitated and was supported by his wife's full-time career as a licensed vocational nurse. He understood his roles as husband, father, and student as ways to provide support at home while advancing the family's long-term goals. As he spoke, he continuously paused and asked, "Am I answering this right?" Enrique's concern to answer the questions "right" indicated that he was still perceiving the hierarchy of his relationship with the author as one of professor-student and not as researcher-participant. It also points to how the evolving roles of interviewer-interviewee are being performed (Briggs, 1997).

The theme of gender emerged more obviously in Enrique's interview. In addition to talking about himself in juxtaposition to his wife, he also spoke about how classes at RSU, particularly the course he had just taken with the researcher, had deepened his understanding of gender and had helped him become comfortable with gender fluidity and different sexualities. He cast this as an example of how schooling and parenting intertwined: this was a new understanding that he and his wife now wanted to instill in their children. Enrique gave follow-up examples of conversations he had with his daughters about gender through the frame of gender equity.

Of course, parents consider how they teach their children about gender. However, given Enrique's concern for answering the interview questions correctly, Jen could not help but wonder whether this example stemmed organically from his lived experiences as a father, or if he was trying to give a "right answer" to the questions. Briggs (1997) explains that participants may have distinct interactional goals during an interview. An interviewee's perception of the interview as a certain type of communicative event will influence what subjects may be discussed and how much information might be given. Participants, like Enrique, judge what will constitute a "right" answer based not only on how questions are asked but how the social situation of the interview is perceived, presumably by the researcher and those around (Briggs, 1997).

Interviewing Enrique added to the understanding of collaborative inter-sectionality as an increasingly complex element in ethnography. Crenshaw (1989) points to the merging of gender and race and their entanglement in power structures as the base for understanding intersectionality. As with Coco, Jen's status as a professor was still perceived as a power differen-tial as she and Enrique negotiated their researcher-participant relationship. Complicating this in a different way was the element of gender.

Enrique was not quite sure how to act with the author outside the school setting, and he recognized their appointment as important but was unsure about how to interact with her during summer vacation, resulting in an awk-ward hug. His offer to buy her a coffee could have stemmed from his respect for her as a professor, from his expectation of gender roles, or, most likely, from the intersection of both. Enrique appeared to be constantly aware of his presentation of gender as the two settled into the researcher-participant relationship during fieldwork.

Interestingly, after the interview was over, Enrique exclaimed, "I totally forgot to talk about my gender!" He went on to explain that he loved being a dad and did not see it as a masculine or feminine responsibility. He reiterated that he was not "machismo" and felt like that mentality was detrimental to parenting. Only then did he state that some of his family members made fun of him for being a stay-at-home dad.

Looking back at Enrique's interview, his reasoning for being a full-time parent and a full-time student was centered on his identity as a Latinx male from Compton, California. He explained how his career in the Army first served as a way to "get out of Compton and that lifestyle [of working at fast-food restaurants and warehouses]" and to afford to raise a young fam-ily. Then, after years of his wife supporting his career, he realized that the army—and living in the state of Washington—was not for him, and he wanted to return to Compton with his family. His use of the G.I. Bill to attend RSU full time permitted him to stay at home with his daughters and support his wife's career but in a different way than he had done so previously.

Enrique reiterated several times that he was not like others. He was not like his other Mexican friends and cousins in Compton who wasted money on a degree right after high school that they did not use. He was not like others in the army who just listened and did what they were supposed to do. He was not like other student-parents because he was male. He mentioned that his ideas about gender had been evolving while attending college. Perhaps, Enrique's need to address the Mexican stereotype of "machismo" after participating in an interview that focused on his identity as a father stemmed from his agency to both capture and distinguish his intersecting identities against the broader sociocultural contexts that he occupies.

Negotiating intersectional identities happens in context, and what emerges is cultural practice reflective of the people in that time and space (Plump and Geist-Martin, 2013). The practice of presenting gender was a clear component of interviewing Enrique as much as it was a cultural matter regarding his current experience as a student-parent. Gender performance coupled with other identities such as ethnicity and age then emerged as a necessary angle from which to understand the student-parent experience at RSU. The distinct dynamic that unfolded during the gaining entry stage with Enrique compared to female student-parents led the researcher to think more analytically about how intersectionality was being captured as a theme across participants during the presentation of self-process and throughout their daily lives as student-parents at RSU.

After writing analytical memos, Jen discovered that she needed to capture the multimodal aspects of intersectionality as they unfolded in the particular nexus of time and space. Multimodality indexes more than a description of what happened or a transcription of what was said. It encapsulates the fuller context to aesthetically represent intersecting identities, power structures, and sociocultural dynamics. As detailed as her field notes were about Enrique's awkward hug, the researcher realized that she struggled to articulate how their actions, reactions, and comments during this moment were melded in a way that was dependent on and responsive to their intersectional social identities. Hence, photo and video documentation of significant moments using mobile technology would be included subsequently in the study.

DISCUSSION

As the author embarked on a new study of undergraduate student-parents at Rancho State University, she found that negotiating her role as researcher with her former students was more complex than she had anticipated. While conducting formal interviews, she was able to pinpoint moments of intersectionality and power imbalance and then attempted to adjust how the process was unfolding. Through data analysis and memo-writing, the ethnographer saw more clearly that collaborative intersectional identity negotiation also emerged as a cultural theme.

Plump and Geist-Martin (2013) note that "the feeling of being betwixt and between our multiple identities is a critical component of being successful in the work we do in our ethnographic research" (p. 61). The puzzlement pushes ethnographers to think analytically about what messages are being sent and interpreted within a particular context and through multiple identities. It permits ethnographers to explore how identities are constructed and how they play out in cultural practices.

Interactions with Coco and Enrique illustrate how the researcher's status as a professor could be influencing the degree of comfort they experienced as they redefined their relationships from professor-students to researcher-participants. Drawing from this data, Jen was able to think more innovatively about research methodology. She made attempts to mitigate power differences so that the participants' cultural practices emerged more accurately.

Initial data analysis also illuminated how intersectionality emerged as a cultural theme: the ethnographer's identities and interactions with the student-parents in multiple roles were intertwined with students' cultural practices. The researcher and the participants connected through Rancho State as a social institution. Their subsequent institutionalized identities (professor, students) along with their myriad social identities intertwined to influence the unique cultural practices that student-parents enacted at RSU.

The author was simultaneously becoming more aware that her role as a professor contributed to the social structures that mediated the student-parent cultural experience at RSU. For example, Coco's reluctance to critique the program might indicate the degree to which students perceive the teacher education program authentically wishes to integrate "who students are" into their practices. Enrique's quest to answer the interview questions correctly may illuminate how students think their professors want them to apply their studies to their lives. It could have been the case that the power dynamics did skew participants' interview responses. Or, most likely, it was a mix of all of these things.

Reconciling Intersectional Social Identities

Ethnography, like culture, is inherently messy. The beginning of a new research project in a familiar context surfaces thick, intertwined semiotic materials (Geertz, 1979) that typically go unnoticed. As the ethnographer enters the field in her home institution, the process of presenting different identity roles also illuminates cultural practices and social structures. Participants' "expectations about what the ethnographer wants to learn—and their decisions about what should be told—will derive from their sense of who he or she is" (Agar, 1996, p. 91) as it unfolds in the social context.

Participants and ethnographers connect through their intersectional social identities within structures of power. The ethnographer's negotiation of self requires being cognizant and critical of how her multiple identities are being perceived and how they are influencing data collection. This should be understood as cultural material, and documented and analyzed. Recognizing early these intersectional puzzles provided a new vantage point and an additional theoretical framing for this study (Erickson, 1989). Collaborative intersectionality permitted Jen to problematize the familiar in way that also captured student-parents' cultural realities. And, she was able to study herself through the lens of her participants.

Understanding the cultural practices of students within familiar contexts is contingent on discovering the nexus of intersectional social identities through the presentation of self. In analyzing this process, ethnographers can learn how they are perceived within the cultural space and how they influence it. Ethnographic understanding of intersectionality is necessary for thick, accurate descriptions that reflect all who co-construct cultural spaces.

REFERENCES

Agar, Michael. 1996. *The Professional Stranger*, 2nd edition. San Diego, CA: Academic Press.

Alim, Samy H. and Django Paris. 2017. "What Is Culturally Sustaining Pedagogy and Why Does It Matter?" In *Culturally Sustaining Pedagogies: Teaching and Learning for Justice in a Changing World*, edited by Django, Paris, Alim, Samy H., and Genishi, Celia, pp. 12–32. New York: Teachers College Press.

Attwell, Paul and David E. Lavin. 2012. "The Other 75%: College Education Beyond the Elite." In *What is College For? The Public Purpose of Higher Education*, edited by Lagemann, Ellen C. and Lewis, Harry, pp. 86–103. New York: Teachers College Press.

Auerbach, Elsa. 1989. "Toward a Social-Contextual Approach to Family Literacy." *Harvard Education Review* 59, no. 2, 165–181. doi: 10.17763/haer.59.2.h237313641283156

Baquedano-López, Patricia, Rebecca Anne Alexander, and Sera J. Hernandez. 2013. "Equity Issues in Parental and Community Involvement in Schools: What Teacher Educators Need to Know." *Review of Research in Education* 37, 149–182. doi: 10.3102/0091732X12459718

Bartolomé, Lilia. 1994. "Beyond the Methods Fetish: Toward a Humanizing Pedagogy." *Harvard Educational Review* 64, no. 2, 173–194. doi: 10.17763/haer.64.2.58q5m5744t325730

Briggs, Charles. L. 1997. *Learning How to Ask: A Sociolinguistic Appraisal of the Role of the Interview in Social Science Research*. New York: Cambridge University Press.

Castillo-Montoya, Milagros. 2017. "Deepening Understanding of Prior Knowledge: What Diverse First-Generation College Students in the U.S. Can Teach Us. *Teaching In Higher Education* 22, no. 5, 587–603. doi: 10.1080/13562517.2016.1273208

Collins, Patricia H. 1993. "Toward a New Vision: Race, Class, and Gender as Categories of Analysis and Connections." *Race, Class, & Sex* 1, no. 1, 26–45.

Collins, Patricia H. 2015. "Intersectionality's Definitional Dilemmas." *Annual Review of Sociology* 41, 1–20. doi: 10.1146/annurev-soc-073014-112142

Crenshaw, Kimberlé. 1989. "Demarginalizing the Intersection of Race and Sex: A Black Feminist Critique of Antidiscrimination Doctrine, Feminist Theory and Antiracist Politics." *University of Chicago Legal Forum* 1, no. 8, 139–167. https://chicagounbound.uchicago.edu/uclf/vol1989/iss1/8

Emerson, Robert M., Rachel I. Fretz, Linda L. Shaw. 2011. *Writing Ethnographic Field Notes*, 2nd edition. Chicago: University of Chicago Press.

Erickson, Frederick. 1984. "What Makes School Ethnography 'Ethnographic'?" *Anthropology and Education Quarterly* 15, 51–66. doi: 10.1525/aeq.1984.15.1.05x1472p

Longwell-Grice, Rob, Nicole Zervas Adsitt, Kathleen Mullins, and William Serrata. 2016. "The First Ones: Three Studies on First-Generation College Students." *NACADA Journal* 36, no. 2, 34–46. doi: 10.12930/NACADA-13-028

Lovell, Elyse D. 2014. "College Students Who Are Parents Need Equitable Services for Retention." *Journal of College Student Retention: Research, Theory & Practice* 16, no. 2, 187–202. doi: 10.2190/CS.16.2.b

Muser, Heather. 2017. "A Parent's Dream Come True: A Study of Adult Students Who Are Parents and Their Academic Engagement with Higher Education." EdD diss., California State University, Stanislaus. https://search-proquest-com.libproxy.csudh.edu/docview/1898822307

National Center for Education Statistics. 2019. "The Condition of Education: Undergraduate Enrollment." Retrieved from: https://nces.ed.gov/programs/coe/indicator_cha.asp#info

National Center for Education Statistics. 2018. "[Rancho State University*]." Retrieved from: https://nces.ed.gov/globallocator/

Nieto, Sonia. 2010. *The Light in Their Eyes: Creating Multicultural Learning Communities*. New York: Teachers College Press.

Plump, Brielle and Patricia Geist-Martin. 2013. "Collaborative Intersectionality: Negotiating Identity, Liminal Spaces, and Ethnographic Research." *Liminalities: A Journal of Performance Studies* 9, no. 2, 59–72.

Spradley, James P. 1979. *The Ethnographic Interview*. New York: Wadsworth Cengage Learning.

Yosso, Tara. 2005. "Whose Culture has Capital? A Critical Race Theory Discussion of Community Cultural Wealth." *Race, Ethnicity and Education* 8, no. 1, 69–91. doi: 10.1080/1361332052000341006

Chapter 9

Being a Researcher-Teacher in an Action-Oriented School Research Project on Welding

Perspectives, Positions, and Ethical Dilemmas

Stig-Börje Asplund, Nina Kilbrink,
and Jan Axelsson

In response to the increased demand for more practice-based school research to ground teaching in scientific evidence, a growing trend in educational research includes teachers in the actual research process. In this work, action-oriented learning studies, in which teachers themselves have been involved in defining the research focus, have proven to be effective in changing and developing teachers' teaching practices and professional learning (Brante et al., 2015; Lo, 2012). However, this close cooperation between teachers and researchers also involves ethical as well as analytical dilemmas. These dilemmas are connected to power relations in the collaborative process (cf. Baath, 2009; Biesta, 2007; Gelling and Munn-Giddings, 2011). The issue is further complicated in the case of action-oriented ethnographic research conducted in a context familiar to the participating actors—especially for teachers performing dual roles of educator and researcher in their local context (often in their own classrooms).

This chapter highlights and discusses some of the challenges that a teacher has to face and deal with when participating as a researcher in an ongoing ethnographic research project running over three years which involves close cooperation between two university-based researchers, Stig-Börje Asplund and Nina Kilbrink, one vocational teacher, Jan

Axelsson (Teacher 1, henceforth T1), and a teaching team at an upper secondary vocational school in Sweden. Both researchers teach in the VET (Vocational Education and Training) teacher program at Karlstad University and do research in the field of VET. However, neither of the researchers has experience or skills in welding. T1, on the other hand, has worked as a welder and has more than ten years of experience in welding education. As a former teacher colleague of Axelsson, Asplund asked him if he and his teaching team would like to join the research project, which they did.

The fact that the teacher takes an active part in the study and the specific methodological approach used in the research project entails shifting positions for the teacher during the research project. These shifting positions highlight shifts in perspectives and create ethical challenges for the teacher-as-researcher that also intersect with issues of power. By examining excerpts from the teacher's logbook notes that were kept during the project and bringing those notes into focus in relation to the shifting positions during the second year of the project, the chapter intends to shed light on some of the challenges a teacher-as-researcher has to manage in a familiar context.

LEARNING TO WELD IN VOCATIONAL EDUCATION—A LEARNING STUDY

The research project *Learning to Weld in Vocational Education*, which received funding from the Swedish Institute of Educational Research (Dnr: 2017-00056), examines the relationship between teaching and learning in vocational education with a specific focus on learning to weld. The study is conducted as an action-oriented study based on the Learning study method, and it combines Conversation Analysis with Variation Theory Approach (CAVTA). This approach draws attention to fine-grained interactional evidence of the learning processes that take shape when vocational teachers and upper secondary students interact in relation to the object of learning to weld in the vocational workshop at school (cf. Asplund and Kilbrink, 2020).

The basis of the study is the close cooperation between the researchers and the teacher and his teacher team regarding the development of teaching a specific learning content in a three-year study. One important criterion for school-based action research is that the research methods harmonize with the aim of teaching practice and the participating teachers (cf. Posch, 2019). Just like in most Learning studies (cf. Kilbrink et al., 2014; Pang and Ling, 2012; Posch, 2019), an important aspect of this study was to involve the teacher (T1) early in the process of deciding what to teach.

During the first year of the study, the teaching was planned, executed, and analyzed by one teacher (T1) and two researchers, in three iterative cycles, inspired by the Learning study method (cf. Kilbrink et al., 2014; Pang and Ling, 2012). The lessons were video recorded, then analyzed by the researchers at a preliminary stage, and subsequently analyzed by the researchers and the teaching vocational teacher (T1) together. Based on these analyses, new teaching strategies were incorporated into the teacher's didactic approach in the next cycle.

After the first three successive cycles, the study was relaunched for a second year, during which another teacher (Teacher 2; henceforth T2) from the teaching team (Teachers 1–4) was responsible for planning, executing, and analyzing the teaching in three new iterative cycles. Like the first year, teaching was performed in collaboration with the researchers and in consultation with the teaching team, based on the results from the first year of the study. In the third year of the project, the teaching team (T1–T4) will assume increased responsibility as regards the implementation of the three final cycles of teaching, while the researchers will take a step back and serve as the teacher team's sounding board. Throughout the project, T1 embodies the ethnographic role of being and working in a pedagogical practice and being actively involved in the research project. This dual role in the research project, which is intended to develop teaching practice based on the theoretical framework CAVTA, will be presented and discussed in relation to perspectives, positions, and ethical dilemmas.

Teacher 1 and Shifting Positions during an Action-Oriented Research Project

In this section, the action-oriented school research project on welding will be described in relation to the role of the teacher-as-researcher (T1) and the shifting positions of the various actors participating in the project. T1's role has changed during the past two years in relation to the researchers and the teaching team. This shifting position has led to several ethical and analytical dilemmas for T1. The dilemmas are also linked to issues of power. Before that discussion, and an account of how these dilemmas have been addressed more specifically by T1 in the project, some central methodological elements of the research process will be presented, with a focus on the role of the teacher-as-researcher.

YEAR 1—IMPLEMENTING THEORIES
IN TEACHER 1'S TEACHING

An important base for the continuous work with the action-oriented research study presented here was to involve T1 early in the research process. Thus, already in formulating the focus of the Learning study, T1 had an important role. Furthermore, it was important in the project to maintain a dialogue between T1 and the university-based researchers. Therefore, in the initial phase of implementing the Learning study, the scientific approach and theoretical perspectives were suspended, and the approach was to let T1 have full control of his teaching. Thereafter, in collaboration and dialogue between the researchers and T1, the theories were implemented, and the teaching was developed on a scientific basis involving close collaboration between the actors in the project.

Before implementing the first cycle, T1 read some research on welding education (Asplund and Kilbrink, 2018) and a text on Variation Theory (Carlgren, 2017). An interview conversation was then conducted with the teacher with the purpose of providing the two researchers with some insights into the specific teaching context and into the teacher's didactic approach to teaching a specific welding method (TIG welding). The first cycle lesson was then implemented and then video recorded. During this lesson, the teacher gave a lengthy and detailed lecture before providing the students with a demonstration of how to TIG-weld. Thereafter, the students TIG-welded on their own for the very first time in school, in separate welding booths, and the teacher monitored their work. Before the lesson ended, the teacher and the students discussed their experiences of the lesson.

The video recordings were then analyzed by the researchers at a preliminary stage and then analyzed by the researchers and T1 together. Based on these analyses, employing a CAVTA perspective, the teacher, together with the researchers, worked on new teaching strategies that were to be incorporated into the teacher's didactic approach for cycle 2. The process of the second and third cycles was the same as the first one, with the exception of the interview conversation that did not take place during the second and third cycle (see figure 9.1).

The results from the first year of the study show that the content of teaching was made more visible in the interaction between the teacher and the students. Furthermore, the aspects of TIG welding that the students were supposed to learn were displayed more explicitly in teaching in the second and third cycles. The example below shows how the teacher encourages the student to verbalize what happens when the melt

Interview
conversation

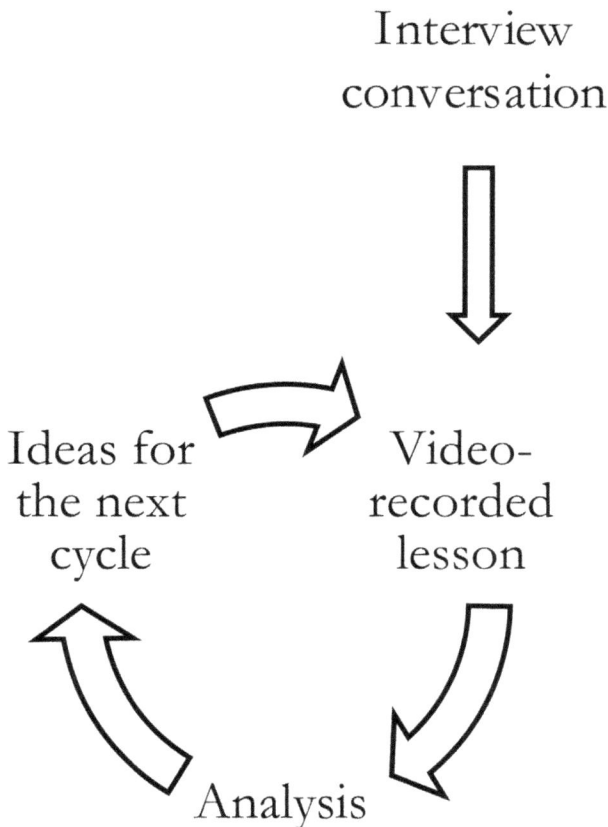

Figure 9.1 Learning Study 1 (Year 1); Cycle 1–3. *Source*: Stig-Börje Asplund, Nina Kilbrink, and Jan Axelsson.

is created in order to establish a shared understanding of the learning content.

This example in Figure 9.2 highlights a sequence from the third cycle, and in contrast to the first cycle where there was nearly no interaction between the teacher and the students when the students welded on their own, the student in the example above is given the opportunity to verbalize what happens when the melt forms. Encouraging the students to verbalize their understanding, as in the example above, creates increased opportunities and conditions for the teacher to interact with the students and to adapt the teaching in relation to the students' displayed understanding of the object of learning.

1. T1:   tell me what you see
           berätta för mig vad du ser

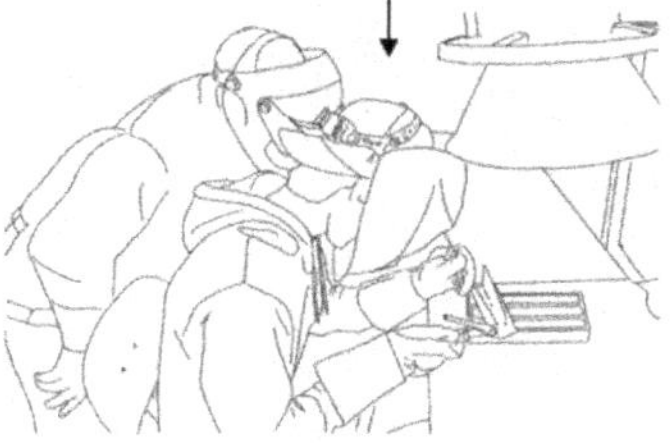

2. S: yes now it gets fluid here ((leans forward))
           ja nu börjar det bli flytande här ((lutar sig framåt))

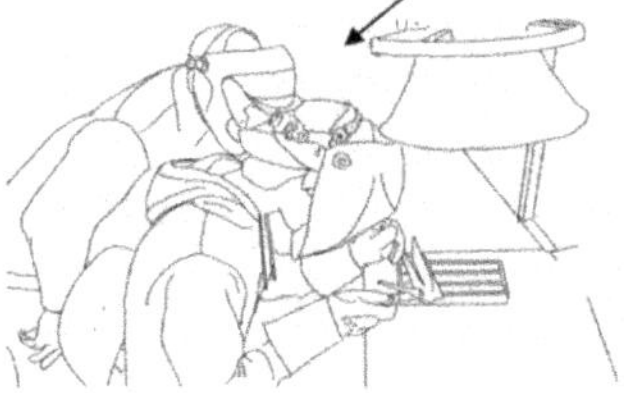

3. T1:   where do you have fluid
           vart har du flytande
4. S: on there ((points with the additive material))
           på där ((pekar med tillsatsmaterialet))

5. T1:   on the wall like
           på väggen liksom
6. S: yes (.) now it melts together here
           ja (.) nu smälter det ihop här
7. T1:   there it melts good
           där smälter det bra

Figure 9.2 Establishing a shared understanding of the object of learning. *Source*: Stig-Börje Asplund, Nina Kilbrink, and Jan Axelsson.

Year 2—Teacher 1 as a Link between the Researchers and Teacher 2

During the second year of the project, three new cycles were implemented, this time with a new teacher (T2). The role of T1 changed during year 2 into a link between the researchers on the one hand, and the teaching teacher (T2) and other teachers in the teaching team (T3 + T4) on the other.

The first cycle began with a meeting where the researchers, with input from T1, presented the theories used for the study and the results of the first year's three cycles to the teaching team (T2 + T3 + T4). T2 was then asked to plan and conduct the teaching as usual, but he was also encouraged to try to incorporate results from the first year's cycles that he would like to build upon.

During this process, T1's experience of participating as teacher-as-researcher during the first year proved to be significant, and he thus served as a discussion partner and support for T2 in his preparation for the upcoming lesson. In relation to the researchers and the research project as such, T1 was given the task of keeping logbook notes from the discussions with T2 and the teacher team (T2–T4) about T2's lesson plans. The researchers were then able to read through these notes before the lesson was conducted and video recorded.

These video recordings were analyzed by the researchers at a preliminary stage and then analyzed by the researchers and the vocational teachers (T1+T2+T3+T4) together. Based on these analyses, using the CAVTA perspective, the teacher (T2), together with the researchers and T1, worked on new teaching strategies that were to be incorporated into the teacher's didactic approach for cycle 2. The process of the second and third cycles is the same as the first one, with the exception of the presentation of results from the first year's three cycles, which did not take place during the second and third cycles (see figure 9.3).

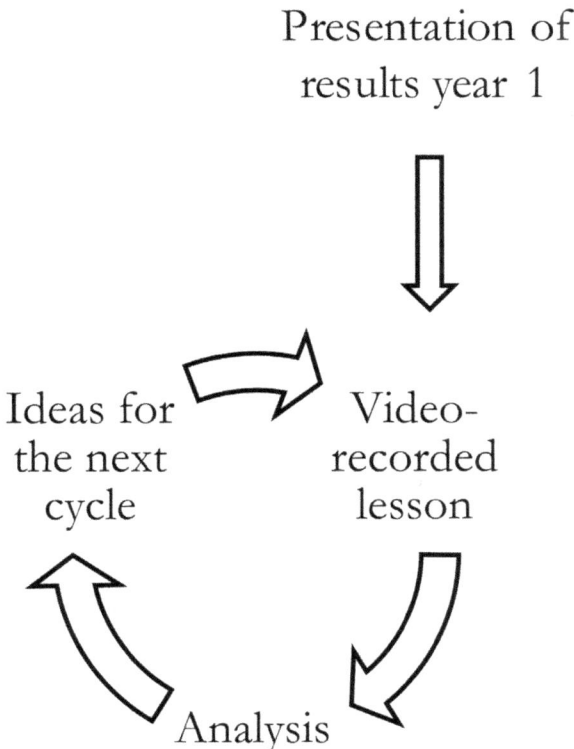

Figure 9.3 Learning Study 2 (Year 2); Cycle 1–3. *Source*: Stig-Börje Asplund, Nina Kilbrink, and Jan Axelsson.

SHIFTING POSITIONS FOR TEACHER 1

The transition to the second year of the project led, as mentioned earlier, to an altered position for T1 in the project. It was no longer his own teaching that constituted the basis for analysis and revision, but instead the planned and completed teaching of another teacher (T2) in the teaching team. Into this process, T1 brought his own experiences of participating as a teacher-as-researcher from the first year, which he had to deal with in collaboration with the research team, on the one hand, and T2 and other colleagues in the teacher team (T3+T4) on the other.

This shift in year 2 in terms of position induced a major change and resulted in a shift in perspectives, when T1 was suddenly placed adjacent to the teaching activities that were about to be conducted, analyzed, and revised. Despite the immediate (and emotional?) proximity to the teaching—how it would be executed, what learning content would be focused, and why, in this particular way with these particular students—these were issues over which T1 no longer had his own mandate.

At the same time, this new position and the shift in perspectives allowed T1 to distance himself from the teaching that was being researched. This distancing was more difficult to achieve for T1 during the first year, since his own teaching was the focus of the study. From this point forward, T1 took on the role of an ethnographic participant observer and analyst at the cost of the teaching role. However, while the change of positions involved a rapprochement toward the research team and a more theoretical, analytical approach, the movement also resulted in a degree of tension in T1's relationship with T2 (and with other teachers in the teacher team) with regard to instruction as well as its pedagogical content.

The following questions arose: To what extent can and should T1 highlight his own experiences and the results that the research project produced during its first year in conversation with T2? And how much autonomy in terms of planning and executing teaching about a specific learning content should T2 get? Should T2 start from scratch without using or taking advantage of the lessons learned by T1 and the project during the first year?

This reasoning could also be turned the other way: How ethically justifiable is it not to let T1 share the experiences and lessons of the first year (both the emotional experiences of "exposing" oneself to be examined in this way and the experience of implementing scientific theories to reflect on teaching practice)? And what does it mean for the project not to use the results from the first year during year 2? These questions became important aspects of the new positions for T1 in relation to ethical dilemmas caused by the shifted roles and positions in the project.

T1 and the Handling of the Shifted Positions

The concrete work with cycle 1 during the second year of the project began with a teacher team meeting in which T1 started the meeting by giving an account of his own experiences of participating in the study:

> *I briefly described how I planned the sessions which were filmed, how I gradually had learned more about the theoretical perspectives. My colleagues posed questions, now and then we drifted into didactic issues.* (From T1's logbook, 01 April 2019)

Through this short excerpt we can see how T1 takes on the role of a link between the researchers and the practice. In concrete terms, this meant that T1 positioned himself as a colleague who was able to share important experiences from participating in a research project. T1 did not only make himself and his own learning process available to his colleagues, but he also paved the way for scientific and theoretical concepts to become less abstract and thus more accessible to his colleagues.

Thereafter, T2 talked about his thoughts regarding the teaching he intended to do in the first session. It turned out that T2 had planned a slightly different arrangement compared to the format T1 used in his teaching:

> *For the first welding session, T2 plans a somewhat different design, although the focus on a selected amount of critical aspects is still there, keeping in line with my experiences of the first year's cycles. T2 plans to start with overlay welding, no joint welding, in welding position PA, since he anticipates he can visualize the melt best by doing so. In the discussion we agreed on the melt being as central in the fusion welding process as becoming an object of learning of its own.*
>
> *The discussion moved to a conversation about the complex interplay between critical aspects (where we on several occasions used body language to express ourselves!) and T2 emphasized how hard it can be to isolate one from the other. Certain critical aspects I had left out in my sessions, or at least I had not focused on them. T2 ended up focusing on the following critical aspects.* (From T1's logbook, 01 April 2019)

The fact that T2 initially said he wanted to change parts of the teaching that has already been carried out in the project, and openly relayed his ideas for change to his colleagues, not only testifies that he felt independent enough in relation to T1's teaching and the project itself, but also that he had the agency to propose these changes. The excerpt also shows how the teachers discussed together the importance of the melt as a central content (object of learning) in the specific welding method, and how the discussion then culminated in a discussion about the interaction and interplay between the aspects of TIG welding that the students are supposed to learn (critical aspects). We can see how the project as such also gave the teachers space and opportunity to conduct didactic discussions about the content and form of the welding education.

> *For the first time in years, we discuss specific didactic details in the actual learning contents of our welding education. On a regular basis, often every day, we discuss issues concerning our practices, but these discussions tend to deal with anything but specific didactic details. In the more formal and thoroughly documented conversations in scheduled meetings the teaching team analyzes the progression of individual students, including aspects such as absence, challenges linked to the learning process, etc.*
>
> *Class dynamics, informal leadership of the class and different ways of stimulating motivation in the class are other aspects which surface in the meetings as is the development of the curriculum and new exercises. In the informal chat during recesses all kinds of questions are brought up; parents have called, educational material needs to be ordered; machines have to be mended. Being part of this research project has enabled us to get to the core of our practices—finally getting to discuss the **what, how** and **why** of our welding education.* (T1, written reflections, 30 September 2019)

After the joint discussion on content issues regarding how to teach welding, T2 presented his thoughts about the teaching process itself—what could be termed as the different phases of the lesson. It also became clear that T2 had not really decided how certain concepts would be taught and that he needed more time to plan for this:

> *Furthermore, T2 plans to show the welding exercise, individual welding by the students and an assembly including a discussion about the outcome of the welding. T2 wanted to reflect further upon the details of his display of the welding, the individual feedback in the welding booths and the response at the assembly with all of the students.* (From T1's logbook, 01 April 2019)

The meeting ended with the teacher team agreeing that the teaching should focus on the "person-dependent parameters," that is, how to "physically weld," rather than the equipment-dependent parameters (equipment settings).

Overall, the extracts from T1's logbook notes show T2's independent position in relation to T1, T3, and T4, the research team, and the results and experiences from the first year of the project. At the same time, the excerpts show that there was a dialogue between the teachers about the experiences gained during the first year of the project and how these experiences were woven into a didactic discussion wherein questions about the specific content of the welding education were highlighted. Furthermore, it emerges clearly how T2 aimed to build further on the results and experiences from the first year of the project. This indicates that there already existed an openness at this early stage during year 2 to change his own teaching practice, and to do this in front of colleagues, students, and the researchers (with their video cameras).

A worry of mine has been that my colleagues would treat the results of the study so far, the findings of the video recordings of the welding sessions I have taught, as some kind of key or a blueprint to copy. These apprehensions have come to naught, though. As the experienced teacher T2 is, he would have no such limitations. He has listened carefully to my experiences. I have informed him about the integration of CAVTA and he has asked constructive questions about my assessments of the recorded sessions.

To my relief he has done all this while keeping his critical eye and asserting his individual right to frame his own teaching. I guess we both, even before our participation in this project, had noticed the differences in the way we teach TIG welding, although we have never come to discuss it in depth; "his way is as good as mine" being the general idea. By now confronting each other with the ideas regarding our designs of the learning processes, we are forced to question them openly; thus, a completely new element has been introduced in the evaluation process of our teaching practices.

A great potential for enhancement of our professional skills is found in this collaboration; by the implementation of two scientific theories, two experienced teachers, in full respect of the other's integrity, have made their practices transparent and in the encounter with a colleague's ideas and thoughts new insights may be gained. (T1, written reflections, 30 September 2019)

In the joint analytical work that took place, after cycle 1 year 2, when the researchers visited the teaching team at the current school, they presented their analyses of the recorded lesson. In connection with this, the researchers were also given the opportunity to ask questions to the teaching team about specific content aspects which the teachers know better than the researchers. Based on these discussions, possible teaching strategies for T2 to execute in the next teaching session (cycle 2) were discussed.

During the meeting it was also decided that T2 and T1 would meet shortly to discuss how T2, based on the joint analytical work and the experiences of cycle 1, could proceed in his teaching before cycle 2. T1's logbook notes show that T1 and T2 met several times before the teaching of cycle 2 took place. During these discussions, content aspects of welding were discussed, and it was clear that T2 wanted to continue to change and develop the teaching by, among other things, clarifying the central content even more, and he also announced a desire to approach the theories used in the study.

T2 plans to modify the actual exercise to the welding of a corner joint in the welding position PA, material thickness 2 mm, in order to reduce the amount of critical aspects to two—the arc length and the travel speed. The actual object of learning will be the melt. The additive material is in this exercise omitted, thus further focus can be put on the melt and the two critical aspects mentioned before.

A third critical aspect might be added—the electrode angle. In that case it will be briefly presented, since it has shown to be dealt with kind of instinctively by the students. Possibly, this critical aspect will be brought up in the individual welding if a student does not use the correct electrode angle.

T2 will also try to implement the variation theory and the conversation analysis to a larger extent, although he has not finalized those reflections yet. How will the variation patterns be made visible regarding the arc length and the travel speed? Will T2 himself show these patterns in practice, will the students after the interaction in the individual welding show the variation patterns, or will they be displayed both ways?

T2 figures he will let the students find the right values of the critical aspects and then, in the following discussion verbalize the correct values, either individually, at the general assembly, or on both occasions. He finds that much is gained by letting the students find the correct values in the learning situation.

In what way will the interaction regarding the variation patterns be designed? Verbalized, or merely by showing the students and then by letting them carry out the variation patterns? What will the follow-up of the critical aspects in the general assembly look like? (From T1's logbook, 24 May 2019)

During these sessions, T1 did not interfere with the plans of T2 to any great extent. This can be seen as motivated by the wish that last year's lessons should not be seen as a blueprint to be copied but a baseline to be reconsidered and modified. T1's approach was to pose questions to T2, in order for him to understand that the study was not a question of whether or not to implement the theories, but how to do it. T2 did not have the same opportunity as T1 to study the theories; therefore, it was important for T1 to explain the theories, general ideas, and the terminology.

In line with what was stated in the application for the project, the researchers gradually stepped back during the second year. The researchers briefed T1 about their reflections on cycle 2, and in the follow-up, T1 and T2 discussed the findings and how to move on to cycle 3. Mutual experiences unfolded as well as detailed didactic aspects of the welding exercises. T1 recognized T2's ambitions to focus on the chosen aspects of the object of learning in cycle 2, and T2's struggle to maintain that focus throughout the welding lesson was also familiar to T1. Unexpected issues that arise in the lessons must be addressed instantly; decisions on whether to stick to the planned focus or to digress must be made. The question of the students' verbalizations was another topic where the teachers shared the same experience. The actual exercise and the change of joint in order to better visualize the melt were evaluated, and the teachers agreed on the improvement and even suggested how to take it one step further by changing both the material and the settings of the equipment:

Frequently other aspects in the learning process emerge and one must imme-diately decide if one should bring them up with the student. We both feel an ambiguity and one has to bite one's tongue regarding these aspects in order to stick to the planned focus on critical aspects. [. . .] T2's exercise seems to be a hit. We plan to develop it further by changing both the material thickness and the setting of the equipment in order to visualise the melt as an object of learn-ing even further. (From T1's logbook, 30 September 2019)

Two other issues that surfaced in this meeting included (1) how to imple-ment the findings of the project in a regular classroom and (2) how to implement theories that underpin the research effectively. In the study, the video-recorded sessions were conducted with the teacher completely dedicat-ing himself to three or four students, whereas the class in everyday education consisted of up to sixteen students.

We also end up in discussions about how we can identify the enhancement of quality regarding shared understanding with the students, but how this stands in stark contrast to the implementation in our daily practices. [. . .] We end up talk-ing about how to use our time with the individual student/entire class in the most efficient way. Furthermore, we both express how the ideas about the current exercise, but also the transfer to other exercises and other welding methods, are growing like seeds. (From T1's logbook, 01 October 2019)

DIALOGIC APPROACH TO BRIDGE THE GAP

As stated earlier in this chapter, action-oriented Learning studies, where teachers are involved in formulating the research focus, have proven to be effective approaches in which teachers can change and develop their teaching practices as well as their professional learning, based on a theoretical frame-work. And, as Biesta (2007) puts it, teacher and researcher collaborations can also be a way of bridging the gap between educational practice and academic research.

However, this bridge can be rather complex and delicate to manage. Teachers and researchers can have different aims and expectations, and the different stakeholders can contribute to different competences in the collaborative process. A dialogic approach is important for addressing this complexity and for fostering collaboration between research and teaching practices. Communication and reflection during the process of collaboration are important, and as Biesta (2007) argues, some differences between research and practice can also be fruitful to keep:

> Attempts to bridge gaps between research and practice are therefore generally laudable, it is also important to remain aware of differences in expertise and responsibility between the stakeholders. This, in sum, reveals that it is as important to try to bridge gaps between research and practice as it is to keep a critical distance between the two, both from the side of educational research and from the side of educational practice. (Biesta, 2007, 300)

During the iterative cycles conducted in the second year, new premises for participating teachers (T1 and his teaching team T2–T4) as well as for the researcher team were created. In this chapter, the changed position of T1 during this second year has been highlighted. Based on the aim of the action research project to develop welding teaching on a scientific basis and relying on the Learning study method, the question of how the results and experiences of the first year can be used by a new teacher in his teaching has been in focus.

The main challenge of the project, in relation to the change of positions, different perspectives, and ethical dilemmas, has been to use the results and experiences from the first year of the project, without interfering with the agency of T2 in relation to his teaching practice. This has enabled T2 to contribute new perspectives and experiences, as well as his specific competences in welding education. It becomes evident that T1's presence at the school where the research was conducted and his relationship to T2 as a colleague has become important for the project in several ways.

During the second year of the project, T1 assumed greater responsibility for the research. Hence, a link to bridge the gap between educational science and school practice was established. It is obvious that T1 already at an early stage in the second year of the project highlighted the importance of the scientific approach and how the theories can be implemented in welding education. He increased the possibilities for the scientific approach to achieve legitimacy in the eyes of the teaching team. Hence, T1 used his positive experiences of the project and positioned himself with the legitimacy and authority to share this with his colleagues. At the same time, T1's logbook notes and written reflections show that in spite of the positive results from the first year's cycles, T1 was very much concerned about giving T2 space to design his own teaching, just as he himself was able to do during the first year of the project. After making sure that T2 had this agency, this design was discussed in light of the experiences and results from the first year.

In the second year of the project, the relationship established between T1 and T2 on the one hand and T2 and the teaching team on the other built further on the same dialogical premises as those which structured the relationship between the university-based researchers and T1. This dialogic approach is something that has permeated the whole research project, from research application to implementation and continuously during the action research process.

In the second year, T1, in collaboration with his colleagues, actively drew up requirements for creating conditions for content-related didactic discussions in the teaching team. Those discussions were based on theoretical perspectives (CAVTA) and had analytical intentions, which enabled the necessary critical distance, emphasized by Biesta (2007).

As Posch (2019) writes, it is important for research methods to harmonize with school practice. In a Learning study, a cornerstone of iterative cycles includes connecting learning content with the aims of the practice and the participating teachers (cf. Holmqvist, 2017; Kilbrink et al., 2014; Pang and Ling, 2012). Consequently, the aim of the teaching practice has a central role already in formulating the research questions in the welding project.

Moreover, teaching can always be unexpected and professional judgment can, as Biesta puts it, be more fruitful than "mechanical application of research-based rules for action" (2007, 298–299). Therefore, the aim of the research project must not be privileged over teaching and what is best for learning (cf. Asplund, 2010), something that was also emphasized before implementing the project. Through T1's active and deliberate work in positioning himself as the link between educational science and school practice, this ethical approach was an ongoing part of the teacher-researcher-pact in this project. The dialogical approach emphasized in this chapter served as a central part of T1's work. Adjusting to the shifts of perspectives and positions as well as the ethical challenges that arise when collaborating with researchers and one's own colleagues requires critical attention to practice in familiar contexts.

REFERENCES

Asplud, Stig-Börje. 2010. *Läsning Som Identitetsskapande Handling: Gemenskapande och Utbrytningsförsök i Fordonspojkars Litteratursamtal* [Reading as Identity Construction. Practices and Processes of Building a Sense of Community in Literary Discussions among Male Vehicle Engineering Students]. (Diss.) Karlstad: Karlstad University.

Asplund, Stig-Börje and Nina Kilbrink. 2018. "Learning How (and How Not) to Weld: Vocational Learning in Technical Vocational Education." *Scandinavian Journal of Educational Research* 62, no. 1, 1–16.

Asplund, Stig-Börje and Nina Kilbrink. 2020. "Lessons from the Welding Booth: Theories in Practice in Vocational Education." *Empirical Research in Vocational Education and Training* 12, no. 1, 1–23.

Bath, Caroline. 2009. "When Does the Action Start and Finish? Making the Case for an Ethnographic Action Research in Educational Research." *Educational Action Research* 17, no. 2, 213–224.

Biesta, Gert. 2007. "Bridging the Gap between Educational Research and Educational Practice: The Need for Critical Distance." *Educational Research and Evaluation* 13, no. 3, 295–301.

Brante, Göran, Mona Holmqvist Olander, Per-Ola Holmquist, and Marta Palla. 2015. "Theorising Teaching and Learning: Pre-service Teachers' Theoretical Awareness of Learning." *European Journal of Teacher Education* 38, no. 1, 102–118.

Carlgren, Ingrid (ed). 2017. *Undervisningsutvecklande Forskning: Exemplet Learning Study* [Teaching Developing Research: The Learning Study Example]. Gleerups: Malmö

Gelling, Leslie and Carol Munn-Giddings. 2011. "Ethical Review of Action Research: The Challenges for Researchers and Research Ethics Committees." *Research Ethics* 7, no. 3, 100–106.

Holmqvist, Mona. 2017. "Models for Collaborative Professional Development for Teachers in Mathematics." *International Journal for Lesson and Learning Studies* 6, no. 3, 190–201.

Kilbrink, Nina, Veronica Bjurulf, Ingela Blomberg, Anja Heidkamp, and Ann-Christin Hollsten. 2014. "Learning Specific Content in Technology Education: Learning Study as a Collaborative Method in Swedish Preschool Class Using Hands-on Material." *International Journal of Technology and Design Education* 24, 241–259.

Pang, Ming Fai and Lo Mun Ling. 2012. "Learning Study: Helping Teachers to Use Theory, Develop Professionality and Produce New Knowledge To be Shared." *Instructional Science* 40, no. 3, 589–606.

Posch, Peter. 2019. "Action Research–Conceptual Distinctions and Confronting the Theory–Practice Divide in Lesson and Learning Studies." *Educational Action Research* 27, no. 24, 496–510.

Tan, Yuen Sze Michelle and Imelda Santos Caleon. 2016. "Problem Finding in Professional Learning Communities: A Learning Study Approach." *Scandinavian Journal of Educational Research*, 60, no. 2, 127–146.

von Schantz Lundgren, Ina, Mats Lundgren, and Victoria Svensson. 2013. "Learning Study i Gymnasial Yrkesutbildning: En Fallstudie Från ett Hantverksprogram" ["Learning study in secondary vocational education: A case study from a craft program"]. *Nordic Journal of Vocational Education and Training* 3, no. 4, 1–16.

Chapter 10

Teachers as Ethnographers in Schools

Research Dynamics at a Waldorf School in the Philippines

Thijs Jan van Schie

This chapter discusses challenges and opportunities that arise when teachers become ethnographers in schools. The discussion draws on examples of ethnographic research dynamics, presented as vignettes, from fieldwork in a school setting in the Philippines. Central questions are: Is it possible to do research while teaching? What are the challenges and opportunities that emerge from a dual role in the field? And, is it desirable or not that teacher-researchers become co-producers of data and are active agents for change in their research settings?

These interrelated and overlapping topics are linked to classical dilemmas related to the ethnographic method of *participant observation* (as described by many scholars, for example Spradley, 1980; Agar, 1980; and Bernard, 2006). In many ways, all participant observation—whether it is done in a remote tribal community or in a high school classroom—shares similar characteristics and requires similar skills and techniques. Researchers are always striving to "experience the lives of the people you study as much as [one] can," (Bernard 2006, 343–344) but, at the same time, "being able to switch back and forth between the insider's view and that of an analyst" (Bernard 2006, 371).

The primary dilemma, presented in the first vignette, is about becoming a participant observer, instead of an ordinary participant (Spradley 1980, 53–58); in other words, becoming a teacher-researcher instead of just a teacher. The second dilemma, in the next vignette, is about gaining access to the field. How does one present him- or herself and how does one deal with the multiple roles that are ascribed in addition to the researcher's role? (Agar

1980 54–62). Lastly, the third dilemma, in the final vignette, is about forging a research partnership with research participants and working together to improve education. This chapter argues that the teacher-ethnographer is uniquely positioned to carry out ethnographic research from an insider perspective, including eliciting in-depth information from multiple perspectives with great potential for empirical impact.

ETHNOGRAPHY IN FAMILIAR
EDUCATIONAL SETTINGS

The strange-familiar dichotomy has a long tradition in anthropology and beyond (Myers 2011). Traditionally, ethnographers aimed "to make the strange familiar" by doing fieldwork in faraway exotic cultural contexts, distinct from their own backgrounds, and, once back in their home contexts, by introducing unknown cultural practices to home audiences. In these classic colonial ethnographies, the strange was made familiar by focusing on universal human themes such as ritual, kinship, and exchange. They showed us that, despite cultural differences, people everywhere deal with similar issues in life.

Current ethnography also tries "to make the familiar strange." This concept is especially important in the growing number of ethnographic studies carried out in more or less familiar settings to the ethnographer, such as the ethnographer's own locality or one's own workplace (Gmelch and Gmelch 2018, 238; Shore 2012, 90). Underlying structures, assumptions, and values are pointed out in order not to take things for granted (Delamont 2016, 34–37). In educational research, for example, designing better tests without questioning the assumption that standardized mass testing is valuable should be avoided, as should coming up with recommendations for classroom management without any discussion of the underlying structure of uniformly graded classes.

The trend for ethnography in familiar settings coincides with another tendency: the *professional as researcher*, as opposed to the *researcher as professional* (Mosse 2006, 938; Shuttleworth 2004, 46). Undertaking such *insider-ethnography* provides an interesting new perspective (Brannan et al. 2007, 399–400), also in education (inter alia Klippel, 2017; Bakbie and Provost, 2004), with teachers positioned as ethnographers *in* education, as opposed to ethnographers *of* education. The doctoral research upon which this chapter is based is an example of the professional becoming a researcher. It is funded by the Doctoral Grant for Teachers of NWO, the Dutch Organization for Scientific Research.

ETHNOGRAPHIC RESEARCH DYNAMICS AT A WALDORF SCHOOL IN THE PHILIPPINES

The examples used in this chapter originate in a research project on the globalization of Waldorf education. Waldorf education is an alternative educational approach based on the pedagogic and didactic ideas of its founder, Rudolf Steiner, who espoused a specific spiritual worldview called *anthroposophy*. Since the turn of the century, Waldorf education has spread globally; consequently, its educational philosophy and practice was transformed and adapted to fit the new local contexts (see e.g. the studies of Boland, 2015 or Hoffmann, 2016). The research project investigates this process, the local manifestation of Waldorf education as a globalizing phenomenon, via an ethnographic case study in the Philippines.

The fieldwork serving as the basis for the research project was planned in several short periods (of about one to two months) in 2017 and 2018, and it continued into 2020. In practice, doing ethnographic fieldwork in a specific Filipino Waldorf school means hanging out in the teachers' lounge; chatting with students in the schoolyard; sitting in the back of classrooms observing; interviewing teachers, parents, and students; participating in various school activities, such as school camps, festivities, and teacher meetings; taking notes of casual conversations with parents and villagers; and, also, teaching occasionally.

Despite the fact that the research location used as an example in this chapter, namely the Philippines, is not home to the teacher-researcher (who lives and works in the Netherlands), the research setting is familiar, in the sense that research about Waldorf education is combined with the profession of being a Waldorf teacher. The notion of Waldorf is de-territorialized in the sense that ideas about it circulate within an international Waldorf network. It is also territorialized, in the sense that it is practiced and reformulated in a particular school in a particular locality. De-territorialized and territorializing notions of familiarity therefore go hand in hand in international (educational) networks (Inda and Rosaldo, 2008, 12–15).

In the case study used in this chapter, the research setting is familiar to the teacher-researcher insofar as numerous school practices at the Filipino Waldorf school show similarities with Waldorf schools in the Netherlands. To some extent, the researcher and the research participants (especially the Filipino teachers) share the same knowledge and experiences. They are both familiar with the Waldorf philosophy and with numerous practices in the school, including curricular content, pedagogical principles, and didactics.

More generally, many aspects of school life are more familiar and thus easier for the teacher-researcher to identify with than those of non-teacher-researchers, including typical classroom and schoolyard dynamics and efforts and struggles of teachers and students. However, the assumption of such familiarity may also mask seeing potential differences and distract from the fact that day-to-day school practices are undeniably embedded in their local context and that Filipino culture is evident in teaching, in working together, and in interacting with students.

RESEARCH SETTING 1: STUDYING ONESELF

When teachers do research, it might be the case that—sooner or later—they study themselves. That is to say, they study the pedagogical and didactical approaches they use as well as educational ideologies that they themselves follow and put into practice. This may occur in the school setting in which they are employed or in a different school. For example, teachers may be asked to temporarily replace a teacher or to participate in other occasional work activities, such as guidance during a school camp or class trip, making or grading tests, etc.

This was the case during the research on Waldorf education in the Philippines, when a request was made to co-teach a series of geography lessons on the topic of meteorology. As a result, participant observation partly turned into self-observation.

Diary excerpt:

Every day we start the lesson with a morning verse. Because the students were rattling off that verse quite monotonically and mechanically, the co-teacher of the course, John [note that all names in this article are pseudonyms] *asked me to experiment a bit to gain more awareness of the verse lines. So, we tried various things. For example, just saying the word "I" out loud but reciting the rest of the verse in our heads. Or standing backwards, while reciting. Today, we stand in a circle.*

After the verse, the lesson usually proceeds with an inspiring story. Today, it is the story of the photo "earth rise," the first photo of the earth made from space. It is supposed to make the students aware of the vulnerability of our planet. It is typical of the Waldorf way of teaching, to use images and stories without being explicit about the underlying message of those images and stories. John does that very well. A bit too extensive perhaps, but the scope is clear: We must be careful with our planet.

[. . .] Now it is my turn to elaborate on the revolutions of the earth in space, causing day and night, different seasons, and different climate zones on earth. As difficult as it may be to distinguish four seasons in the Philippines, students still have to learn about the tilted axis of the earth, the angle of incidence of solar radiation, the solstice, and the latitudes of the tropics and polar circles. Everyone listens attentively, even when I use students to demonstrate the earth's

revolutions in space by walking these movements through the classroom or when I let someone shine the torch on his smartphone on the blackboard to depict the bundling of the sun's rays in different angles.

But, no matter how animated the lesson, or how great the enthusiasm and attention of the students, when they have to process their notes into their lesson books, they apparently find it difficult to articulate things well. This is partly due to some students' low-level knowledge of English, which isn't their native tongue, while it is the language of instruction in almost all lessons at school. They also seem to experience a heavy homework burden, even though, in my opinion, they get little homework compared to my Dutch students. Apparently, they are not used to it.

In the example above the teacher has become a participant observer while teaching. That means that he has a dual purpose, both engaging with his work as a teacher and observing like an ethnographer (Spradley 1980, 54). In addition to the dual purpose, the role of participant observer also requires *explicit awareness* of the class situation, a *wide-angle lens*, and personal skills in order to distance oneself from one's own teaching practices and allow for being *introspective* (Ibid., 55–58). Lastly, and obviously, one should *record objective observations and subjective feelings* (Ibid., 58). One has become an "*active participant*," but should guard against becoming a *complete participant* (Ibid., 60–61).

The many challenges related to the method of participant observation, and to becoming or being a participant observer in an educational setting, include incidental confusion about what is observed, biases related to one's educational ideology and frame of reference, and suffering from the so-called *homeblindness*, meaning that certain blind spots are neglected. Three related examples to these challenges from the diary entry are explained.

First, the diary entry above provides an example of confusion about what is observed, as noted when the teacher-researcher was asked to think about experiments to make students more aware of the contents of a morning verse. Do these experiments such as standing backward or in a circle reveal anything about the educational practices of this particular school because they resulted from a pedagogical question raised by one of the teachers of the school? Or, should they be seen as the outcome of a creative approach by the teacher-researcher; in other words: an observation of the self?

Similarly, the above example also reveals potential biases related to being a Waldorf teacher. Agar (1980) suggests that biases are not only personal and cultural, but "[they] also have been programmed with some powerful professional ones" (42). Inevitably, one has profound ideas about professional competence: about good or bad lessons, capable or non-capable teachers, and so on. It was stated in the diary excerpt, for example, that the

Filipino teacher used a typical *Waldorf way of teaching* and that he did this *very well*. One must inquire on what basis the teacher-researcher is observing and judging certain professional competences and on what basis is teaching *well done* in *a Waldorf way*? To some extent, it can be said that the use of strong images is typical for the Waldorf pedagogy, since it is mentioned in many Waldorf resource books that are used both in the Philippines and in the Netherlands. On the other hand, this judgment is also one of personal taste and interpretation.

Third, there may be *homeblindness*, a classical anthropological concept referring to a very small analytical distance between observer and observed, causing certain blind spots. A famous analogy attributed to Kluckhohn (1949) is that of a fish forgetting about the water around it because the water is always there. Spradley (1980) is especially cautious of homeblindness in cases of ethnography in familiar settings: "The more you know about a situation as an ordinary participant, the more difficult it is to study it as an ethnographer" (61).

In the diary entry, such a blind spot can be observed in relation to the contradiction between the students' enthusiasm for and involvement with the subject matter and the difficulties they experienced with processing their notes and managing their homework. Does this say something about a specific learning culture, or does it instead speak to the learning abilities of the students? Does the teacher's non-native background make him simultaneously interesting and difficult to understand, for example? In fact, there can be many reasons, but certain blind spots can easily influence analysis of such a contradiction.

How should teacher-ethnographers approach these challenges of potential confusion, biases, and blind spots? It is important to understand that ethnographic research is subjective by definition, and its quality does not depend on neutrality, but rather on a reflexive epistemological stance. "[Ethnography] has always meant the attempt to understand another life world using the self [. . .] as the instrument of knowing" (Sherry Ortner 1995, in Shuttleworth 2004, 47) in which "subjective experiences and selfhood are part and parcel of fieldwork and its results" (Robben and Sluka 2007, 63).

Reflexivity, then, includes the art of "making the familiar strange," meaning that one is able to see oneself from a distance when operating in the field and navigate between different identities, for example, teacher or researcher, man, White, European, a father, Dutch. Another method for transcending one's own viewpoints is to imagine new viewpoints by empathizing with the other actors in the school, that is, students, parents, or support staff. Thus, defamiliarization is not just a technique, it provides a range of new experiences and perspectives.

Above all, studying one's own familiar educational context provides opportunities. Specific professional competences and knowledge not only provide the teacher-ethnographer with easier access to the field but also allow for a more profound exploration: "The insider is potentially better positioned [. . .] to reveal the 'true story'" (Alvesson, 2003, 178). The positioning of ethnographers in familiar settings facilitates in-depth research, allows for an easier grasp of sensitive issues, and grounds theories in practice in a more or less natural way, resulting in thorough empirical accounts (Ibid., 2003, 181).

In addition to easy access and in-depth information, there are a number of practical advantages to ethnography done in familiar settings, compared to ethnography in less familiar settings: It is usually less costly, easier to set up, and less time-consuming (Ibid., 2003, 172).

RESEARCH SETTING 2: DUAL ROLES

The previous example in which the researcher is submerged in his own research setting as a result of teaching practices, clarifies how teacher-researchers can take on dual roles in the field. To a certain extent, all ethnographers deal with multiple roles in the field and must continuously navigate between them. There are many more possible roles in addition to those of researcher and teacher. For example, the teacher-researcher might have and/or might be perceived as having the role of project manager, advisor, colleague, coach, trainer, supporter, donor, policymaker, sparring partner, confidante, and/or friend.

As the diary excerpt below illustrates, there was confusion about the role of the researcher in the Filipino research setting.

Diary excerpt:

After I had introduced myself during the plenary meeting, I wondered how people saw me: As a Waldorf teacher? A Waldorf consultant? A supporter of the school? A potential donor? Or as a researcher? I had the feeling that my background as a Waldorf teacher was more valued than my intended role as researcher. [. . .]

I even wondered if everyone really realized that I was a researcher. I had stressed the fact that I—unlike most foreign visitors [the school had been frequently visited by foreign advisors and sympathizers]— did not come to bring things, such as money or advice, but that—instead—I had come to get things from them, namely research data. [. . .]

Despite my firm and clear introduction, I noticed, quite quickly, that teachers regularly saw me as an advisor and colleague rather than as researcher. They also asked for feedback about their teaching after I had observed their classes. They pretty much expected it. They asked, for example: Did I do it right? How would you do it? Do you have any tips? I repeatedly reminded them that I was not here to judge. But that didn't stop them from asking time and again for my opinion. [. . .] Like Ms. Kristine. Based on my casual feedback of the day before, she had chosen a different approach in her lesson today.

The example above deals with the theme of entering the field and presenting oneself as a researcher, an issue of access that all ethnographers are confronted with. Agar (1980) explains that what one is doing in the field is very important in relation to research ethics, but people initially "will draw on their own repertoire of social categories to find one that fits [them]" (54). Sometimes, research participants value other roles more than that of the researcher.

In the context of ethnography in familiar educational settings, and especially in cases of dual roles in those settings, entering the field is often relatively easy. But such a smooth connection to the field comes with its own set of challenges. The challenges inherent to having dual roles include fostering multiple loyalties and having an engaged insider's perspective, making it difficult to distance oneself analytically. Moreover, if the role of the researcher is overruled by other roles, dual roles can conceal the fact that there is actually research being conducted for those who are part of it. These challenges will now successively be discussed on the basis of the above example from the field.

First, multiple loyalties relating to multiple roles can come into conflict with each other. The loyalty of the researcher toward research outcomes, for example, can be in conflict with the loyalty of the professional toward the institution in which she or he works or is associated with. In fact, "the more roles and statuses ethnographers occupy in relation to their informants, the higher the likelihood that conflicts of interest, ethical dilemmas, and/ or points of contention will occur" (Shuttleworth 2004, 46). Moreover, some roles could lead to "too strong of an identification with one's research subjects" (Ibid., 51). This can result in self-restraint with respect to research outcomes, such as omitting sensitive information in order to prevent the organization from being shown in a bad light (Alvesson 2003, 167).

Furthermore, critique of Waldorf education can be marginalized in the research, even unconsciously, in order to present a positive image of the Waldorf school under investigation. This happens especially when one identifies too strongly with the educational ideology of Waldorf education as a core element of one's professional identity. This is not obvious in the example above, but it is applicable to the research literature on Waldorf education, which is often accused of being biased. It is seen as being too positive about the educational approach or too negative, with almost no middle ground or neutral considerations (Dhondt et al., 2015).

In classical ethnography, when an amalgamation of roles occurs, it is sometimes referred to as "going native" (Bernard 2006, 348–349). When one is too close, one might become reluctant to talk about sensitive issues or taboos. And even when one tries to be as neutral as possible, sometimes research environments or participants put pressure on the researcher—explicitly or implicitly—to choose sides in a conflict. This occurred, for example, in the research of Forsey (2004), *He's Not a Spy; He's One of Us*.

Teachers who conduct research in schools are already familiar with or are "native" in their research setting. Their challenge is to adapt a non-teacher lens in their research setting by questioning everyday commonalities, underlying structures, assumptions, and values. Instead of getting close by "breaking into" their "field," they might distance themselves by "breaking out" (Alvesson 2003, 176), by simultaneously being "immersed and estranged" (Ybema and Kamsteeg 2009, 103), and alternately "social" and "anti-social," in order to be able to be both socially connected to research participants and be analytical toward the research outcomes (Mosse, 2006). "In fact, closer relations in the field [. . .] have made exit rather than entry the significant shift in location" (Ibid., 936).

The diary excerpt shows how difficult this is in practice. Despite the researcher's conscious attempts to present himself as a researcher, people continued to treat him as a colleague, as another teacher, or as an advisor. On the one hand, this is about how one presents oneself. Bernard (2006) is clear about the rules related to such presentation: "Be honest, be brief, and be absolutely consistent [and] understand that not everyone will be thrilled about your role as researcher" (358). On the other hand, it is also about how people understand your message. Agar (1980) noted: "I tried to tell everyone who I was, but [. . .] the message does not always get across to everyone" (1980, 60)

How can these challenges of multiple loyalties and identities, sufficient analytical distance, and an unambiguous presentation of the self be overcome? First, a balance must be found between issues that require openness and those issues that require prudence. On the one hand, it is useful to reflect openly on one's role in the research, including the personal sympathies, intentions, loyalties, and complications that emerge with multiple roles in the field and becoming a participant observer. On the other hand—also from an ethical perspective—one must be aware of power differences and be prudent about sensitive information that could possibly harm research participants.

Second, there must be a combination of closeness and distance. Closeness is essential to be able to empathize with research participants in order to obtain in-depth information and even to "understand what goes without saying" (Ybema and Kamsteeg 2009, 101). However, in order to analyze and theorize research outcomes, a degree of distance must also be maintained and the researcher must also avoid "staying native" by "breaking out" (Alvesson 2003, 176) or by becoming involved in a way that has been characterized as "detached involvement" (Nash 1963, in Agar 1980, 50–51).

Third, voluntary and prior informed consent must always be pursued, and it must not be assumed that one's role as a researcher is immediately clear to anyone in the field. Therefore, however frustrating it may be, repetition is necessary. One should constantly be clear and open about one's role as a researcher.

The challenges linked to having multiple roles in the field may have down sides, but they certainly also entail excellent opportunities for good ethnographic insight. Multiple roles imply that there are also multiple perspectives. Indeed, the research topic is then approached, in a relatively natural way, from different angles and through multiple, bottom-up, "insider" views.

RESEARCH SETTING 3: CO-PRODUCING DATA

Dual roles can be confusing not only for research participants but also for researchers themselves. When researchers switch smoothly between their roles in the field, boundaries may become blurred and more hybrid. A possible result is that researchers become co-producers of research data as a side effect of being active agents attempting to improve their research and educational settings as they move toward the participant side of the participant-observer spectrum. This is almost inevitable in any research in which participant observation is used as a method (Spradley 1980, 58–62; Bernard 2006, 347).

This occurred in the Filipino research setting when a group of Dutch Waldorf consultants joined a trip to the Philippines. They were responsible for a series of Asian Waldorf Teacher Training sessions. This event turned out not only to be an opportunity to meet Filipino Waldorf teachers from all over the country, but it was also a way to discuss various aspects of Waldorf education with them and to think collectively about improvements in teaching practices and the curricula in their schools. In such a situation, a researcher could easily act as a consultant, even if one is not officially assigned to that role. Or, one may even be asked to substitute for a trainer who suffered from sunstroke in the tropical heat at the end of the Philippines dry season.

Diary excerpt:

> *Trainer Henk invited me to his workshop in order to facilitate a discussion on the history curriculum in grade 7 and 8. Teachers from different Filipino Waldorf schools joined the discussion. All participants considered*

the discussion relevant, and it became clear that most of them were not fully satisfied with the current history curriculum, which was evaluated as being too general, too unspecific, and too Eurocentric in relation to the national and local contexts of the schools. Various options for change became part of the conversation.

Gradually, I joined the discussion by making suggestions and coming up with alternative ideas. I did so partly because my opinion was asked for by the participants, but also partly due to my own enthusiasm for the topic. After all, I am a teacher myself and I know the Waldorf history curriculum of grade 7 and 8 quite well.

This third and last example deals with the dilemma of forging a research partnership with research participants. Could one cooperate with them to make things better? Why would one do this? "Increasingly, anthropologists today involve the people whom they study in their fieldwork" (Gmelch and Gmelch 2018, 240). Such questions relate to the increase of anthropological studies in familiar settings, in which close proximity between researchers and research participants makes cooperation easier.

Usually, ethnography is more focused on describing social realities rather than on changing them. But the researcher's influence on the research setting is considered implicit to the research process, not something to be avoided per se, but something to be open about and reflect upon. Anthropological knowledge is always "inseparable from their relationship with those they study" (Mosse 2006, 935) and "socially negotiated" (Ibid., 946). Furthermore, research plans are usually open to change during the research, since the data are collected inductively and there is a certain openness to serendipitous (unintentional) findings.

In the example above, the possibility to co-produce a newly adjusted history curriculum can be considered serendipitous because it had not been anticipated. Like the *Three Princes of Serendip*, ethnographers find all kinds of things they weren't looking for. So, even though an action-oriented method is less conventional in ethnographic research, it leaves the option open, often in cooperation with research participants (Down and Hughes 2009). The challenge in such research is not necessarily to minimize one's influence as a researcher, but to ensure that all participants recognize their contributions.

Ultimately, all social researchers strive for validation of their research outcomes. This usually happens by giving critical accounts of underlying structures, that is, ethnography of education, or by action-oriented cooperation from the inside, that is, ethnography in education. Teachers who study schools are able to be *ethnographers in education*, since they are familiar with teaching and research practices. This gives them the tools to rapidly convert research outcomes into practical change. This is illustrated by the third vignette, which shows how the researcher is readily drawn into potential curricular change.

A RATIONALE FOR ETHNOGRAPHIC
RESEARCH BY TEACHERS IN SCHOOLS

What opportunities are provided by ethnographic research conducted by teachers in schools? This question must be asked while taking into account that teachers-ethnographers partly study themselves, play multiple roles in the field, and often co-produce data with research participants. There are clearly a number of challenges related to ethnographic research conducted by teachers in schools, but there also some good reasons to make a case for it. First, an insider perspective is founded on an organic closeness to research participants and offers a considerable chance to yield in-depth information. Second, the research is approached from multiple grounded insider perspectives. Lastly, it implies the potential for practical empirical impact.

REFERENCES

Agar, Michael H. 1980. *The Professional Stranger: An Informal Introduction to Ethnography*. New York: Academic Press.
Alvesson, Mats. 2003. "Methodology for Close Up Studies: Struggling with Closeness and Closure." *Higher Education* 46, no. 2, 167–193.
Bakbie, Andrea M. and Mary C. Provost. 2004. "Teachers as Researchers." *Intervention in School & Clinic* 39, no. 5, 260–268.
Bernard, Harvey Russell. 2006. *Research Methods in Anthropology: Qualitative and Quantitative Methods*, 4th edition. Walnut Creek, CA: AltaMira
Boland, Neil. 2015. "The Globalisation of Steiner Education: Some Considerations." *Research on Steiner Education Journal* 6, 192–202.
Brannan, Matthew, Geoff Pearson, and Frank Worthington. 2007. "Ethnographies of Work and the Work of Ethnography." *Ethnography* 8, no. 4, 395–402.
Delamont, Sara. 2016. *Fieldwork in Educational Settings: Methods, Pitfalls and Perspectives*, 3rd edition. Oxford: Routledge.
Dhondt, Pieter, Nele van de Vijver, Pieter Verstraete, Moritz Föllmer, Moritz, and Mark B. Smith. 2015. "The Possibility of an Unbiased History of Steiner/Waldorf Education?" *Contemporary European History* 24, no 4, 639–649.
Forsey, Martin. 2004. "'He's not a Spy; He's One of Us': Ethnographic Positioning in a Middle-Class Setting." In *Anthropologists in the Field: Cases in Participant Observation* edited by Lynne Hume and Jane Mulcock, pp. 59–70. New York: Columbia University Press.

Gmelch, George and Sharon Bohn Gmelch. 2018. *In the Field: Life and Work in Cultural Anthropology.* Oakland, CA: University of California Press.

Hoffmann, Vera. 2016. "Creating Place-based Waldorf Festivals: An Ethnographic Study of Festivals in Two Non-European Waldorf Schools." *Research on Steiner Education Journal* 7, no. 2, 88–104.

Inda, Jonathan X. and Rosaldo, Renato (eds). 2008. *The Anthropology of Globalization,* 2nd edition. Malden: Blackwell.

Klippel, Friederike. 2017. "Teachers as Researchers," *Language Teaching* 50 (2): 297-98.

Kluckhohn, Clyde. 1949. *Mirror for Man: The Relation of Anthropology to Modern Life.* New York: McGraw-Hill Book Company.

Mosse, David. 2006. "Anti-social Anthropology? Objectivity, Objection, and the Ethnography of Public Policy and Professional Communities." *Journal of the Royal Anthropological Institute* 12, no. 4, 935–956.

Myers, Robert. 2011. "The Familiar Strange and the Strange Familiar in Anthropology and Beyond," *General Anthropology* 18, no. 2, 1–9.

Robben, Antonius C.G.M. 2007. "Fieldwork Identity". In *Ethnographic Fieldwork. An Anthropological Reader,* edited by Antonius C.G.M. Robben and Jeffrey A. Sluka, pp. 59–63. Malden: Blackwell.

Shore, Cris. 2012. "Anthropology and Public Policy." In *The Sage Handbook of Social Anthropology,* pp. 89–104. https://www.researchgate.net/publication/2929 14436.

Shuttleworth, Russell. 2004. "Multiple Roles, Statuses, and Allegiances: Exploring the Ethnographic Process in Disability Culture." In *Anthropologists in the Field; Cases in Participant Observation,* edited by Lynne Hume and Jane Mulcock, pp. 46–58. New York: Columbia University Press.

Spradley, James P. 1980. *Participant Observation.* New York: Holt, Rinehart and Winston.

Ybema, Sierk and Frans Kamsteeg. 2009. "Making the Familiar Strange: A Case for Disengaged Organizational Ethnography." In *Organizational Ethnography: Studying the Complexities of Everyday Life,* edited by Sierk Ybema, Dvora Yanow, Harry Wels, and Frans Kamsteeg, pp. 101–119. London: Sage.

Chapter 11

The Familiar and the Foreign

The Schooling of System-Involved Youth

Sarah Staples-Farmer

While taking a tour through any neighborhood school environment, visitors would probably see inspirational signs, brilliant bulletin boards, reading and textbooks, maps, equipment for science experiments, art or pottery classes, wood working, and artifacts of student achievement. Students walk freely through these halls, navigating forty-eight-minute class periods, long lunch lines, and catching up on the latest news during passing time. Teachers wait expectantly outside their open doors for students, sharing "Good morning!" fist bumps or "How are you today?" waves. Some students will enter, warm and familiar with age-appropriate behaviors and skillsets, while others will posture a mysterious hard-shelled exterior difficult to crack.

Students take their seats. A broad range of experiences awaits the classroom teacher, impacting the class dynamic and academic achievement: student trauma, high mobility, socioeconomic status, cultural differences, immigrant status, and/or learning abilities/disabilities. Despite designing the classroom and curriculum to invite and inspire learning for *all* students, the teacher may not be prepared for an oft-overlooked population of young people: the system-involved, the detained, or those who have spent time in confinement or total lockdown. The lack of preparation may stem from little (if any) exposure to professional development programming addressing the unique learning needs of court-affiliated youth. The researcher, a veteran teacher of secondary English, recognized this struggle, understanding her most challenging students as well as her discomfort around them. Strategies were absent because real knowledge was absent. The only way to increase her own comfort was to enter the foreign space of a detention center classroom.

By visiting multiple detention centers throughout a Midwestern state, the researcher tried to answer how, like her, educators in a typical, familiar school environment can engage the student who is "bad ass" or delinquent, or, who, just the day before, slept in a locked cell that was monitored by cameras and juvenile detention officers. A juvenile detention facility could be intimidating to many, given the extreme fencing and the knowledge that some youth who are inside have committed violent crimes. Nevertheless, observations exposing the schooling experiences of teacher participants and how they viewed their lives teaching in a detention center school revealed how professionals can approach a mysterious student demographic despite limitations of a secured environment. If teachers and administrators in neighborhood schools could gain a comprehensive understanding of the culture and teaching in the juvenile detention/youth center, that knowledge could translate to addressing obstacles found in mainstream "home" classrooms.

They Are Still "Kids"

Research seeks to learn about this student demographic, to consider the factors that contribute to their circumstances, including those within the public education system, and to inform specific professional development for educators. Numbers from 2010 indicate that 2.18 million students were involved in the U.S. juvenile justice system, and 93,000 were incarcerated. More recently, the Office of Juvenile Justice and Delinquency Prevention (OJJDP) posted that 43,580 students are housed in residential placement facilities (O'Cummings, Bardack, and Gonsoulin 2010, 1; Puzzanchera and Hokenberry, 2019).

These declining numbers illustrate that juvenile justice policy reform and pre-adjudicated types of intervention now work to keep youth out of lockdown. Instead, students are placed in their communities: in group homes, other alternative settings, and of course in neighborhood schools. However, system-involved youth are just that: youth. Historically, education has not been a positive experience for these young people. Traditional schooling may not suit their learning styles nor needed accommodations, and many experience multiple transitions. These disruptions along their educational journey result in low attendance, gaps in learning sequence, and extreme skill deficiency (Read and O'Cummings, 2011). Subsequently, low literacy, low academic performance, and stigma labeling characterize most court-affiliated youth.

Ironically, for these students, the familiar may be the detention center school where they receive various health services, experience small class sizes, and individualized instruction. In detention, they are removed from outside circumstances like negative home environments that create anxiety. Beyond the razor wire, however, the unfamiliar experience may be that of navigating a typical eight-period day and multiple classes. An estimated 45–70 percent of youth in custody suffer from learning disabilities and emotional behavior disorders, and 75 percent of incarcerated juveniles nationwide are high school dropouts (Guerra, 2010; Tannis 2014, p. 13). Students are typically three to four years below their grade level (Nurse 2010, p. 57; Coulter 2010, p. 321), and more than one-third of incarcerated youth are illiterate (Guerra, 2010).

Moreover, Hooper-Arana (2019) emphasizes the increased potential for ongoing stigmatization of youth who return to classrooms, noting low internal motivation, social-emotional struggles, maltreatment at home, and even unidentified learning disabilities or inhibitors, all of which can manifest in poor behaviors and subsequent removal from classroom settings (4). Red flags follow these youth wherever they go. Unable to escape their label, they are arguably the most vulnerable population of young people. Surrounding them with adult advocates who are connected, caring, and informed can make the difference between staying in school and experiencing success or reoffending and repeating failure.

ACCESSING FORGOTTEN SPACES: HOME AWAY FROM HOME PART 1

Despite the challenges and trepidation of studying youth in a detention center, this realm of education that not many people understand can become as much of a home as any other. Using ethnographic tools, this study explores the foreign culture of "doing school" in a detention center, with the intent to create and improve curriculum, instruction, and the comprehensive education of adjudicated youth. Second, the study examines the misperceptions housed in familiar spaces about system-involved students, that is, how labeling in a traditional classroom can impact student behavior and academic performance. The schools on either side of the razor wire are not dissimilar, except perhaps in the way each chooses to accept or change the narrative about youth offenders.

Over a period of three years, ethnographic observations occurred in three different youth detention centers, representing urban, suburban, and rural communities, ranging in size from a 130-bed facility to an 80- and 35-bed facility, respectively. Ethnography, through its narratives and thick descriptions, offers a way to present "a credible argument that what one learned should be believed by others who were not present" and bring "ways of understanding into awareness" (Agar 2008, 1). Ultimately, the focus of data collection was to "reduce the puzzlement" and mystery of a detention school setting not only for the researcher but for everyone in the home community (Geertz 1973, 16). Both the general public and educators in traditional learning environments are often unaware that such schools even exist and that within them, students can and do learn.

Faculty and staff within two sites were interviewed, teaching materials and student work examples were collected to serve as artifacts, and over 200 hours were spent in the classroom taking field notes. Formal interviews with participants included administrators, lead teachers, and faculty in each building. Informal interview participants included students, detention officers, volunteer trainers, aides, transition specialists, medical staff, literacy coaches, and volunteers with security clearance.

Gaining access to youth who are confined presented multiple challenges. One roadblock rested in the highly mobile nature of court-affiliated youth. Students come and go, limiting opportunity for repeated observation of approved student subjects. During informal interviews with administration and teachers, stories of youth returning, even as high as fifteen or twenty times throughout their adolescence, were shocking. While no national recidivism rate exists, youth with no prior court referrals experience a recidivism rate of 40 percent; for those who have prior court referrals, the number jumps to 60 percent (Snyder and Sickmund 2006, 235). A second roadblock was gaining parent/guardian consent for student participation. Guardians and parents tend to be highly mobile themselves or not present, thus getting signatures of consent was nearly impossible.

In addition, the presence of a researcher outsider, albeit one who was a fellow educator, illuminated conflicts between the primary nature of security and the secondary concern of education. Security's presence drew a line between curricular philosophy and allowed practice. The familiar classroom grew distant as the researcher faced tensions between her own pedagogy and what teaching strategies were observed within the culture, essentially, of a prison "home": inappropriate discourse, mannerisms, and physical proximity. Bright, comfortable, and inviting spaces were replaced with bland cement block walls, cold tiled floors, plastic chairs and tables bolted to the floor, and juvenile detention officers with their loud, interruptive radios stationed in every classroom.

Perhaps the greatest limitation presented itself in one of the three facilities observed: the director of educational programming was the researcher's husband. Access to certain teachers and classrooms was prohibited because he was the appraising administrator. Concerns arose of compromised ethics, of conversations sharing confidential information occurring at home. This barred opportunity to talk in the home as two veteran educators with time and flexibility to dig in and collaborate on valuable student-centered research was an unfortunate loss. Nevertheless, the research and data gathered within two other sites still offered a solid spectrum of youth, adults, and environments to observe.

BECOMING AND BELONGING: HOME
AWAY FROM HOME PART 2

During intake, students are stripped of everything that makes them an individual: clothing, piercings, fake nails, hair weaves, jewelry. Students are cleaned and provided state-issued clothing, often consisting of undergarments, socks, elastic-waisted pants, sweatshirts, polos, and shoes with Velcro closures. Issued clothing is usually color-coded according to status and security risk. Students are assigned a suicide-proofed cell with a rigid bed and a thin, plastic mattress and pillow. Stools and desks are permanent, unmovable fixtures. Small windows allow in some natural light but are difficult to see out of or reach. Students are alone. They are separated from family. They are as young as eleven in this new home with detention officers as surrogate parents.

Students in detention are grouped in living units according to their security risk, not by their academic grade level or age. In detention, school is required, just like everywhere else. So, students of different ages and wide-ranging abilities sit in one classroom at the same time for math, English, social studies, and science, because of their individual "score" given at the time of intake—whether they are a low-, medium-, or high-intensity risk. Sometimes students travel to class, and sometimes, they remain at home, on the unit. As one teacher shares, "My classes may have a 12-year-old and an 18-year-old. Both may have a 4th grade reading level, but the home schools consider one a senior and the other a 7th grader . . . the objectives may be too abstract for the 12-year-old and the medium may be too juvenile for the 18-year-old." Each classroom then, differentiates for multi-age, multi-level, and multi-ability. Each teacher, then, must unlock the minds of students who are afraid and uncertain of their own future.

Labels that Limit: Our Part in Their Failure

One question to consider is whether or not education aids in the social construction of the youth offender. How does a child reach this point? Labeling theory proposes that, yes, student deviants are socially constructed by the labels education and society assign to them. And, such labeling can lead to a self-fulfilling prophecy (Rist, 2011/1998; Rankin, 1974). Because system-involved youth typically have had early experiences with school discipline and/or have unmet needs addressing learning disabilities, they possess negative reactions and feelings about school. The idea is that labeling impacts not only professional educators' perceptions of student ability and potential but also that of the community and students themselves.

During informal interviews with detained youth, students shared their self-awareness. They have made mistakes, and they know they should be held accountable. However, they also know that they need chances, multiple chances. They know they will make more mistakes, but their message was simply "Don't give up on me." The researcher was forced to reflect: When do teachers give up on students? When do students give up on themselves? When, if ever, do adults pause to acknowledge how the language of labeling could limit children in their own classrooms? And, further, how do educators perceive youth who come in one day, plop into a chair before them, having been detained only the day prior? The familiar space of school suddenly became a potential cause; the foreign space, the detention center school, became the paradigm shift.

The Teachers: The Platform

Randy, the school administrator (and my husband), pulled out his keys and unlocked the door. We exited the living unit and entered the commons where youth can play foosball, ping pong, cards, or simply relax. Behind the security desk, a giant window gave view to a small outside recreation area—octagonal in shape—about a 40–50 feet diagonal. The cement flooring had no markings despite the single basketball hoop standing to one side. The sky could be seen through the chicken-wire-like covering, enforced with criss-crossed slender white beam-like structures.

Randy pointed to the top right corners of the "cage" as he said the kids called it. There, a small white platform, approximately 10 x 6 inches, hung suspended from the caged covering. He explained that the birds wiggled through the wire holes to make nests in the rec area, but then were unable to poke back through and fly away, essentially being trapped. Seeing their struggle, a maintenance man hung sturdy platforms just inches below the wired ceiling. Now, the birds could fly up to this perch and find the leverage they needed to push back through the small openings and be free.

Randy's face revealed that he had never before made the connection between the maintenance worker and his teachers or between the students and the birds. But, in this moment, his English-teacher-wife did: the platform created by this one individual symbolizes the philosophy of their school and the hope of juvenile justice education itself. Randy responded:

The culture we try to create here is that every room that you go into would be someone who cares about you and will work with you to make you successful . . . kids are unsuccessful in regular schools all the time and don't know why . . . [here] every possible accommodation is offered to change. My favorite phrase is "What do we need to do to make you [the student] successful? You tell us what you need."

I think that sometimes they [students] are in an emotional place where there is no answer . . . maybe this [learning] just isn't possible right now. . . . Sometimes it's "I just need to sit and read my book—I love this book, and it's the only thing

I think that will keep my mind off of court for the next two hours if I can just sit here and read my book." Why wouldn't you let kids sit and read their book, which is at least something productive, when he's telling you, "I won't be successful in your classroom, I'm gonna cause trouble, I'm going to have a problem?"

Teachers in Randy's school face not only a broad spectrum of learners within a single classroom but also restrictions characteristic of a lockdown environment and all of the emotions that come with it. Therefore, the platform, that is, solutions, can be discovered by simply asking "What do you need today?" Because they do not know what each day brings, these education professionals must be masters of differentiation and scholars of street life. They know and are fluent in both youth culture and youth lingo. They must be creative with the tools they are given, be prepared for anything, and shocked by nothing.

Ms. Black, a.k.a. "Ms. B"

Schools within detention centers appear to be what they are, i.e., schools experiencing the usual tensions many educators experience on a daily basis: rote routines, dictated curriculum, administrative decisions, policy and its implementation, legislation and law, and frustration with the detainees they hope to teach and inspire. Library books, technology and computers, calculators, maps, art supplies, and so on make the school look "normal" despite the institutional smell and security presence. Nevertheless, many usual items are absent due to security risk, for example, scissors, hardback books, popsicle sticks, paper clips, staples, wired binders and/or notebooks. Pencils are counted daily. As a matter of fact, everything is counted daily. If one pencil is missing, everything goes into lockdown until it is found.

Regardless, these courageous educators have chosen to teach here in their home, their familiar space, and more importantly, to remain there over the years. A teacher who "radically encourages the human spirit," and who possesses "confident, independent thought and action in an uncertain world," can prepare students for "a world of difference" (Clarke 1995, 7). Enter Ms. Black, a teacher in the largest facility observed, whose sometimes radical ways are those that inspire students to think and to write, which may be easier said than done, especially when the setting is one full of emotion, risk, and uncertainty.

She laughs uncontrollably with her students, celebrates their words of wisdom or profound moments, and listens intently to their stories of home, school, and trouble, simultaneously honoring their experiences while also helping them to see and analyze the error of their ways. Day and Gu (2010) comment that "there are teachers everywhere who resist being molded into functionaries or hired hands" (Hansen 2010, 118). This perfectly describes Ms. Black. Employing tactics of hospitality and reverence (Rud and Garrison, 2010), she exposes her students to what they do not know as well as invites them to share themselves. Ms. Black respects her students and their individual contribution to the learning space, maintaining a sense of awe and wonder about them. She understands that "the student as a person is as important as the student as a learner," and she has the courage and perseverance to fight for and preserve her own personal pedagogy (Day 2004, 12).

Ms. Black was one of the most favored teachers by the students. According to one Juvenile Detention Specialist, Ms. Black challenged the students, and no matter what the kids tried to say or do, she didn't skip a beat. Her quick wit matched those of the students before her and this was her strength in this place: humor, sarcasm, talking smack in a way that students understood and a way that did not offend. Certainly, many high school teachers can attest to the fact that sarcasm is their greatest tool, but in a detention center, it can be a lifesaver.

As Ms. Black shared, "I pick on kids, sure, to make them laugh—but I pick on something they can control like a zit or their hair or body odor—or what they say. I never pick on them about why they are here or their family/home life. Sarcasm keeps them awake and keeps the lesson lively." Through her sarcasm and comments directed toward students, Ms. Black notices *them*. She notices students as individuals, giving them positive attention, demonstrating that someone cares about their day and their problems, albeit in an unusual manner. She makes connections, and laughter was the best way to handle the darkness of detention.

Ms. Black certainly had a way with students, getting them to consider complicated texts such as *Beowulf* and *The Kite Runner*. Despite her comment "They don't care about education because they can't see themselves doing anything other than what they're doing. Five years in the future is incomprehensible," she persevered. Her favorite unit was poetry, often using herself as the brunt of jokes, on the chopping block, fair game for students to make their own comments. As long as they were learning the concept/objective, Ms. Black didn't care what came her way.

For example, a lesson about metaphors led to a poetry exercise during which Ms. Black was compared to a bus and then a station wagon. The conversation was lively about the metaphor.

Ms. B: "If I'm a bus, what does that mean?"
Boy 1: "Transporting kids . . . like from being dumb to being smart."
Boy 2: "The bus bounces so you are . . . like . . . moody."
Boy 3: "You got big lights . . . you do nasty stuff on the bus."

Ms. B: (responding with sarcastic warning, yet still within the metaphorical context): "You're gonna get kicked off that bus!"

Ms. Black's ability here to keep the metaphor going, to address the student's inappropriate and obviously sexual comment, and still maintain authority illustrates her skill and polished tactics needed for teaching in this environment. She gets on their level in a way that both motivates and slaps the wrist at the same moment.

Turning quickly to another example, Ms. B asks, "What is Miss P?" Miss P, a para-educator, is middle-aged, stands about 5'2," and has wavy brown hair reaching her shoulders. The students replied:

. . .she is a pit bull
. . .she is protective
. . .she is aggressive
. . .she is cute but vicious
. . .she has a loud bark

Despite the stereotyping here (pointed out by Ms. Black) and chatter about pit bulls, these youth shared what their experiences may have been. Next, she read poems written by previous youth from a publication she and Miss P had put together a few years prior.

Ms. B: "I am a rearview mirror/ I only see my mistakes once they are behind me/ my past is closer than it appears."
Ms. B: "I am a street corner / where rocks are sold /and lives get stole."

She then told the boys that they would now make a poem out of all these descriptions. She selected one youth to serve as an example for a class poem. The student smiled and willingly became the object of this activity.

Ms. B: "If Blake were a weather condition, what would he be?"
Boy 1: "a thunderstorm"
Boy 2: "a tornado"
Ms. B: "What is thunderstormish about Blake?"
Crowd response: "he is spontaneous. . .loud and obnoxious . . . he rumbles but nothing happens . . . I like thunderstorms, but I don't like Blake (in jest)."
Ms. B: "Work with the question here," Ms. B said while looking at the boy who made the previous comment.

Next, Ms. B wrote on her portable white board: "Start with 'I am' . . . you get the idea . . . but no 'I'm a pimp' or 'I'm a thug'—I don't want crap like that

. . . cars, animals, weather conditions, a weapon, are you sly and sneaky like a knife . . . are you laid back like marijuana? Use your imagination."

Students began to work; some were drawing, some doodling. Ms. B floated from table to table to help boys get started, stopping at one table to comment: "interesting concept guys." During the time students worked, the normal interruptions ensued: phone calls, radio transmissions, students being escorted in and out by security, and so on. The creativity of these young men was inspiring and also the depth of their understanding of the metaphor as a literary device was impressive. The freedom with which they wrote suggested that they were not worried what others here in prison thought and enjoyed the opportunity to write creatively:

I am a sidewalk—people walk over me all day. . .
I am an ocean because I am full of life—
Inside me is a deep abyss with a hatred
for tiny fish.

On this unit, Ms. Black had youth write limericks, haikus, and metaphorical pieces. Students were engaged and creative, though not all. Some were inattentive, distracted, or simply observant, just like in the researcher's home classroom, but essentially, students were learning about poetry, writing, and developing their own literacy skills and sense of style.

Throughout the lesson, Mr. B was comical, patient, and encouraging. She never suggested to any student that his poem was not worthy. Her voice inflection, her movement around the room, the gentle poking of the students to keep them focused, use of proximity, and maintaining composure were all classic teaching moves. Ms. B provided the students with a meaningful classroom experience; she inspired adolescent boys *in detention* to write powerful poetry and have the courage to share their work.

Poetry is a perfect teaching tool in an ever-changing environment such as detention; the readings are short, diverse, creative, and manageable for many ability levels. And, with the popularity of rap, slam poetry, and the writing of both, students are more easily engaged. Here, Ms. Black uses poetry to empower student voices, to illustrate for them that writing can serve as a means to acknowledge the identity that led them to destructive behaviors, develop a deeper understanding of that identity, and to explore/discover a better "self" and purpose. Poetry helps to reframe thinking and allows students to use writing to suit the purpose of self-exploration and potential change. They can experience the redemptive and self-altering power of sharing one's voice and having it received by the other.

In Ms. B's classroom, students learn that "existence is the event of cobeing" (Holquist 2002, 41). Even Nebraska author Mary Pipher (2006) adds to this notion quoting a Zulu belief: "A person is a person through other persons" (63). For Ms. Black and her students, the first step was finding their voice and identity—a self. The second step comes from Bahktin's position that "nothing means anything until it achieves a response" (Holquist 2002, 48), which takes form when the audience shares a reaction or a critique. Essentially, Ms. Black provided such opportunities for students to share their work and to receive and enjoy that response, empowering students and providing a sense of "I matter."

For youth in a detention center, having affirmation in their experiences, feelings, and reasons for their negative behaviors can increase confidence in their overall literate selves. Students learn in Ms. Black's classroom that their writing, that their existence, is part of a social/world structure—that theirs is not a "lonely event" (Holquist 2002, 38). The poetry activities allowed for students to engage in a dialogue regarding their writing. This was a non-threatening situation in which they shared ideas, opinions, and conversation and learned to edit, and revise, as well as practice humor, irony, wit, rhyme, and of course, to learn about the experiences of their fellow classmates.

Holquist (2002) emphasizes that "we see the world by authoring it, by making sense of it through the activity of turning it into a text" (84). In the end, teaching young people to write is to teach them to see the world from multiple perspectives, to author and write it to make a change—even if that change is within their own lives. Students—youth offenders—were "doing school" and the familiar language of English curriculum. In those epiphanic moments, they could be learners in any school and potentially seated one day in the researcher's own home classroom.

When entering a detention facility, security cameras, detention officers, locked doors, the blended odors of musty, smelly adolescent bodies, and rose-scented-gone-rancid cleaners are overwhelming. The fear of triggering an alarm or standing in the wrong space never subsides. Yet, in the classroom, even one that exists on the unit where students live, eat, shower, and sleep, the act of teaching and learning feels like home, organic with its familiarity. This juxtaposition of home and homelessness, of being within and without, of knowing yet not knowing, is unique to the juvenile detention environment.

UNLOCKING DOORS AND OPENING WINDOWS

William Ayers (1993) asks: "When teachers look out over their classrooms, what do they see?" (26). In any classroom, when teachers look over it, what they "see" is what they will get. Ms. Black could see losers and deviants, but instead, she sees thinkers and learners. Yet, when both teacher and student embrace the home of the classroom and the promise of engagement, what they both "see" also determines what they both will become. Ms. Black and her colleagues in juvenile justice education *become* the platform, the leverage and stability youth need to rehabilitate. Youth become students again, scholars even, who can become free and stay free.

Educators beyond lockdown can learn much from Ms. Black and her colleagues, the experts who know these youth better than anyone. When one witnesses patience, humor, faith in youthful spirits, and a commitment to working with perhaps the most intimidating and vulnerable students in education today, inspiration results, but so does the quest for further inquiry. To some degree, these educators face the same marginalization as their students. They are often absent or excluded from district professional development. What is worse is their invisibility. Marginalized youth, marginalized teachers, and marginalized schools—none are recognized or taken seriously behind that razor wire. Ms. Black noted that they [the teachers] were "public school cast-outs." Palmer (1998) asserts that "if we continue to demean and dishearten the human resource called the teacher on whom so much depends . . . if we fail to cherish—and challenge—the human heart that is the source of good teaching," then students lose and our communities lose (3).

During the study of each facility, a connection was clear between the struggle to find a fitting curriculum suited for the unique dynamics of a school within a confined setting and the gap in teacher preparation and continuing education programs. Whereas talented and caring professionals could be found in each facility, each teacher expressed frustration and fatigue due to inadequate training or access to resources designed specifically for this area of education, noting their invisibility and even their homelessness. The faculty, administrators, and students struggle to find a compromise between the rules of the detention center and goals of the curriculum.

Because research in these settings is restricted, a lack of understanding limits programming potential and consequently spins the revolving door of recidivism. These youth and their teachers live in the home of the community, thus they belong to *everyone*. Their voices and participation could create more multidisciplinary approaches for adjudicated or behaviorally challenged youth.

Tannis (2014b), veteran educator and coach/consultant with the Center for Educational Excellence in Alternative Settings emphasizes, "We cannot throw away the keys to a better future by denying these children the right to a good education" whether in an alternative or traditional setting. Addressing the particular needs of system-involved youth is both a mystery and a challenge, especially given the negative educational history they carry as baggage paired with the labels assigned to them.

Ultimately, schools try to *be schools*—despite the locked doors, standard issue clothing, bland food, and looming JDS/JDOs. And, they try to *be homes* for youth who are removed from their own. During class, students could forget for a time their status as delinquents and focus on their potential as learners. They could read books they selected from the library, write poetry, debate about politics, or learn to figure out mathematical concepts.

Beyond the school day, they had access to life skills classes, mentoring, tutoring, and counseling. The staff was encouraging. They were supportive, and they gave the students what they needed: grace—in the opportunity to be successful and start the process of feeling positive about themselves. As Randy, school administrator, emphasizes, "We make the school fit the needs of the individual student; not try to force the student to fit the needs of the school."

JOINING FORCES INSIDE AND OUTSIDE OF DETENTION

Observing stimulating classroom activities and close interaction with creative professionals and goal-oriented youth illustrated how a classroom environment is not defined by labels and incorrect assumptions, but, rather, by a relentless belief in the potential of every young person. Tannis (2014b) emphasizes:

> We must seize the opportunity to capture the hearts and minds of our nation's incarcerated youth while many of their distractions from the outside have been removed . . . we must not lose hope in what we've all been led to believe—that education is the key. If this is the case, we must use this important tool to free the minds and lives of our nation's most disenfranchised and educationally neglected youth.

Somewhere, the public education setting participated to some extent in the failure of these students. Thus, the education community has the responsibility to remove whatever labels may have impacted learning experiences and to build student cultural capital through meaningful, creative, and individualized curriculum.

After so much time spent passing through multiple layers of security just to witness life for youth in confinement, returning to the comfort of one's own classroom was profound. As the ethnographer, the researcher weighed the words of William Ayers (1993) to consider what *she* sees. Her students could walk freely every day and go home after school. Her students were clothed, fed, warm, safe, and accepted. Yet, some were not. Home is a place where one feels valued and validated, where one is loved unconditionally, where fear does not exist. It can be wherever one is surrounded in support. Ultimately, students just want others to notice and validate their lives, to confront their own biases and recognize that past decisions do not determine future success. They want to feel *at home* in the classroom and that can make all the difference.

REFERENCES

Agar, M. H. 2008. *The Professional Stranger*, 2nd edition. Emerald Press.

Ayers, William. 1993. *To Teach*. New York: Teachers College Press.

Clarke, Christopher. 1995. *Thoughtful Teaching*. London: Cassell.

Coulter, G. 2004. "Using One-to-One Tutoring and Proven Reading Strategies to Improve Reading Performance With Adjudicated Youth." *The Journal of Correctional Education* 55, no. 4, 321–333.

Day, Christopher. 2004. *A Passion for Teaching*. New York: Routledge Falmer.

Day, Christopher and Qing Gu. 2010. *The New Lives of Teachers*. London: Routledge.

Drakeford, William. 2002. "The Impact of an Intensive Program to Increase the Literacy Skills of Youth Confined to Juvenile Corrections." *Journal of Correctional Education* 53, no. 4, 139–144.

Guerra, Stephanie. 2010. "Reaching Out to At-risk Teens: Building Literacy With Incarcerated Youth." *PNLA Quarterly* 75, no. 1. Pacific Northwest Library Association. http://libraryservicestoincarceratedyouth.pbworks.com/f/lib_serving_inc_youth.pdf

Hanson, D. T. 2011. *The Teacher and the World*. New York: Routledge.

Holquist, Michael. 1990. *Dialogism*. New York: Routledge.

Hooper-Arana, Erica. 2019. "Lessons Learned from a Multidisciplinary Collaborative Supporting Juvenile Reentry." *Journal of Applied Juvenile Services*. Online. National Partnership for Juvenile Services 1–14.

Nurse, Anne. M. 2010. *Locked Up, Locked Out: Young Men in the Juvenile Justice System*. Nashville: Vanderbilt University Press.

O'Cummings, Mindee, Sarah Bardack, S., and Simon Gonsoulin, S. 2010. *Issue Brief: The Importance of Literacy for Youth Involved in the Juvenile Justice System*. Washington, DC: National Evaluation and Technical Assistance Center for the Education of Children and Youth Who Are Neglected, Delinquent, or At Risk (NDTAC).

Palmer, Parker J. 1998. *The Courage to Teach. Exploring the Inner Landscape of a Teacher's Life*. San Francisco: Jossey-Baas.

Pipher, Mary. 2006. *Writing to Change the World*. New York: Riverhead Books.

Puzzanchera, Charles and Sarah Hockenberry. 2019. "Trends and Characteristics of Youth in Residential Placement, 2017." National Center for Juvenile Justice. Office of Juvenile Justice and Delinquency Prevention. https://www.ojjdp.gov/ojstatbb/snapshots/DataSnapshot_CJRP2017.pdf

Read, Nicholas W. and Mindee O'Cummings. 2011. *"Factsheet: Juvenile Justice Education."* Washington, DC: National Evaluation and Technical Assistance Center for the Education of Children and Youth Who Are Neglected, Delinquent, or At Risk. (NDTAC).

Rist, Ray C. 2011/1998. "On Understanding the Processes of Schooling: The Contributions of Labeling Theory." In A.R. Sadovnik, *Sociology of Education: A Critical Reader*, 2nd edition, pp. 71–82. New York: Routledge.

Rud, A. G. and James Garrison. 2010. "Reverence and Listening in Teaching and Leading." *The Teachers College Record* 112, no.11, 2777–2792.

Snyder, Howard and Melissa Sickmund. 2006. *Juvenile Offenders and Victims: 2006 National Report*. Washington, DC: U.S. Department of Justice, Office of Justice Programs, Office of Juvenile Justice and Delinquency Prevention.

Tannis, Lynette. 2014a. *Educating Incarcerated Youth: Exploring the Impact of Relationships, Expectations, Resources, and Accountability*. New York: Palgrave Macmillan.

Tannis, Lynette. 2014b. "Punishing Young Offenders Twice." *Education Week*. Online 33, no. 19, 28. https://www.edweek.org/leadership/opinion-punishing-young-offenders-twice/2014/01

Onward

Loukia K. Sarroub

This volume's realistic accounts of fieldwork in contexts that either constitute or become "home" for researchers and research participants alike index a turn toward shared relational meanings that have great potential for further extension and application to places that are familiar. Each chapter in this volume discusses how ethnographers and researchers' knowledge and assumptions about "being" at home in the field invite more nuanced understandings of familiar patterns and "ah ha" moments. Importantly, the authors in this volume argue strongly for a scholarship of ethnography and education that is grounded in everyday familiar contexts. They also acknowledge their own past and present positions as subjects and agents of those cultural scenes in which they continue to learn with their research participants.

As such, the insider/outsider opposition in doing fieldwork at home is juxtaposed with a continuum of experiences that flexibly bind researchers and those with whom they work, study, and collaborate. As Pierre Bourdieu noted in his afterward to Paul Rabinow's (1977) *Reflections*, "Ethnology will have taken a giant step forward when all ethnologists understand that something similar is taking place between their informants and themselves" (167). The ambiguity of "something similar" is well-founded as it proposes that relationships in the field are mercurial, growing out of context-dependent interactions that are mediated by language, symbols, power, and the everyday doings of a cultural scene.

Ultimately, researchers reconstruct "home" dialogically with research participants over time because they never leave the field. The field is phenomenologically and literally there, and "being there" in a Geertz-minded way is a question of degree and focus rather than time in the field. When "home" becomes familiar and is no longer a strange option, alternating between the familiar and strange requires reconstituting home and embodying it differently as interactions and the field site are reimagined by all social actors together as they sometimes co-produce the fieldwork data.

As of this writing, fieldwork at home became all the more estranging as people around the world negotiated different kinds of interactions in spaces that they no longer inhabited socially as they had prior to the COVID-19 pandemic. For example, everyday routines such as greetings and paralinguistic elements, sitting, standing, talking, and walking (among others) became objects within the "social distancing" trope, which was indexed by the maintenance of a physical distance of six to eight feet that pervaded all institutions, including schools. People were inadvertently expected to say so much more with their eyes now that their expressions were partly masked by facial coverings.

Importantly, "masked" communication disadvantaged some people more than it did others on the basis of social factors such as health conditions, age, stigmas, or profiling founded on perceived (or actual) ethnic, racial, political, and national identities. How fieldwork practices might change under conditions imposed by a pandemic as researchers and informants convened via technological means such as Zoom remains to be seen. Culture "at home" resides outside the screens of communication and the quotidian practices that shaped people's home lives, wherein they both lived and worked. In other words, in many places, fieldwork at home changed again in a literal sense—it took place in the researcher's own domicile, and access to sites vulnerable to a pandemic, such as schools, refugee camps, community centers, hospitals, prisons, and corporate or government buildings was not possible.

At the same time, education, in one form or another, continues to be enacted, which begs the question: How should ethnographers of education study remote and hybrid educational contexts? If education in the time of a pandemic is itself the object of study, and much of it is likely to be occurring in "home" spaces of teachers, students, parents, as well as "residential" sites of institutions such as schools and prisons, how should ethnographers begin to map, describe, and account via "thick description" the increasingly complex lived world that exists beyond traditional physical boundaries?

At times like these, this looming question inspires finding innovative, multiscale ways (cf. Eisenhart, 2016) to uncover and make visible everyday structures beyond the computer screens and smartphones that facilitate education and communication on the one hand but also mask the lived experiences of those who are not visible as social actors on the other hand. Participant observation along with listening, collaborating, and working with various interlocutors "at home" to foster understanding as part and parcel of ethnography and education continue to be essential and innovative means of doing fieldwork.

Bibliography

Abu El-Haj, Thea. 2009. "Becoming Citizens in an Era of Globalization and Transnational Migration: Re-imagining Citizenship as Critical Practice." *Theory into Practice* 48, no. 1, 274–282.

Agar, M. H. 2008. *The Professional Stranger*, 2nd, revised edition. Emerald Press.

Agar, Michael H. 1980. *The Professional Stranger: An Informal Introduction to Ethnography*. New York: Academic Press.

Agar, Michael H. 1996. *The Professional Stranger: An Informal Introduction to Ethnography*, 2nd edition. San Diego, CA: Academic Press.

Ainscow, Mel, and Margarida César. 2006. "Inclusive Education Ten Years after Salamanca: Setting the Agenda." *European Journal of Psychology of Education* 21, no. 3, 231–238.

Alim, Samy H., and Django Paris. 2017. "What Is Culturally Sustaining Pedagogy and Why Does It Matter?" In *Culturally Sustaining Pedagogies: Teaching and Learning for Justice in a Changing World*, edited by Django, Paris, Alim, Samy H., and Genishi, Celia, pp. 12–32. New York: Teachers College Press.

Allen, Danielle. 2004. *Talking to Strangers: Anxieties of Citizenship Since* Brown v. Board of Education. Chicago, IL: University of Chicago Press.

Alvesson, Mats. 2003. "Methodology for Close Up Studies: Struggling with Closeness and Closure." *Higher Education* 46, no. 2, 167–193.

Asplund, Stig-Börje. 2010. *Läsning som Identitetsskapande Handling: Gemenskapande och Utbrytningsförsök i Fordonspojkars Litteratursamtal* [Reading as Identity Construction. Practices and Processes of Building a Sense of Community in Literary Discussions Among Male Vehicle Engineering Students] (Diss.) Karlstad: Karlstad University.

Asplund, Stig-Börje, and Nina Kilbrink. 2018. "Learning How (and How Not) to Weld: Vocational Learning in Technical Vocational Education." *Scandinavian Journal of Educational Research* 62, no. 1, 1–16.

Asplund, Stig-Börje and Nina Kilbrink. 2020. "Lessons from the Welding Booth: Theories in Practice in Vocational Education." *Empirical Research in Vocational Education and Training 12, no. 1*, 1-23.

Atkinson, Paul Anthony. 2015. *For Ethnography*. London: SAGE Publications Ltd.

Attwell, Paul, and David E. Lavin 2012. "The Other 75%: College Education Beyond the Elite." In *What is College For? The Public Purpose of Higher Education*, edited by Lagemann, Ellen C. and Lewis, Harry, pp. 86–103. New York: Teachers College Press.

Auerbach, Elsa. 1989. "Toward a Social-Contextual Approach to Family Literacy." *Harvard Education Review* 59, no. 2, 165–181. doi: 10.17763/haer.59.2.h237313641283156

Ayers, William. 1993. *To Teach*. New York: Teachers College Press.

Bakbie, Andrea M., and Mary C. Provost. 2004. "Teachers as Researchers." *Intervention in School & Clinic* 39, no. 5, 260–268.

Baquedaño-Lopez, Patricia, Rebecca Anne Alexander, and Sera J. Hernandez. 2013. "Equity Issues in Parental and Community Involvement in Schools: What Teacher Educators Need to Know." *Review of Research in Education* 37, 149–182. doi: 10.3102/0091732X12459718

Bartolomé, Lilia. 1994. "Beyond the Methods Fetish: Toward a Humanizing Pedagogy." *Harvard Educational Review* 64, no. 2, 173–194. doi: 10.17763/haer.64.2.58q5m5744t325730

Basque Government. 1982. *10/1982 Basic Law for the Normalization of the Use of Basque*. Vitoria/Gasteiz: Official Gazette of the Basque Country. https://www.boe.es/eli/es-pv/l/1982/11/24/10/con

Basque Government. 2007. *Decree 175/2007, Curriculum for Basic Education in the Basque Autonomous Community*. Vitoria/Gasteiz: Official Gazette of the Basque Country. http://www.euskadi.eus/gobierno-vasco/contenidos/decreto/bopv200706182/es_def/index.shtml

Basque Government. 2014. *Heziberri 2020. Pedagogical Framework in Education*. Vitoria/Gasteiz: Basque Government. http://www.euskadi.eus/contenidos/informacion/heziberri_2020/es_heziberr/adjuntos/Heziberri_2020_c.pdf

Basque Government. 2016. *Decree 235/2015, Education for the Basic Curriculum in the Basque Autonomous Community*. Vitoria/Gasteiz: Official Gazette of the Basque Country. http://www.euskadi.eus/eli/es-pv/d/2015/12/22/236/dof/spa/html/web01-ejeduki/es/

Bath, Caroline. 2009. "When does the Action Start and Finish? Making the Case for an Ethnographic Action Research in Educational Research." *Educational Action Research*, 17, no. 2, 213–224.

Beach, Rick, and David O'Brien. 2007. "Adopting Reader and Writer Stances in Understanding and Producing Texts." In *Secondary School Literacy: What Research Reveals for Classroom Practice*, edited by Leslie S. Rush, Jonathan A. Eakle, and Allen, Berger, pp. 217–242. Urbana, IL: NCTE.

Benner, Patricia, Molly Sutphen, Victoria Leonard, and Lisa Day. 2010. *Educating Nurses: A Call for Radical Transformation*, 1st edition. San Francisco, CA: Jossey-Bass.

Bernard, Harvey Russell. 2006. *Research Methods in Anthropology: Qualitative and Quantitative Methods*, 4th edition. Walnut Creek, CA: AltaMira.

Biesta, Gert. 2007. "Bridging the Gap Between Educational Research and Educational Practice: The Need for Critical Distance." *Educational Research and Evaluation,* 13, no. 3, 295–301.

Boland, Neil. 2015. "The Globalisation of Steiner Education: Some Considerations." *Research on Steiner Education Journal* 6, 192–202.

Borgnakke, Karen. 1996a. *Pædagogisk Feltforskning Og Procesanalytisk Kortlægning - En Forskningsberetning. Procesanalytisk Teori Og Metode*, Vol. 1. København: Thesis & Akademisk Forlag A/S.

Borgnakke, Karen. 1996b. *Procesanalytisk Metodologi. Procesanalytisk Teori Og Metode*, Vol. 2. København: Thesis & Akademisk Forlag A/S.

Bourdieu, Pierre. 1966. "The Sentiment of Honor in Kabyle Society." In *Honour and Shame: The Values of Mediterranean Society*, edited by Jean G. Peristiany, pp. 191–241. Chicago, IL: University of Chicago Press.

Bowman, Nicholas. 2010. "College Diversity Experiences and Cognitive Development: A Meta-Analysis." *Review of Educational Research* 80, no. 21, 4–33.

Bradburn, Norman, Seymour Sudman, and Brian Wansink. 2004. *Asking Questions: The Definitive Guide to Questionnaire Design-For Market Research, Political Polls, and Social and Health Questionnaires*, Rev. edition. San Francisco, CA: Wiley & Sons.

Brannan, Matthew, Geoff Pearson, and Frank Worthington. 2007. "Ethnographies of Work and the Work of Ethnography." *Ethnography* 8, no. 4, 395–402.

Brante, Göran, Mona Holmqvist Olander, Per-Ola Holmquist, and Marta Palla. 2015. "Theorising Teaching and Learning: Pre-Service Teachers' Theoretical Awareness of Pearning." *European Journal of Teacher Education* 38, no. 1, 102–118.

Brettell, Caroline B. (ed). 1993. *When They Read What We Write: The Politics of Ethnography*. Westport, CT: Bergin & Garvey.

Briggs, Charles. L. 1997. *Learning How to Ask: A Sociolinguistic Appraisal of the Role of the Interview in Social Science Research*. New York: Cambridge University Press.

Brinkmann, Svend. 2012. *Qualitative Inquiry in Everyday Life*. London: SAGE.

Carlgren, I. 2015. *Kunskapsstrukturer och Undervisningspraktiker*. Gothenburg: Daidalos.

Carlgren, Ingrid (ed). 2017. *Undervisningsutvecklande Forskning: Exemplet Learning Study* [Teaching Developing Research: The Learning Study Example]. Gleerups: Malmö.

Carspecken, Phil. 1996. *Critical Ethnography in Educational Research: A Theoretical and Practical Guide*. New York: Routledge.

Castillo-Montoya, Milagros. 2017. "Deepening Understanding of Prior Knowledge: What Diverse First-Generation College Students in the U.S. Can Teach Us. *Teaching In Higher Education* 22, no. 5, 587–603. doi: 10.1080/13562517.2016.1273208

Cenoz, Jasone. 2009. *Towards Multilingual Education: Basque Educational Research from an International Perspective*. Bristol: Multilingual Matters.

Chang, Mitchell, Nida Denson, Victor Sáenz, and Kimberly Misa. 2006. "The Educational Benefits of Sustaining Cross-Racial Interaction Among Undergraduates." *The Journal of Higher Education* 77, no. 3, 430–455.

Chavous, Tabbye, Bridget Richardson, Felecia Webb, Gloryvee Fonseca-Bolorin, and Seanna Leath. 2018. "Shifting Contexts and Shifting Identities: Campus Race-Related Experiences, Racial Identity, and Academic Motivation Among Black Students During Transition to College." *Race and Social Problems* 10, no. 1, 1–18.

Clifford, James, and George E. Marcus (eds). 1986/2010. *Writing Culture: The Poetics of Ethnography*. Berkeley, CA: University of California Press.

Collins, Patricia H. 1993. "Toward a New Vision: Race, Class, and Gender as Categories of Analysis and Connections." *Race, Class, & Sex* 1, no. 1, 26–45.

Collins, Patricia H. 2015. "Intersectionality's Definitional Dilemmas." *Annual Review of Sociology* 41, 1–20. doi: 10.1146/annurev-soc-073014-112142

Council of Europe. 1992. *European Charter for Regional or Minority Languages*. Strasbourg: European Treaty Series. https://www.coe.int/en/web/conventions/full -list/-/conventions/rms/0900001680695175

Crenshaw, Kimberlé. 1989. "Demarginalizing the Intersection of Race and Sex: A Black Feminist Critique of Antidiscrimination Doctrine, Feminist Theory and Antiracist Politics." *University of Chicago Legal Forum* 1, no. 8, 139–167. https:/ /chicagounbound.uchicago.edu/uclf/vol1989/iss1/8

Crow, Chris. 2003. *Mississippi Trial*, 1955. Speak Press.

Day, Christopher. 2004. *A Passion for Teaching*. New York: Routledge Falmer.

Day, Christopher and Qing Gu. 2010. *The New Lives of Teachers*. London: Routledge.

Delamont, Sara. 2016. *Fieldwork in Educational Settings: Methods, Pitfalls and Perspectives*, 3rd edition. Oxford: Routledge.

Delamont, Sara and Paul Atkinson. 1995. *Fighting Familiarity: Essays on Education and Ethnography*. New York: Hampton Press.

Delgado, Richard, and Jean Stefancic. 2012. *Critical Race Theory: An Introduction*. 2nd edition. New York: New York University Press.

Delgado Bernal, Dolores. 2002. "Critical Race Theory, Latino Critical Theory, and Critical Raced-Gendered Epistemologies: Recognizing Students of Color as Holders and Creators of Knowledge." *Qualitative Inquiry* 8, no. 1, 105–126.

Deschenes, Sarah, Larry Cuban, L, and David Tyack. 2001. "Mismatch: Historical Perspectives on Schools and Students Who Don't Fit Them." *Teachers College Record* 103, no. 4, 525–547.

Dhondt, Pieter, Nele van de Vijver, Pieter Verstraete, Moritz Föllmer, and Mark B. Smith. 2015. "The Possibility of an Unbiased History of Steiner/Waldorf Education?" *Contemporary European History* 24, no. 4, 639–649.

DiAngelo, Robin. 2011. "White Fragility." *International Journal of Critical Pedagogy* 3, no. 3, 54–70. https://libjournal.uncg.edu/ijcp

Drakeford, William. 2002. "The impact of an Intensive Program to Increase the Literacy Skills of Youth Confined to Juvenile Corrections." *Journal of Correctional Education* 53, no. 4, 139–144.

Draper, Sharon. 1997. *Forged by Fire*. New York: Atheneum Books.

Duran, Elva, Jo Gusman, and John Shefelbine. 2005. *Access American History: Building Literacy Through Learning*. Wilmington, MA: Great Source Education Group.

Echeverria, Begoña. 2003. "Schooling, Language and Ethnic Identity in the Basque Autonomous Community." *Anthropology & Education Quarterly* 34, no. 4, 351–362.

Echeverria, Begoña. 2010. "For Whom does Language Death Toll? Cautionary Notes From the Basque Case." *Linguistics and Education* 21, 197–209. doi: 10.1016/j.linged.2009.10.001

Eisenhart, Margaret. 2016. "A Matter of Scale: Multiscale Ethnographic Research on Education in the United States." *Ethnography and Education* 12, 134–147.

Emerson, Robert, Rachel Fretz, and Linda Shaw. 2011. *Writing Ethnographic Fieldnotes*, 2nd edition. Chicago, IL: University of Chicago Press.

Erickson, Frederick. 1984. "What Makes School Ethnography 'Ethnographic'?" *Anthropology and Education Quarterly* 15, 51–66. doi: 10.1525/aeq.1984.15.1.05x1472p

Fahrenthold, D. A. (2016, October 8). "Trump Recorded Having Extremely Lewd Conversation About Women in 2005." *The Washington Post*. October 8, 2016. https://www.washingtonpost.com/politics/trump-recorded-having-extremely-lewd-conversation-about-women-in%202005/2016/10/07/3b9ce776-8cb4-11e6-bf8a-3d26847eeed4_story.html?utm_term=.e7251fa0806c

Forsey, Martin. 2004. "'He's not a Spy; He's One of Us': Ethnographic Positioning in a Middle-Class Setting." *In Anthropologists in the Field: Cases in Participant Observation* edited by Lynne Hume and Jane Mulcock, pp. 59–70. New York: Columbia University Press.

Freire, Paulo. 1970. *Pedagogy of the Oppressed*. London: Penguin Books.

Geertz, Clifford. 1973. "Thick Description: Toward an Interpretive Theory of Culture." In *The Interpretation of Culture: Selected Essays*, pp. 3–30. New York: Basic Books.

Gelling, Leslie, and Carol Munn-Giddings. 2011. "Ethical Review of Action Research: The Challenges for Researchers and Research Ethics Committees." *Research Ethics*, 7, no. 3, 100–106.

Gmelch, George and Sharon Bohn Gmelch. 2018. *In the Field: Life and Work in Cultural Anthropology*. Oakland, CA: University of California Press.

Goffman, Erving. (1959) 1990. *The Presentation of Self in Everyday Life*. London: Penguin.

Gray, Tricia. 2017. "'Hear us, see us': Constructing Citizenship in the Margins." Doctoral dissertation, University of Nebraska-Lincoln.

Greenwood, Davydd J., William F. Whyte, and Ira Harkavy. 1993. "Participatory Action Research as a Process and as a Goal." *Human Relations* 46, no. 2, 175–192.

Gregory, Eve and Mahera Ruby. 2011. "The 'Insider/Outsider' Dilemma of Ethnography: Working with Young Children and Their Families in Cross-cultural Contexts." *Journal of Early Childhood Research* 9, no. 2, 162–174. doi: 10.1177/1476718X10387899

Guerra, Stephanie. 2010. "Reaching Out to At-Risk Teens: Building Literacy with Incarcerated Youth." *PNLA Quarterly* 75 (1). Pacific Northwest Library

Association. http://libraryservicestoincarceratedyouth.pbworks.com/f/lib_serving
_inc_youth.pdf

Gupta, Akhil and James Ferguson (eds).1997. *Anthropological Locations: Boundaries
and Grounds of a Field Science*. Berkeley, CA: University of California Press.

Hall, Leigh. 2012. "Rewriting Identities: Creating Spaces for Students and Teachers
to Challenge the Norms of What It Means to be a Reader in School." *Journal of
Adolescent & Adult Literacy* 55, no. 5, 368–373.

Hammersley, Martyn and Paul Atkinson. 1983/1993. *Ethnography: Principles in
Practice*. London: Routledge.

Hammersley, Martyn and Paul Atkinson. 2007. *Ethnography: Principles in Practice*,
3rd edition. London: Routledge.

Hanson, David T. 2011. *The Teacher and the World*. New York: Routledge.

Harré, Rom. 1997. *The Singular Self: An Introduction to the Psychology of
Personhood*. London: Sage.

Hastrup, Kirsten, ed. 2010. *Ind i Verden: En Grundbog i Antropologisk Metode*, 2nd
edition. Kbh.: Hans Reitzel.

Hatch, J. Amos. 2002. *Doing Qualitative Research in Educational Settings*. Albany:
SUNY Press.

Heath, Christian, Jon Hindmarsh, and Paul Luff. 2010. *Video in Qualitative Research—
Analysing Social Interaction in Everyday Life*. London: SAGE Publications Ltd.

Heath, Shirley Brice. 1986. "What No Bedtime Story Means: Narrative Skills at
Home and School." *In Language Socialization across Cultures* edited by B.
Schieffelin and E. Ochs, pp. 97–124. Cambridge: Cambridge University Press.

Heath, Shirley Brice, and Milbrey W. McLaughlin. 1993. *Identity and Inner-City
Youth: Beyond Ethnicity and Gender*. New York: Teachers College Press.

Hemment, Julie. 2007. "Public Anthropology and the Paradoxes of Participation:
Participatory Action Research and Critical Ethnography in Provincial Russia."
Human Organization 66, no. 3, 301–314.

Hoffmann, Vera. 2016. "Creating Place-based Waldorf Festivals: An Ethnographic
Study of Festivals in Two Non-European Waldorf Schools." *Research on Steiner
Education Journal* 7, no. 2, 88–104.

Holmquist, Mona. 2017. "Models for Collaborative Professional Development for
Teachers in Mathematics." *International Journal for Lesson and Learning Studies*
6, no. 3, 190–201.

Holquist, Michael. 1990. *Dialogism*. New York: Routledge.

Hooper-Arana, Erica. 2019. "Lessons Learned from a Multidisciplinary Collaborative
Supporting Juvenile Reentry." *Journal of Applied Juvenile Services*. Online.
National Partnership for Juvenile Services 1–14.

Hurtado, Sylvia and Adriana Ruiz. 2012. "The Climate for Underrepresented Groups
and Diversity on Campus." *Research Brief, Higher Education Research Institute*
(June): Los Angeles, CA: Higher Education Research Institute. https://www.her
i.ucla.edu/PDFs/Discriminination-and-Bias-Underrepresentation-and-Sense-of-
Belonging-on-Campus.pdf

Hurtado, Sylvia and Adriana Ruiz Alvarado. 2015. "Discrimination and Bias,
Underrepresentation, and Sense of Belonging on Campus." *Research Brief, Higher*

Education Research Institute (October): Los Angeles, CA: Higher Education Research Institute. https://www.heri.ucla.edu/PDFs/Discrimination-and-Bias -Underrepresentation-and-Sense-of-Belonging-on-Campus.pdf

Illeris, Knud. 2008. *How We Learn—Learning and Non-learning in School and Beyond*. New York: Routledge.

Inda, Jonathan X., and Renato Rosaldo (eds). 2008. *The Anthropology of Globalization*, 2nd edition. Malden: Blackwell.

Johnson, Dawn R., Patty Alvarez, Susan Longerbeam, Matthew Soldner, Karen Kurotsuchi Inkelas, Jeannie Brown Leonard, and Heather Rowan-Kenyon. 2007. "Examining Sense of Belonging Among First-Year Undergraduates from Different Racial/Ethnic Groups." *Journal of College Student Development* 48, no. 5, 525–542.

Kendall, Brent. "Trump Says Judge's Mexican Heritage Presents 'Absolute Conflict'." *The Wall Street Journal*. June 3, 2016. https://www.wsj.com/articles/donald-trump -keeps-up-attacks-on-judge-gonzalo-curiel-1464911442

Kern, Richard. 2009. *Literacy and Language Teaching*. New York: Oxford.

Kilbrink, Nina, Veronica Bjurulf, Ingela Blomberg, Anja Heidkamp, and Ann-Christin Hollsten. 2014. "Learning Specific Content in Technology Education: Learning Study as a Collaborative Method in Swedish Preschool Class Using Hands-on Material." *International Journal of Technology and Design Education* 24, 241–259.

Klein, Julie. 1996. *Crossing Boundaries: Knowledge, Disciplinarities, and Interdisciplinarities*. Charlottesville, Va: University Press of Virginia.

Klippel, Friederike. 2017. "Teachers as Researchers," *Language Teaching* 50, no. 2, 297–298.

Kluckhohn, Clyde. 1949. *Mirror for Man: The Relation of Anthropology to Modern Life*. New York: McGraw-Hill Book Company.

Kopan, Tal. "What Donald Trump Has Said About Mexico and Vice Versa." *CNN Politics*. August 31, 2016. http://www.cnn.com/2016/08/31/politics/donald-trump -mexico-statements/

Ladson-Billings, Gloria. 2004. "Culture Versus Citizenship: The Challenge of Racialized Citizenship in the United States." In Joseph A. Banks, ed. *Diversity and Citizenship Education*, pp. 99–126. San Francisco, CA: Jossey-Bass.

Lareau, Annette and Jeffrey Schultz (eds).1996. *Journeys Through Ethnography: Realistic Accounts of Fieldwork*. Westview Press.

Levine, Peter. 2007. *The Future of Democracy: Developing the Next Generation of American Citizens*. Lebanon, NH: University Press of New England.

Levinson, Meira. 2012. *No Citizen Left Behind*. Cambridge, MA: Harvard University Press.

Macbeth, Douglas. 1994. "Classroom Encounters with the Unspeakable: 'Do You See, Danelle?'" *Discourse Processes* 17, no. 2, 311–335.

Marcus, George E. 1995. "Ethnography in/of the World System: The Emergence of Multi-Sited Ethnography." *Annual Review of Anthropology* 24, no. 1, 95–117. doi: 10.1146/annurev.an.24.100195.000523

Marvasti, Amir Barzegar. 2010. *Interviews and Interviewing.* London: Elsevier Science.

Mauss, Marcel. 1990. *The Gift: The Form and Reason for Exchange in Archaic Societies.* Translated by W.D. Halls. New York: W.W. Norton.

McNess, Elizabeth, Lore Arthur, and Michael Crossley. 2015. "'Ethnographic Dazzle' and the Construction of the 'Other': Revisiting Dimensions of Insider and Outsider Research for International and Comparative Education." *Compare: A Journal of Comparative and International Education* 45, no. 2, 295–316. doi: 10.1080/03057925.2013.854616

Mehan, Hugh. 1979. *Learning Lessons: Social Organization in the Classroom.* Cambridge, MA: Harvard University Press.

Meneley, Anne. 1996. *Tournaments of Value: Sociability and Hierarchy in a Yemeni Town.* Toronto: University of Toronto Press.

Merriam, Sharon. 2009. *Qualitative Research: A Guide to Design and Implementation.* San Francisco, CA: Jossey-Bass.

Milroy, Lesley. 1987. *Language and Social Networks.* Oxford: Wiley-Blackwell.

Moll, Luis, Cathy Amanti, Deborah Neff, and Norma Gonzalez. 1992. "Funds of Knowledge for Reaching: Using a Qualitative Approach to Connect Homes and Classrooms." *Theory into Practice* 31, no. 2, 132–141.

Mosse, David. 2006. "Anti-social Anthropology? Objectivity, Objection, and the Ethnography of Public Policy and Professional Communities." *Journal of the Royal Anthropological Institute* 12, no. 4, 935–956.

Muser, Heather. 2017. "A Parent's Dream Come True: A Study of Adult Students Who Are Parents and Their Academic Engagement with Higher Education." Ed. D. diss., California State University, Stanislaus. https://search-proquest-com.li bproxy.csudh.edu/docview/1898822307

Myers, Robert. 2011. "The Familiar Strange and the Strange Familiar in Anthropology and Beyond," *General Anthropology* 18, no. 2, 1–9.

Narayan, Kirin. 1993. "How Native is a 'Native' Anthropologist?" *American Anthropologist* 95, 671–686.

National Center for Education Statistics. 2018. "[Rancho State University*]." Retrieved from: https://nces.ed.gov/globallocator/

National Center for Education Statistics. 2019. "The Condition of Education: Undergraduate Enrollment." Retrieved from: https://nces.ed.gov/programs/coe/in dicator_cha.asp#info

Nielsen, Camilla Kirketerp. 2018. "Dyrlæge På Spil... Uddannelsesetnografiske Studier i Professionsorienteret Spilbaseret Læring På Den Danske Dyrlægeuddannelse." Københavns Universitet, Det Sundhedsvidenskabelige Fakultet.

Nieto, Sonia. 2010. *The Light in Their Eyes: Creating Multicultural Learning Communities.* New York: Teachers College Press.

Noddings, Nell. 1984. *Caring: A Feminine Approach to Ethics and Moral Education.* Berkeley, CA: University of California Press, 1984

Noer, Vibeke Røn. 2014. "Zooming in - Zooming out - Using IPad Video Diaries in Ethnographic Educational Research." In *Networked Together - Designing*

Particpatory Research in Online Ethnography, edited by P Landri, A Maccarini, and R De Rosa, pp. 85–96. Napoli, Italien: Istituto di Ricerche sulla popolazione e le politiche sociali. http://bit.ly/310yuHC.

Noer, Vibeke Røn. 2016. *"Rigtige Sygeplejersker". Uddannelsesetnografiske Studier Af Sygeplejestuderendes Studieliv Og Dannelsesprocesser.* Københavns Universitet, Det Humanistiske Fakultet.

Nurse, Anne. M. 2010. *Locked Up, Locked Out: Young Men in the Juvenile Justice System.* Nashville: Vanderbilt University Press.

Ogbu, John U. and Herbert D. Simons. 1998. "Voluntary and Involuntary Minorities: A Cultural-Ecological Theory of School Performance with Some Implications for Education." *Anthropology & Education Quarterly* 29, no. 2, 155–188.

Ong, Aihwa. 1996. "Cultural Citizenship as Subject-Making: Immigrants Negotiate Racial and Cultural Boundaries in the United States." *Current Anthropology* 37, no. 5, 737–751.

Ortner, Sherry B. 2019. "Practicing Engaged Anthropology." *Anthropology of this Century* 25 (May): http://aotcpress.com/articles/practicing-engaged-anthropology/.

O'Cummings, Mindee, Sarah Bardack, S., and Simon Gonsoulin, S. 2010. *Issue Brief: The Importance of Literacy for Youth Involved in the Juvenile Justice System.* Washington, DC: National Evaluation and Technical Assistance Center for the Education of Children and Youth Who Are Neglected, Delinquent, or At Risk (NDTAC).

Packer, Martin J. and Jessie. Goicoechea. 2007. "Sociocultural and Constructivist Theories of Learning: Ontology, Not Just Epistemology." *Educational Psychologist* 35, no. 4, 227–241.

Palmer, Parker J. 1998. *The Courage to Teach. Exploring the Inner Landscape of a Teacher's Life.* San Francisco, CA: Jossey-Baas.

Pang, Ming Fai and Lo Mun Ling. 2012. "Learning Study: Helping Teachers to Use Theory, Develop Professionality and Produce New Knowledge To Be Shared" *Instructional Science* 40, no. 3, 589–606.

Pérez-Izaguirre, Elizabeth. 2018. "'No, I Don't Like the Basque Language.' Considering the Role of Cultural Capital Within Boundary-work in Basque Education." *Social Sciences* 7, no. 15, 1–20.

Pérez-Izaguirre, Elizabeth. 2019. "Educational Inequalities, Teacher Authority and Student Autonomy in Multi-ethnic Basque Secondary Education." *Issues in Educational Research* 29, no. 2, 519–536.

Pipher, Mary. 2006. *Writing to Change the World.* New York: Riverhead Books.

Plump, Brielle and Geist-Martin, Patricia. 2013. "Collaborative Intersectionality: Negotiating Identity, Liminal Spaces, and Ethnographic Research." *Liminalities: A Journal of Performance Studies* 9, no. 2, 59–72.

Posch, Peter. 2019. "Action research–Conceptual Distinctions and Confronting the Theory–Practice Divide in Lesson and Learning Studies." *Educational Action Research* 2, no. 4, 496–510.

Puzzanchera, Charles and Sarah Hockenberry. 2019. "Trends and Characteristics of Youth in Residential Placement, 2017." National Center for Juvenile Justice. Office of Juvenile Justice and Delinquency Prevention. https://www.ojjdp.gov/ojstatbb/snapshots/DataSnapshot_CJRP2017.pdf

Rabinow, Paul. (1977/2007). *Reflections on Fieldwork in Morocco*, 2nd edition. Berkeley, CA: University of California Press.

Read, Nicholas W. and Mindee O'Cummings. 2011. *"Factsheet: Juvenile Justice Education."* Washington, DC: National Evaluation and Technical Assistance Center for the Education of Children and Youth Who Are Neglected, Delinquent, or At Risk (NDTAC).

Rist, Ray C. 2011/1998. "On Understanding the Processes of Schooling: The Contributions of Labeling Theory." In A.R. Sadovnik, *Sociology of Education: A Critical Reader*, 2nd edition, pp. 71–82. New York: Routledge.

Robben, Antonius C.G.M. 2007. "Fieldwork Identity". In *Ethnographic Fieldwork. An Anthropological Reader*, edited by Antonius C.G.M. Robben and Jeffrey A. Sluka, pp. 59–63. Malden: Blackwell.

Roccas, Sonia and Marilynn B. Brewer. 2002. "Social Identity Complexity." *Personality and Social Psychology Review* 6, no. 2, 88–106.

Rosaldo, Renato. 1994. "Cultural Citizenship and Educational Democracy." *Cultural Anthropology* 9, no. 3, 402–411.

Rowan, Leonie, Michele Knobel, Chris Bigum, and Colin Lankshear. 2001. *Boys, Literacies and Schooling: The Dangerous Territories of Gender-based Literacy Reform*. Buckingham, PA: Open University Press.

Rubin, Beth. 2007. "'There's Still Not Justice': Youth Civic Identity Development Amid Distinct School and Community Contexts." *Teachers College Record* 109, no. 2, 449–481.

Rud, A.G. and James Garrison. 2010. "Reverence and Listening in Teaching and Leading." *The Teachers College Record* 112, no. 11, 2777–2792.

Santa Ana, Otto. 2002. *Brown Tide Rising: Metaphors of Latinos in Contemporary American Public Discourse*. Austin, tx: University of Texas Press.

Sarroub, Loukia K. 2007. "Seeking Refuge in Literacy from a Scorpion Bite." *Ethnography and Education* 2, no. 3, 365–380.

Shore, Cris. 2012. "Anthropology and Public Policy." In *The Sage Handbook of Social Anthropology*, pp. 89–104. https://www.researchgate.net/publication/292914436

Shuttleworth, Russell. 2004. "Multiple Roles, Statuses, and Allegiances: Exploring the Ethnographic Process in Disability Culture." In *Anthropologists in the Field; Cases in Participant Observation*, edited by Lynne Hume and Jane Mulcock, pp. 46–58. New York: Columbia University Press.

Snyder, Howard, and Melissa Sickmund. 2006. *Juvenile Offenders and Victims: 2006 National Report*. Washington, DC: U.S. Department of Justice, Office of Justice Programs, Office of Juvenile Justice and Delinquency Prevention.

Spradley, James P. 1979/2016. *The Ethnographic Interview*. New York: Wadsworth Cengage Learning.

Spradley, James P. 1980. *Participant Observation*. New York: Holt, Rinehart and Winston.

Swedish Research Council. 2017. *Good Research Practice*. Stockholm: Vetenskapsrådet.

Tan, Yuen Sze Michelle, and Imelda Santos Caleon. 2016. "Problem Finding in Professional Learning Communities: A Learning Study Approach." *Scandinavian Journal of Educational Research* 60, no. 2, 127–146.

Tannis, Lynette. 2014a. *Educating Incarcerated Youth: Exploring the Impact of Relationships, Expectations, Resources, and Accountability.* New York: Palgrave Macmillan.

Tannis, Lynette. 2014b. "Punishing Young Offenders Twice." *Education Week.* Online 33, no. 19: 28. https://www.edweek.org/leadership/opinion-punishing-young-offenders-twice/2014/01

Theophano, Janet, and Karen Curtis. 1996. "Reflections on a Tale Told Twice." In *Journeys through Ethnography: Realistic Accounts of Fieldwork*, edited by Annette Lareau and Jeffrey J. Schultz, pp. 151–176. Boulder, CO: Westview Press.

Urla, Jacqueline. 2012. *Reclaiming Basque: Language, Nation, and Cultural Activism.* Reno, NV: University of Nevada Press.

Vickers, David Andrew. 2019. "At-home Ethnography: A Method for Practitioners." *Qualitative Research in Organizations and Management: An International Journal* 14, no. 1, 10–26. doi: 10.1108/QROM-02–2017–1492

von Schantz Lundgren, Ina, Mats Lundgren, and Victoria Svensson. 2013. "Learning Study gymnasial yrkesutbildning: En fallstudie från ett hantverksprogram" ["Learning Study in Secondary Vocational Education: A Case Study from a Craft Program"]. *Nordic Journal of Vocational Education and Training* 3, no. 4, 1–16.

Walford, Geoffrey, ed. 2008. *How to Do Educational Ethnography. Ethnography and Education.* London: Tufnell Press.

Ware, Franita. 2006. "Warm Demander Pedagogy: Culturally Responsive Teaching that Supports a Culture of Achievement for African American Students." *Urban Education* 41, 427–456.

Watson, Wanda, Yolanda Sealey-Ruiz, and Iesha Jackson. 2016. "Daring to Care: The Role of Culturally Relevant Care in Mentoring Black and Latino Male High School Students." *Race, Ethnicity and Education* 19, no. 5, 980–1002.

Whitburn, Ben and Vicky Plows. 2017. "Making Sense of Everyday Practice: By Whom, for Whom, for What?" In *Inclusive Education: Making Sense of Everyday Practice*, edited by Ben Whitburn and Vicky Plows, pp. 3–12. Rotterdam: Sense.

Wolf, Marjory. 1992. *A Thrice Told Tale: Feminism, Postmodernism, and Ethnographic Responsibility.* Palo Alto: Stanford University Press.

Woods, Peter and Martyn Hammersley. 2017. *School Experience. Explorations in the Sociology of Education.* New York: Routledge.

Woods, Peter. 2012. *Sociology and the School: An Interactionist Viewpoint.* London: Routledge.

Wortham, Stanton, Jr., Enrique Murillo, and Edmund Hamann, eds. 2002. *Education in the New Latino Diaspora: Policy and the Politics of Identity.* Westport, CT: Ablex Publishing.

Ybema, Sierk and Frans Kamsteeg. 2009. "Making the Familiar Strange: A Case for Disengaged Organizational Ethnography." In *Organizational Ethnography: Studying the Complexities of Everyday Life*, edited by Sierk Ybema, Dvora Yanow, Harry Wels, and Frans Kamsteeg, pp. 101–119. London: Sage.

Yosso, Tara. 2005. "Whose Culture Has Capital? A Critical Race Theory Discussion of Community Cultural Wealth." *Race, Ethnicity, and Education* 8, no. 1, 69–91.

Index

Author Biographies

Stig-Börje Asplund is an associate professor in the Department of Educational Studies at Karlstad University in Sweden. His main research interests are classroom interaction, processes of identity construction, and literacy practices, with a special focus on vocational education and on boys' and men's relations to reading.

Jan Axelsson is a vocational teacher in welding and a Ph.D. Student. He also holds a university degree as a Swedish and English teacher. His Ph.D. studies are closely linked to the research project *Learning to weld in technical vocational education*. He has also taught in the teacher education program at Karlstad University.

Tricia Gray is an assistant professor of practice in the Department of Teaching, Learning, and Teacher Education. She was a postdoctoral research associate for the International Consortium for Multilingual Excellence in Education (ICMEE) at the University of Nebraska-Lincoln. Her fifteen years as a high school Spanish teacher in contested spaces—including an urban context, a public school located on Native American tribal lands, and an exurban community experiencing demographic change—inform her work in meaningful ways. Her research questions aim to center and amplify the experiences of marginalized young people to inform more equitable and justice-oriented schooling.

Nina Kilbrink is an associate professor at the Department of Educational Studies at Karlstad University in Sweden. Her research interests concern vocational learning ICT in education, school workplace relationships, professional learning, and learning studies and narrative research.

Surin Kim develops research-based entrepreneurship education programs and leads initiatives to build entrepreneurship ecosystems as an assistant professor and extension specialist in Entrepreneurship at the University of Nebraska-Lincoln. Her professional focus has been innovative and high-growth product development, which she successfully launched in the tech industry for the past decade.

Camilla Kirketerp Nielsen is a doctor of veterinary medicine (DVM, Ph.D.). While pursuing her Ph.D. at the University of Copenhagen, she conducted extensive fieldwork in the veterinary learning environment. Her main research areas and interests are veterinary education, qualitative research methods, professional identity, study strategies, and clinical teaching and learning.

Claire Nicholas is assistant professor of Textiles and Material Culture in the Department of Textiles, Merchandising & Fashion Design at the University of Nebraska-Lincoln. She holds a Ph.D. in sociocultural anthropology from Princeton University, a DEA from EHESS (École des Hautes Études en Sciences Sociales, Paris), and she has completed a postdoctoral research fellowship in the Department of Human Ecology at the University of Alberta. Her research focuses on the ethnography of craft and design process, pedagogy, and the everyday practices (and politics) of making and interpreting material and visual culture. She has conducted fieldwork in Morocco and across North America in contexts ranging from artisanal textile workshops to university architecture studios.

Elizabeth Pérez-Izaguirre is an adjunct professor of School Organization and Integrated Curriculum and Multilingual Education at the Faculty of Education, Philosophy and Anthropology at the University of the Basque Country (UPV/EHU). Her area of research includes marginalization in multi-ethnic environments and the intersection between language ideologies and identity in Basque education. Her area of expertise include academic learning trajectories and graffiti learning. She has published several articles on Basque education and is a collaborator of the IAS-Research Center for Life, Mind and Society at the University of the Basque Country (UPV/EHU).

Vibeke Røn Noer holds a master's degree in nursing science and a Ph.D. in pedagogy. She is associate professor and head of program for Practice Studies at the Research Centre for Quality of Education, Profession Policy and Practice, VIA University College, Denmark. She has acquired eighteen years of teaching experience and is frequently invited to speak at conferences and seminars. Her main research areas are nursing education, formation, challenges of transitioning school to work, and end-of-life care education.

Mary Anne Poe is dean of the School of Social Work and director of the Center for Just and Caring Communities at Union University in Jackson, Tennessee. She has published *Instructor Resources for Christianity and Social Work* for the last three editions and *Instructor Resources for Congregational Social Work: Christian Perspectives.* She has also contributed chapters and case studies to other books. Poe earned a B.A. from Vanderbilt University, an MDiv from The Southern Baptist Theological Seminary, and an MSSW degree from the University of Louisville.

Charlotta Rönn is a Ph.D. student in the Department of Education, Mid-Sweden University, Sweden. With a background as a teacher in an American language center in Morocco, her main research interests include students' informal social strategies when carrying out formal, individual assignments given by teachers. Rönn is interested in developing research methodology in education with a specific focus on children. She is interested in the use of audio-visual recordings in ethnography research in particular. She teaches undergraduate students in teacher preparation programs as well as supervises student theses.

Phillip Ryan is a professor in the Department of Language and Director of the Center for Intercultural Engagement at Union University in Jackson, Tennessee. He is responsible for undergraduate programs in TESOL, Applied Linguistics, and Intercultural Studies. Most recently, he co-authored two articles—one on the structured integration of interdisciplinary and qualitative research—with program alumni for *Issues in Interdisciplinary Studies.* Ryan completed the Ph.D. in English with an emphasis in Rhetoric and Linguistics at Indiana University of Pennsylvania.

Loukia K. Sarroub is professor and chair of graduate programs in the Department of Teaching, Learning, and Teacher Education at the University of Nebraska-Lincoln, where she also has a courtesy professor appointment in the Department of Anthropology. She is affiliated with the Center for Research on Children, Youth, Families, and Schools; the Quantitative, Qualitative, and Measurement in Education Program, and Women and Gender Studies. She received her A.B. in linguistics at the University of Chicago and her Ph.D. in curriculum and education policy and social analysis from Michigan State University. As an ethnographer and researcher, her research lies at the nexus of adolescent literacies; language and culture and sociolinguistic analyses; and anthropology and education. Her publications range from cross-cultural studies that include fieldwork in immigrant and refugee communities in the United States and Europe to studies about youth cultures, Middle Eastern populations, including fieldwork and research in Yemeni and Iraqi communities, as well as research about ethnography and qualitative research methods, discourse analysis, and language and gender in education.

Jen Stacy is an assistant professor in the College of Education at California State University, Dominguez Hills. Her research focuses on parent-school relations, with an emphasis on how schools perceive Latinx families and how these perceptions influence outreach. Currently, she is working on a multi-year ethnography about undergraduate students who parent.

Sarah Staples-Farmer is a twenty-seven-year veteran of the English classroom who has worked with a diversity of youth, from a private boarding school for economically disadvantaged youth to a rural school in a cornfield to a suburban high school. Earning her Ph.D. in education in 2014, Staples-Farmer creates professional development for education professionals on court-affiliated youth, trauma-informed instruction, cultural proficiency, and the transition of court-affiliated youth back into mainstream schools. Currently, Staples-Farmer teaches high school English and serves as a practice fellow teaching English Methods and Curriculum Inquiry for the University of Nebraska's Department of Teaching, Learning, and Teacher Education.

Thijs Jan van Schie completed his master's degree in cultural anthropology and development sociology at Leiden University in 2006. At that time, he also completed his educational master's in social studies education at the Leiden University Graduate School of Teaching. He has worked at the Catholic University of Malawi, Hanoi Medical University, and Leiden University. Currently, he is a Ph.D. student in the Institute of Cultural Anthropology and Development Sociology and the Institute of Education and Child Studies of Leiden University in the Netherlands. His Ph.D. project is about the globalization of Waldorf education, in which he focuses on the Philippines as case study. He is also a high school teacher in social studies at Marecollege, a Dutch secondary Waldorf school.